C000277430

By the same author

The Wealth Elite

A groundbreaking study of
the psychology of the super rich

Published by
LID Publishing Limited
The Record Hall, Studio 204,
16-16a Baldwins Gardens,
London EC1N 7RJ, UK

524 Broadway, 11th Floor, Suite 08-120,
New York, NY 10012, US

info@lidpublishing.com
www.lidpublishing.com

A member of:

BPR
Business Publishers Roundtable

www.businesspublishersroundtable.com

© Rainer Zitelmann, 2019
© LID Publishing Limited, 2019

Printed by in Great Britain by TJ International
ISBN: 978-1-912555-00-0

Originally published in Germany as:
Kapitalismus ist nicht das Problem, sondern die Lösung
FinanzBuch Verlag, Munich (2018)

The English Language Edition was arranged by Maria Pinto-Peuckmann,
Literary Agency, World Copyright Promotion, Kaufering, Germany

Translation: Silke Lührmann (with support from Sebastian Taylor)
Cover and page design: Matthew Renaudin

RAINER ZITELMANN

The Power *of* Capitalism

**A JOURNEY THROUGH RECENT HISTORY
ACROSS FIVE CONTINENTS**

LONDON   NEW YORK   SHANGHAI
MADRID   BARCELONA   BOGOTA
MEXICO CITY   MONTERREY   BUENOS AIRES

Contents

INTRODUCTION

Field Experiments in Human History

For many people, the collapse of one socialist regime after another in the late 1980s firmly established market capitalism as the superior system. Nevertheless, anti-capitalist resentment – sometimes latent, sometimes expressed openly – not only still persists in some quarters but has gained a lot of ground in the wake of the 2008 financial crisis. Policy makers, media commentators and intellectuals almost unanimously interpret the crisis as a failure of the market, or of the capitalist system, that can only be resolved by more government intervention.

This book was written as a response to these views and was driven by the worry that we are about to disown the foundations on which our economic prosperity is based. For many people, 'capitalism' is a dirty word. Although these negative connotations frequently date back to well before the financial crisis, the proponents of a genuinely free market increasingly find themselves on the receiving end of accusations of 'market radicalism'.

A modern economy can be organized according to one of two basic principles. In the first scenario, there is no private ownership of land or means of production. Instead, all of these assets are owned by the state. Government agencies in charge of economic planning decide what and how much is manufactured. In the second scenario, the right to private ownership is guaranteed and entrepreneurs operate within a legal framework to manufacture products they believe consumers will want. The prices they are able to charge for their products serve as a measure of the extent to which their assumptions were right – in other words, the extent to which their supply of products was aligned to the consumers' demand for these products. The first definition describes a socialist system, the second a capitalist one. Throughout this book, the latter term will be used to designate a genuinely free-market economy rather than a watered-down version sometimes defined as a 'social' or 'eco-social' market economy.

In reality, neither of the two systems exists today, or has ever existed, in a pure form. Even in socialist countries such as the German Democratic Republic

(GDR), or even North Korea, some individuals did or do own private property, while the overarching economic plan has never completely suppressed all elements of the free market. Without these elements, the economies of the countries in question would have been even more dysfunctional. While prices nominally exist in socialist economies, the function they perform is radically different from their function in capitalist economies. In fact, they more closely resemble taxes, as the economist Zhang Weiying has noted.[1]

In capitalist economies, on the other hand, a degree of both public ownership and regulatory intervention exists, while taxes essentially represent a system of redistribution that takes from the rich and gives to the middle classes and the poor. Sweden in the 1970s is an extreme example of this kind of redistribution, while the UK during the same period makes a sobering case study that shows the negative economic outcomes of disproportionate government intervention and proves that limiting such intervention is crucial to increasing prosperity.

None of the countries presented in this book operate a 'pure' form of capitalism. In each case, the important issue is the proportion or balance between regulatory intervention and entrepreneurial freedom. The central argument proposed in this book is that increasing the proportion of capitalist elements in a given economy generally leads to more growth, which increases the well-being of a majority of people living within that economy. China's development over the past few decades is a case in point.

Plenty of books seek to marshal theory in order to prove that either of the two economic systems is superior to the other. This is not one of them. Rather than approaching its subject from a theoretical angle, this book takes economic history as its starting point. Unlike socialism, capitalism is not a system invented by intellectuals. Instead, it has evolved organically over centuries, much in the same way in which plants and animals have evolved in nature and continue to do without requiring any centralized planning or theorizing. Among the economist and philosopher Friedrich August von Hayek's most important insights is the realization that the origin of well-functioning institutions is to be found "not in contrivance or design, but in the survival of the successful",[2] with the selection process operating "by imitation of successful institutions and habits".[3]

The biggest error that unites socialists of various stripes with the men and women running the central banks is the belief that a few designated master planners are better able to determine what the people need than the millions of entrepreneurs, investors and consumers whose individual decisions, when added together, are in fact far superior to those of any governmental planning agency, central bank or other organ of state control.

This is why 'top-down' attempts to impose a market-based economy remain largely unsuccessful – although politicians will always need to be involved to some extent. A closer look at China will show that its successful transition towards capitalism was substantially due to the 'bottom-up' growth and widespread adoption of capitalist economic practices – none of which would have been possible without the top-down tolerance of such practices by political leaders such as Deng Xiaoping. Deng and his fellow reformers were smart enough not to invent a new system based on ideals. Instead, they did two things: firstly, rather than attempting to ban or rein in spontaneous developments across that vast country, they allowed them to evolve organically. Secondly, they took a hard look at many other countries to see what was working and what wasn't – and then implemented this knowledge at home.

In this book, I take a similar approach: looking at what has worked and what hasn't. I compare countries that invite comparison because they have a lot of shared history and culture: North and South Korea, the GDR and the Federal Republic of Germany, Venezuela and Chile. The book also shows how the advance of capitalism and the retreat of socialism turned China from a dirt-poor country, where tens of millions of people starved to death less than 60 years ago, into the world's largest export nation, where famine has been eradicated.

While left-wing critics of capitalism and globalization blame capitalism for causing hunger and poverty in various parts of the world, the recent history of the African continent furnishes plenty of examples to prove that the opposite is true: capitalism is not the problem but the solution. Capitalism has proved more effective at fighting poverty than financial aid. Studies show that the more market-oriented developing countries have a poverty rate of only 2.7%, compared to 41.5% in developing countries without a free market.[4]

In general, more state intervention means lower, in some cases even negative, growth rates, while the recent economic history of the US and the UK provides compelling evidence that more capitalism leads to a faster increase in prosperity for the majority of people. In the 1980s, Ronald Reagan and Margaret Thatcher – two political leaders who firmly believed in the benefits of the free market – introduced reforms that reduced the influence of the state on the economy and significantly improved economic prospects in both countries. As the example of Sweden – discussed in Chapter 7 – shows, welfare-state programmes can sometimes stifle economic growth and need to be curtailed.

Over the past 70 years, these real-world experiments have consistently produced similar outcomes – overwhelming evidence pointing to the conclusion that more capitalism means greater prosperity. Still, in many quarters a remarkable reluctance or inability to learn from these outcomes persists. In his *Lectures on the Philosophy of History*, the German philosopher Georg Wilhelm Friedrich Hegel said: "But what experience and history teach is this, – that peoples and governments never have learned anything from history, or acted on principles deduced from it."[5]

Even if his verdict may be too harsh, it does seem that a majority of people are unable to abstract and draw general conclusions from historical experience. Despite the numerous examples of more capitalist economic policies leading to greater prosperity (some of which are discussed in this book, while others, such as India, are not) and the failure of *every single* variant of socialism that has ever been tested under real-world conditions, many people still refuse to learn the obvious lesson.

Following the collapse of the majority of socialist systems in the early 1990s, attempts to implement socialist ideals are still happening in various parts of the world in the vain hope that 'this time' the outcome will be different – most recently in Venezuela. Just as they were captivated by similar earlier experiments, many intellectuals across the Western world were enthralled by Hugo Chávez's attempt to take socialism into the 21st century.[6] As with previous large-scale socialist experiments, the consequences were disastrous, as shown in Chapter 6.

Even in the US today, many young people cling to the 'socialist' dream – although the system they have in mind is an idealized and misguided version of Scandinavian-style socialism rather than Soviet-era communism. However, this book demonstrates that this variant, too, has been thoroughly discredited by its comprehensive failure in the 1970s and 1980s (Chapter 7).

I am not too worried about large-scale nationalization of assets and enterprises sweeping across industrialized Western nations any time soon. Rather, what concerns me is the far greater and more immediate danger of a gradual curtailment of capitalism concomitant with an increase in states' powers of planning and redistribution. Central banks are already acting as if they were planning authorities. Originally set up to guarantee the stability of monetary value, they now see themselves as engaged in the task of neutralizing market forces. By de facto abolishing market interest rates, the European Central Bank partially deactivated the pricing mechanism that is an essential feature of any functioning market economy. Rather than containing excessive public debt, this has only exacerbated the issue.

"The policy of keeping interest rates low over an extended period of time will increasingly distort asset prices and exacerbate the danger of another economic collapse followed by a financial crisis as soon as this policy is jettisoned," the economist Thomas Mayer warns.[7] It does not take a crystal ball to predict that these crises will be blamed on 'capitalism', even though they are in fact the result of a violation of capitalist principles. A wrong diagnosis inevitably leads to the wrong treatment being prescribed – in this case, even more governmental intervention in an even more weakened market.

Once upon a time, socialists simply used to nationalize commercial enterprises. Today, elements of a planned economy are introduced in other ways – increasing governmental intervention in commercial decision-making processes and a range of fiscal and regulatory measures, subsidies and legal restrictions that curtail the freedom of entrepreneurs. In this way, the German energy market has gradually been transformed into a planned economy.

This is possible only because many people are simply unaware – or have forgotten – that the free market is the foundation on which our current level of prosperity is based. This is particularly true of the millennial generation, whose only experience of the socialist regimes in the Soviet Union and other Eastern Bloc countries comes through history books, if at all. 'Capitalism' and 'free market' have become dirty words.

In a GlobeScan poll published in April 2011, respondents in a number of different countries were asked to rate the extent to which they agreed with the following statement: "The free enterprise system and free market economy is the best system on which to base the future of the world."[8] In the UK, which a mere 30 years earlier had been transformed from a desperate economic situation to more growth and prosperity thanks to Margaret Thatcher's uncompromising free-market reforms, only 19% of respondents agreed strongly. Across Europe, these figures were highest in Germany, with 30% of respondents agreeing strongly. In France, many of whose problems are directly related to the population's low opinion of the free market, this number dropped to only 6%.

It is reassuring to note that these percentages significantly increase if we include respondents who agreed "somewhat" with the proposition quoted above: 68% in Germany, 55% in the UK and 52% in Spain. In France, on the other hand, a whopping 57% of respondents expressed disagreement. In the US, the survey showed a drop in approval of the free-market system from 80% in 2002 to only 59% in 2011. Among lower-income tiers of society, this dropped again to 45%. The economist Samuel Gregg quotes these statistics in *Becoming Europe*, a book that serves as a dire warning to Americans against following the model of the European welfare states.

Younger generations of Americans in particular express a strong affinity with anti-capitalist ideas. A 2016 YouGov poll showed that 45% of Americans between the ages of 16 and 20 would consider voting for a socialist, while 20% would even give their vote to a communist candidate. Only 42% of Americans in that age bracket were in favour of a capitalist economy (compared to 64% of Americans over 65). Even more worryingly, in the same poll a third of young Americans revealed the belief that more people had been killed under the George W. Bush administration than under Stalin.[9] In another poll conducted by Gallup in April 2016, 52% of Americans agreed that "our government *should redistribute wealth by heavy taxes on the rich*".[10]

In an Infratest dimap poll conducted in Germany in 2014, 61% of respondents agreed with the view that "we don't live in a real democracy because the power lies with business interests rather than voters".[11] Moreover, 33% of Germans (41% in the former GDR) agreed that capitalism "inevitably causes poverty and starvation",[12] while 42% (59% in the former GDR) agreed that "socialism/communism is a good idea that has been badly executed in the past".[13]

As the collapse of the socialist systems gradually retreats from living memory, many people across the Western world appear to be at risk of losing their awareness of the superior benefits of the free market. This is particularly true of younger people, whose history lessons barely touched on the economic and political conditions in socialist countries.

This book focuses on a single question: Which economic system delivers the greatest quality of life for a majority of people? Quality of life is determined, especially though not exclusively, by the individuals' level of economic wealth and also by their level of political freedom. While history provides many examples of democracy and capitalism going hand in hand, there are other cases of authoritarian regimes with a capitalist economy: South Korea had yet to become a democracy at the time it adopted capitalism, as did Chile. For all its economic success as a capitalist economy, China is still governed by an authoritarian regime. Any comparisons drawn between countries in this book are based only on the criteria of their respective economic systems and economic performance. This is not to say that political freedom is a less important aspect of quality of life – however, it is beyond the scope of this book and would merit a separate investigation.

Much as I disagree with the premises of, and the arguments developed in, Thomas Piketty's *Capital in the Twenty-First Century*, in many respects I do share his criticism of much current research in economics, which demonstrates a "childish passion for mathematics and for purely theoretical and often highly ideological speculation, at the expense of historical research and collaboration with the other social sciences".[14] Instead, Piketty argues for "a pragmatic approach" that uses "the methods of historians, sociologists, and political scientists as well as economists" and describes his book as "a work of history [as much] as of economics".[15] My own first degree is in history and political science and I went on to obtain two PhDs, respectively in history and sociology. Accordingly, my approach in this book is that of a historian.

Piketty's main complaint is that economics and social sciences no longer focus on the "distributional question": "It is long past the time when we should have put the question of inequality back at the center of economic analysis."[16] Other authors have published comprehensive critiques of Piketty's dataset and methodological errors,[17] forcing him to retract some core tenets of his book.[18] My objective here is merely to point out that I am asking a completely different question – one that, in my view, for the majority of people holds far greater significance than Piketty's concern with "inequalities of wealth". Whether capitalism tends to raise or lower the overall standard of living strikes me as far more important than any putative increase in the inequality of wealth.

Piketty bemoans a widening of the gap between the poor and the rich in terms of income and wealth in the period from 1990 to 2010. However, the fact is that during the same period hundreds of millions of people – predominantly in China as well as in India and other parts of the world – escaped from abject poverty as a direct result of the expansion of capitalism.

What is more important to these hundreds of millions of people – that they are no longer starving or that the wealth of multi-millionaires and billionaires may have increased to an even greater degree than their own standard of living? As the first chapter of this book will demonstrate, the increase in the number of millionaires and billionaires in China over the past decades and the massive improvements in the standard of living of hundreds of millions of people are two faces of the same coin. Both can be directly traced back to the same process, i.e. the transition from socialism to capitalism, from a planned towards a free-market economy.

Beyond any doubt, capitalist globalization has reduced poverty worldwide. Whether the rise of prosperity in previously underdeveloped countries has led to losses in prosperity among lower-income strata in industrialized nations in the West, i.e. Europe and the US, is a more controversial issue. Let me point out two things in response. First of all: if this is the case because lower-income earners are now directly competing with workers in emerging countries, it follows that – contrary to their self-styled role as defenders of the rights of the poor in countries across Africa, Asia and Latin America – the anti-capitalist, anti-globalization movement in the West is primarily upholding the privileged status quo of Europeans and Americans. Secondly, the hypothesis that globalization has impoverished swathes of the population in Europe and the US is itself controversial. A 2011 study by the Organisation for Economic Co-operation and Development (OECD) showed a decrease in real incomes among the poorest 10% of the population since the 1980s in only two member states – Japan and Israel.[19]

In many cases, media reports on the alarming rise of poverty in developed Western nations are based on studies that define and measure poverty in relative terms. The official reports on poverty and prosperity published by the German government, for example, apply a definition of poverty that includes anybody who earns less than 60% of the median income. A simple mental experiment shows this definition to be dubious at best: let's assume an across-the-board tenfold increase in income while the value of money remains stable. Those in the lower income bracket who previously made 1,000 euros a month are now getting 10,000 euros. All their money worries would be over. Life would be great for everyone. Nonetheless, the 60% formula would still apply, and the number of people living below the official poverty line would remain the same.

For critics of capitalism of Piketty's ilk, the economy is a zero-sum game in which the rich win what the middle classes and the poor lose.[20] This isn't how the market works, though. Critics of capitalism are always looking at how the pie is split; in this book, I am looking at the conditions that make the pie grow or shrink in size.

Here's yet another mental experiment – I'll leave it up to you to decide which of the following outcomes you'd prefer. Let's assume you live on an island where three rich people have a fortune of 5,000 dollars each, while 1,000 others only have 100 dollars each. The total wealth of the island's residents is 115,000 dollars. Now you decide between two alternatives: due to economic growth, the total wealth of the island's residents doubles to 230,000 dollars. The wealth of the three rich people triples to 15,000 dollars each; they now own 45,000 dollars between them. Meanwhile, the wealth of the island's remaining 1,000 residents grows by 85% to 185 dollars per capita. The inequality gap between the richest and the poorest residents has widened considerably.

In the alternative scenario, let's take the total wealth of 115,000 dollars and split it evenly between all 1,003 residents – 114.66 dollars per capita. As one of the poor with a baseline wealth of 100 dollars, which of the two societies would you prefer – economic growth or equal distribution? And what would happen if, as a consequence of economic reforms aimed at creating greater equality, the island's total wealth were to shrink to a paltry 80,000 dollars, or less than 79.80 dollars per capita?

Of course, you may well object that the best outcome would be economic growth and a higher general standard of living *in tandem with* greater equality. And that's exactly what capitalism achieved in the 20th century, as even Piketty admits. The above mental experiment is still useful as a way of demonstrating a fundamental difference between two competing value systems. Somebody who prioritizes fighting inequality over raising the standard of living for the majority will make a different choice from somebody who believes the opposite.

If you are primarily interested in equality, this is the wrong book for you. If you care about identifying the conditions under which a majority of people are better off – if you believe it *does* matter whether a society as a whole is rich or poor – please join me on my journey through time across five continents in search of answers. Karl Marx was right in his assertion that the means of production (technology, equipment, organization of the production process etc.) and the conditions of production (the economic system) are not just inextricably linked but mutually dependent on each other.[21] However, contrary to Marx's contention, the crucial point is not that the development of the means of production precedes changes in the conditions of production. Much more importantly, changes in the conditions of production can sometimes cause the means of production to develop.

Capitalism is the root cause of a global increase in living standards on a scale unprecedented in human history before the emergence of the market economy. It took humanity 99.4% of its 2.5-million-year history to achieve a per-capita GDP of 90 international dollars about 15,000 years ago (the international dollar is a unit of calculation based on buying-power levels in 1990). It took another 0.59% of human history to double the global GDP to 180 international dollars in 1750. Between 1750 and 2000 – in a period that represents less than 0.01% of the total span of human history – the global per-capita GDP grew 37-fold to 6,600 international dollars. To put it differently, 97% of the total wealth created throughout human history was produced within those 250 years.[22] Global life expectancy almost tripled in the same short period of time (in 1820, it was only 26 years). None of this happened because of a sudden increase in human intelligence or industry – it happened because the new economic system that emerged in Western countries about 200 years ago proved superior to any other before or since: capitalism. It was this system based on private property, entrepreneurship, fair pricing and competition that made the unprecedented economic and technological advances of the past 250 years possible – a system that, for all its successes, is still young and vulnerable.

CHAPTER 1

China:
From Famine
to Economic
Miracle

For millennia, China suffered famine after famine. Today, almost everybody has enough to eat and, in 2016, China overtook the US and Germany to become the world's largest exporter.

As recently as the late 19th and early 20th centuries, 100 million people died of starvation in China. While these famines were caused by natural disasters, what followed during the second half of the 20th century was a man-made, politically motivated crisis. Following his ascent to power in 1949, Mao Zedong wanted to turn China into a shining example of socialism. In late 1957, he proclaimed the Great Leap Forward as a shortcut to the supposed workers' paradise. According to Mao, China would be able to overtake the UK within 15 years, thus proving once and for all that socialism was superior to capitalism. Via the Communist Party's official newspaper, the population was informed of the plan "to overtake all capitalist countries in a fairly short time, and become one of the richest, most advanced and powerful countries in the world".[23]

THE GREAT FAMINE

The most ambitious socialist experiment in history started with tens of millions of farmers across the country being forced into working on massive irrigation projects without sufficient food or rest. Soon, one in six Chinese was busy digging for large-scale dam- and canal-building projects.[24] The removal of a massive part of the agricultural workforce was one of several reasons for the famines that started spreading across China. Party officials were ruthless in their efforts to get results: villagers were tied up for stealing vegetables or stabbed to death for not working hard enough. Recalcitrant peasants were sent to labour camps. Military patrols armed with whips went through the villages to make sure everybody worked as hard as they possibly could.[25]

At the time, agriculture was the primary source of income in China and peasants made up the majority of its population. During the Great Leap Forward, private ownership of any kind was abolished, and peasants were forced to leave their properties and live in factory-like barracks with up to 20,000 fellow sufferers. Across China, there were 24,000 of these collectives or 'people's communes' with an average of 8,000 members.

Mao himself edited – and praised as a 'great treasure' – the charter of the first commune in Henan, which obliged all 9,369 households to "hand over entirely their private plots ... their houses, animals and trees" and live in dormitories "in accordance with the principles of benefiting production and control". Homes were to be "dismantled ... if the commune needs the bricks, tiles or timber".[26]

Mao went so far as to consider "replacing [people's names] with numbers. In Henan and other model areas, peasants worked in the fields with a number sewn on their backs ... Peasants were not only banned from eating at home, their woks and stoves were smashed." Instead, their food was served in canteens, which were "sometimes hours' walk away from where people lived or worked", forcing them to "move to the site of the canteen", where they "lived like animals, crammed into whatever space was available, with no privacy or family life".[27] Every morning, workers' brigades would march into the battlefields of production under red flags and motivational slogans blaring from speakers.

This experiment resulted in what was probably the worst famine – and definitely the worst man-made famine – in human history. Based on official figures, the Chinese demographer Cao Shuji estimates that around 32.5 million people died of starvation across China in the period between 1958 and 1962. According to his calculations, Anhui province suffered the worst, with a total death toll of more than 6 million, or over 18% of the population, followed by Szechuan, where 13% of the population (9.4 million people) perished.[28]

Based on analyses carried out by the Chinese security service and the extensive confidential reports published by party committees during the final months of the Great Leap Forward, the German historian Frank Dikötter arrives at a significantly higher estimate of around 45 million people across China who died prematurely between 1958 and 1962. The majority died of starvation, while another 2.5 million were tortured or beaten to death.[29] "Other victims were deliberately deprived of food and starved to death ... People were killed selectively because they were rich, because they dragged their feet, because they spoke out or simply because they were not liked, for whatever reason, by the man who wielded the ladle in the canteen."[30]

People were punished in large numbers for expressing criticism. According to a report from Fengyang county in Anhui province, 28,026 people (over 12% of the population) were sentenced to corporal punishment or had their food rations reduced; 441 died as a consequence, while a further 383 sustained severe injuries.[31]

In the preface to *Tombstone*, his two-volume investigative study of the Great Famine, which was published in Hong Kong in 2008 and banned in mainland China, the Chinese journalist and historian Yang Jisheng remembers: "The starvation that preceded death was worse than death itself. The grain was gone, the wild herbs had all been eaten, even the bark had been stripped from the trees, and bird droppings, rats and cotton batting were used to fill stomachs. In the kaolin clay fields, starving people chewed on the clay as they dug it."[32] There were frequent cases of cannibalism. At first, desperate villagers would only eat the cadavers of animals, but soon they started digging up dead neighbours to cook and eat. Human flesh was sold on the black market along with other types of meat.[33] A study compiled – and promptly suppressed – after Mao's death for Fengyang county "recorded sixty-three cases of cannibalism in the spring of 1960 alone, including that of a couple who strangled and ate their eight-year-old son".[34]

A victim of its own reign of terror, the leadership of the Communist Party preferred to take at face value the false reports of phenomenal harvests submitted by the people's communes. Communes that submitted realistic figures were given white flags as a form of punishment for lacking revolutionary zeal, accused of lying and subjected to violence. In previous years, peasants had actually submitted false reports in some cases in an act of defiance against grain tax increases. Now anybody who claimed not to have enough to eat was considered an enemy of the socialist revolution and an agent of capitalism. Simply stating "I'm hungry" became a dangerous act of insurgence.[35]

Fleeing to a place that still had food was prohibited, leading to a situation that was "worse than under the Japanese occupation" (1937–1945) according to an eyewitness report: "Even when the Japanese came ... we could run away. [Now] we are simply shut in to die at home. My family had six members and four have died." Party cadres also had the job of stopping people 'stealing' their own food. Horrific punishments were widespread; some people were buried alive, others strangled with ropes, others had their noses cut off. In one village, four terrorized young children were saved from being buried alive for taking some food only when the earth was at their waists, after desperate pleas from their parents. In another village, a child had four fingers chopped off for trying to steal a scrap of unripe food ... Brutality of this kind crops up in virtually every account of this period, nationwide."[36]

According to official government propaganda, the Chinese economy was going from strength to strength, constantly achieving record-breaking results across all industries and delivering compelling proof of the socialist system's inherent superiority. Mao was particularly obsessed with steel production as a measure of the progress of socialism, to the point of memorizing the steel production volumes achieved by almost all other countries and setting unrealistic goals in his attempts to exceed them. In 1957, China produced 5.35 million tons of steel. In January 1958, the government set a goal of 6.2 million tons, which was almost doubled to 12 million tons in September of the same year.[37]

At the time, Chinese steel was largely produced in small blast furnaces (many of which did not work properly and produced materials that were unfit for purpose) operated by villagers in the backyards of agricultural communes. Piles of iron ingots made by rural communes, which were too small and brittle to be usable in modern rolling mills, were a familiar sight across China.[38]

This led to absurd scenes happening across the country, with party cadres going from door to door to confiscate household and agricultural equipment. "Farm tools, even water wagons, were carted off and melted down, as were cooking utensils, iron door handles and women's hair-clips. The regime slogan was: 'To hand in one pickaxe is to wipe out one imperialist, and to hide one nail is to hide one counter-revolutionary.'"[39]

Anybody who failed to muster the requisite level of enthusiasm was "verbally abused, pushed around or tied up and paraded" in public.[40] Experts advocating reason and moderation were persecuted. "Mao set the tone for discrediting rationality by saying the 'bourgeois professor's knowledge should be treated as a dog's fart, worth nothing, deserving only disdain, scorn, contempt.'"[41]

In late December 1958, Mao himself was forced to admit to his inner circle that "only 40 per cent is good steel", all of which came from steel mills, while the backyard furnaces had produced 3 million tons of useless steel – "a gigantic waste of resources and manpower [that] triggered further losses".[42]

Despite the fact that an increasing number of peasants were conscripted for large-scale irrigation and steel production projects instead of working the land, agricultural communes continued to report record yields that were grossly exaggerated. In September 1958, the Communist Party's newspaper, the *People's Daily*, reported an average grain productivity of 65,000 kilograms per mu (660 square metres) in Guangxi, when 500 kilograms would have been a more realistic estimate.[43]

These inflated claims were known as 'sputniks'. Sputnik fields, "usually created by transplanting ripe crops from a number of fields into a single artificial plot",[44] mushroomed across China. As a consequence, the government increased its grain exports from 1.93 million tons in 1957 to 4.16 million in 1959. "In 1959 when Mao announced that grain output had reached 375 million tons in China, the actual output was probably 170 million."[45]

Pressured by the Communist Party's insistence on achieving its economic targets whatever the cost, communes would pledge large amounts of 'surplus grain' to the state. "With inflated crops came procurement quotas which were far too high, leading to shortages and outright famine."[46] To make matters worse, the planned economy created a logistical chaos that in turn led to large parts of the harvest being destroyed by crop disease, rats and insects.[47]

Mao attempted to tackle this problem with another large-scale campaign, this one aimed at ridding China of the 'Four Pests': sparrows, rats, mosquitoes and flies. To this end, he mobilized the entire population to wave sticks and brooms in the air and create a racket that would scare the sparrows off until they were so exhausted from flying that they would fall out of the sky. This campaign proved so effective that pests "once kept down by sparrows (and other birds) now flourished, with catastrophic results. Pleas from scientists that the ecological balance would be upset were ignored." Eventually, the Chinese government sent a "top secret" request for 200,000 sparrows from the Soviet Far East to the Soviet Embassy in Beijing.[48]

Despite the worsening famine, the Chinese were loath to lose face by asking their Russian allies to suspend grain exports and defer repayments of their debts. Likewise, they were too proud to accept Western offers of aid.[49] On the contrary, even during the most severe famines, China generously supplied, and in some cases even donated, wheat to Albania and other allies. The 'export above all else' policy adopted in 1960 meant that, at the height of the famine, all provinces were forced to hand over more food than ever before to the state.[50] Whether directed to domestic or foreign audiences, the regime's official propaganda was a desperate attempt to keep up appearances by denying the existence of famine in a socialist system. Subsequent calculations show that a change in policy could potentially have saved up to 26 million human lives.[51]

Desperate citizens wrote letters to Mao and the head of state, Zhou Enlai, assuming they did not know about the famine. One such letter read: "Dear Chairman Mao, Zhou Enlai and leaders of the central government, best wishes for the Spring Festival! In 1958, our fatherland has achieved a Great Leap everywhere ... but in the eastern part of Hainan, in the districts of Yucheng and Xiayi, people's lives have not been good during the past six months ... The children are hungry, the adults are in distress. They are emaciated to skin and bones. The cause is the false reporting of productivity figures. Please listen to our cry for help!"[52]

Party officials investigating the situation on the ground were faced with terrible scenes. In Guangshan county, they found survivors squatting in the rubble of their homes, crying silently in the bitter cold. All across China, houses had been torn down to provide fuel for blast furnaces and fertilizer. In Guangshan, a quarter of the population of 500,000 had perished and been buried in mass graves.[53] Food shortages were aggravated by the death from starvation of millions and millions of animals.

Mao and his fellow party leaders were aware of the problems, but for a long time attempted to whitewash or deny them. The official party line was that, as in war, these sacrifices were a necessary and inevitable step in the glorious creation of a communist society in the near future. Three years of sacrifice were not too high a price to pay for 1,000 years of living in a communist paradise. In July 1959, Mao proclaimed: "The situation in general is excellent. There are many problems, but our future is bright!"[54]

He was well aware that millions might have to die in order to bring about this bright future, telling Soviet leaders during his 1957 visit to Moscow: "We are prepared to sacrifice 300 million Chinese for the victory of the world revolution."[55] In November 1958, "talking to his inner circle about the labor-intensive projects like waterworks and making 'steel' ..., Mao said: 'Working like this, with all these projects, half of China may well have to die. If not half, then maybe one-third or one-tenth – 50 million – die.'"[56]

Lin Biao, whom Mao had designated as his successor for his purportedly unswerving loyalty, coined a popular slogan: "Sailing the seas depends on the helmsman. Making revolution depends on Mao Zedong thought." But in his private diary, he confided his belief that the Great Leap Forward was "based on fantasy, and a total mess".[57] Mao was eventually forced to abandon his Great Leap Forward – which did not stop him from setting in motion another equally disastrous political programme a few years later. Proclaimed in 1966, the Cultural Revolution was an even more radical attempt to transform Chinese society, in the course of which millions of people accused of propagating capitalist ideas or criticizing the Great Leap Forward were sentenced to forced labour or tortured, and hundreds of thousands killed.

The tens of millions of human lives lost as the consequence of another failed socialist experiment should not have come as a surprise to the Chinese communists, who had after all seen a disaster of similar proportions unfold in the Soviet Union in the 1930s. As in China, attempts at collectivizing agricultural production had caused the deaths from starvation of millions. Unfortunately, the history books are full of instances of failed socialist experiments leading communists elsewhere in the world to believe that their own experiments – in another country and another era – are bound to succeed.

The economic fallout from Mao's reign was disastrous. Two in three peasants had lower incomes in 1978 than during the 1950s. A third even saw their incomes fall below pre-Japanese invasion levels. Following Mao's death in 1976, his successors were more pragmatically inclined. Sensing that the Chinese people had had enough of radical socialist experiments, Mao's immediate successor, Hua Guofeng, paved the way for a man who was to play a crucial role in China's transformation – Deng Xiaoping. Mao's successors, Deng in particular, were smart enough to take some Confucian words of wisdom to heart: "By three methods we may learn wisdom: first, by reflection, which is noblest; second, by imitation, which is easiest; and third by experience, which is the bitterest."

CHINA'S ROAD TO CAPITALISM

Having learned their lesson the hard way, the Chinese now started looking at what was happening in other countries. For leading Chinese politicians and economists, 1978 marked the beginning of a busy period of foreign travel to bring back valuable economic insights and apply them at home. Chinese delegations made over 20 trips to more than 50 countries including Japan, Thailand, Malaysia, Singapore, the US, Canada, France, Germany and Switzerland.[58] In the run-up to the first visit by Chinese government officials to Western Europe since the foundation of the People's Republic, Deng met with the delegation's leader, Gu Mu, and several of its over 20 members, "asking them to see as much as they could and to ask questions about how the host countries managed their economies".[59]

The members of the delegation were greatly impressed by what they saw in Western Europe: modern airports such as Charles de Gaulle in Paris, car factories in Germany and ports with automated loading facilities. They were surprised to see the high standard of living even ordinary workers enjoyed in capitalist countries.[60]

Deng himself travelled to destinations including the US and Japan. After an eye-opening visit to the Nissan plant in Japan, he commented, "now I understand what modernization means".[61] The Chinese were especially impressed by the economic successes in other Asian countries. "Although barely acknowledged, the economic dynamism of the neighboring countries in particular was seen as a role model. The Japanese economy, which went from a state of destruction in 1945 to break all growth records from the 1950s onwards, creating a modern consumer society as well as competitive export industries, made Mao's achievements pale by comparison."[62]

On his visit to Singapore, Deng was particularly impressed by the local economy, which was far more dynamic than the Chinese economy. Lee Kuan Yew, Singapore's founding father and long-time prime minister, remembers: "I had told Deng over dinner in 1978 in Singapore that we, the Singapore Chinese, were the descendants of illiterate landless peasants from Guandong and Fujian in South China ... There was nothing that Singapore had done that China could not do, and do better. He stayed silent then. When I read that he had told the Chinese people to do better than Singapore, I knew he had taken up the challenge I quietly tossed to him that night fourteen years earlier."[63]

The delegations' findings were widely circulated in China, both within the Communist Party and among the general public. Having seen with their own eyes the high standard of living enjoyed by workers in Japan, for example, members of the delegations started to realize the extent to which communist propaganda about the benefits of socialism as compared to the misery of the impoverished working classes in capitalist countries had been based on lies and fabrication. It was obvious to anybody who actually travelled to these countries that the exact opposite was true. "The more we see [of the world], the more we realize how backward we are," Deng repeatedly avowed.[64]

However, this newfound enthusiasm for other countries' economic models did not lead to an instant conversion to capitalism, nor did China immediately ditch its planned economy in favour of a free-market economy. Instead, there was a slow process of transition, starting with tentative efforts to grant public enterprises greater autonomy, that took years, even decades, to mature and relied on bottom-up initiatives as much as on top-down, party-led reforms.

After the failure of the Great Leap Forward, peasants in an increasing number of villages began to circumvent the official ban on private farming. Since they were quickly able to achieve far greater outputs, party cadres allowed them to carry on. Initially, these experiments were restricted to the very poorest villages, where almost any outcome would have been better than the status quo. In one of these villages, "widely known in the region as a 'village of beggars'", the cadres "decided to allocate only marginal land to households in two production teams, while keeping collective farming intact elsewhere. That year, the output of the marginal but privately cultivated land was three times higher than that of the collectively cultivated fertile land. The next year, more land was privatized in more production teams."[65]

Long before the official ban on private farming was lifted in 1982, peasant-led initiatives to reintroduce private ownership against socialist doctrine sprang up across China.[66] The outcome was extremely successful: people were no longer starving and agricultural productivity increased rapidly. By 1983, the process of de-collectivizing Chinese agriculture was almost complete. Mao's great socialist experiment, which had cost so many millions of lives, was over.

China's economic transformation was by no means restricted to agriculture. Across the country, many municipal enterprises increasingly operated like private businesses, although they were still formally under public ownership. Liberated from the restrictions of the planned economy, these companies frequently outperformed their less agile state-run competitors. Between 1978 and 1996, the total number of people employed in these companies rose from 28 million to 135 million, while their share of the Chinese economy grew from 6% to 26%.[67]

The 1980s saw the establishment of an increasing number of collectively owned enterprises (COEs) and township and village enterprises (TVEs) – de facto privately-run companies in the guise of collective enterprises.[68] Legally owned by municipal authorities, these blurred the distinction between state and private ownership.

Accordingly, the German political scientist and China expert Tobias ten Brink argues that "actual control" over access to specific resources is more important than formal ownership.[69] In his analysis of Chinese capitalism, ten Brink distinguishes between formal legal status and actual economic function.[70] However, in the course of China's subsequent wave of privatizations, these COEs have since become considerably less important compared to genuine private businesses.

Initially, the growth in private ownership across China was driven by increasing numbers of small-scale entrepreneurs setting up businesses, which were only allowed to employ a maximum of seven people. Under Mao, China – like other socialist countries – had boasted an official unemployment rate of zero. 'Solutions' for the prevention of unemployment included the resettlement of millions of young people from the cities to the countryside for 're-education'. During the 1980s, a growing number of people took the opportunity to set up small businesses instead.

Initially, they suffered hardship and discrimination. Parents wouldn't let their daughters marry somebody who owned or worked in one of these small businesses because their economic prospects were considered uncertain. Any business owner who employed more than seven people was considered a capitalist exploiter and thus in breach of the law. "To get around this and other restrictions, many private firms were forced to put on 'a red hat' – affiliating themselves with a township and village government and thus turning into a township and village enterprise, or with a street committee or other local governmental branches in cities and thus becoming a collective enterprise."[71]

Eventually, more and more people came to realize that running a business as a self-employed entrepreneur conferred considerable financial advantages as well as a greater level of freedom. In many cases, self-employed barbers were earning more than surgeons in state hospitals, street vendors more than nuclear scientists. The number of self-employed household businesses and single proprietorships increased from 140,000 in 1978 to 2.6 million in 1981.[72]

However, the proponents of socialism refused to give up so easily, and in 1982 the Standing Committee of the People's Congress passed the "Resolution to Strike Hard Against Serious Economic Crimes", which saw over 30,000 people arrested by the end of the year.[73] In many cases, their only crime was making profits or employing more than seven people.

The increasing erosion of this socialist system that exclusively permitted public ownership under the management of a state-run economic planning authority was accelerated by the creation of Special Economic Areas. These were areas where the socialist economic system was suspended and capitalist experiments were permitted. The first Special Economic Area was created in Shenzhen, the district adjacent to capitalist Hong Kong, which was then still a British crown colony. Much like in Germany, where an increasing number of people fled from the East to the West prior to the building of the Berlin Wall (see Chapter 3), many Chinese tried to leave the People's Republic for Hong Kong. The district of Shenzhen in Guangdong province was the main conduit for this illegal emigration.

Year after year, thousands of people risked their lives attempting to cross the heavily guarded border from socialist China into capitalist Hong Kong. The majority either were captured by border patrols or drowned in the attempt to swim across the maritime border. The internment camp close to the border, where those captured by the Chinese were held, was hopelessly overcrowded.

As in the German Democratic Republic, anybody who attempted to flee communist China was denounced as a public enemy and traitor to socialism. However, Deng was smart enough to realize that military intervention and stricter border controls would not solve the underlying issue.

When the party leadership in Guangdong province investigated the situation in more detail, it found refugees from mainland China living in a village they had set up on the opposite side of the Shenzhen River on Hong Kong territory, where they were earning 100 times as much money as their erstwhile compatriots on the socialist side.[74]

Deng's response was to argue that China needed to increase living standards in order to stem the flow.[75] Shenzhen, then a district with a population of fewer than 30,000, became the site of China's first free-market experiment, enabled by party cadres who had been to Hong Kong and Singapore and seen at first hand that capitalism works far better than socialism.

From being a place where many put their lives at risk to leave the country, this former fishing village has today become a thriving metropolis with a population of 12.5 million and a higher per-capita income than any other Chinese city except for Hong Kong and Macau. The electronics and communications industries are the mainstays of the local economy. Only a few years into the capitalist experiment, the Shenzhen city council had to build a barbed-wire fence around the Special Economic Zone in order to cope with the influx of migrants from other parts of China.[76]

Soon, other regions followed suit and tried the Special Economic Zone model. Low taxes, land lease prices and bureaucratic requirements made these Special Economic Zones extremely attractive to foreign investors.[77] Their economies were less heavily regulated and more market-oriented than those of many European countries today. Following a reform in 2003, China had around 200 government-controlled National Economic and Technological Development Zones extending far into the country's interior, as well as up to 2,000 Development Zones under regional or local supervision that were not directly controlled by the central government. "Over time, the boundaries between Special Zones and the rest of the economy became increasingly blurred."[78]

Nevertheless, the economic reforms were half-hearted. The public enterprises of the socialist planned economy continued to co-exist with private businesses of various kinds and Special Economic Zones. In a capitalist economy, entrepreneurs take their cues from the fluctuation of prices and invest accordingly, whereas in a socialist economy prices are set by civil servants working for the planning authorities. In China, the coexistence of both models led to a chaotic pricing situation. In the late 1980s, inflation increased rapidly, with the price index jumping from 9.5% in January 1988 to 38.6% in August of the same year.[79]

Those in favour of the reforms interpreted this as evidence that the measures undertaken so far had not been far-reaching enough, while their critics clung to the belief that the problems had been caused by the abandonment of socialist principles. Political turmoil culminating in the brutal suppression of a student demonstration in Beijing in June 1989, which according to estimates by Amnesty International resulted in the loss of several hundreds or even thousands of lives,[80] only aggravated the situation – as did the events leading to the collapse of the communist regimes in the Soviet Union and across socialist Eastern Europe. China's communist leadership feared a similar loss of power.

Against this background, proponents of more far-reaching reforms struggled to defend themselves against accusations that they were trying to abolish socialism and turning China into a capitalist country. Although Deng held no public office at the time, he decided to intervene. The interviews he gave during a visit to Shenzhen and Shanghai attracted a lot of attention across China. He spent five days in Shenzhen and expressed his amazement at the extent of the region's transformation since his last visit in 1984. He was impressed by the magnificent boulevards, resplendent high-rise buildings, busy shopping streets and seemingly infinite number of factories. The people were dressed in fashionable clothes and were the proud owners of expensive watches and other luxury items. Their income was three times higher than in the rest of China.[81] Deng's 'Southern Tour' made history and his open criticism of those who opposed further reforms featured prominently in the Chinese media. On 21 February 1992, the day before Deng was due to return to Beijing, the *People's Daily* published a much-discussed opinion piece under the headline "Be Bolder in Reform". [82]

Although Deng and his fellow proponents of free-market reforms continued to pay lip service to socialism, they redefined the term to mean something quite unlike a state-controlled planned economy. For them, socialism was an "open system that should 'draw on the achievements of all cultures and learn from other countries, including the developed capitalist countries'". [83]

Unlike political leaders in the Soviet Union and other former member states of the Eastern Bloc, where Marxist ideology was subject to harsh criticism after the collapse of socialism, Deng and his fellow reformers in China did not denounce Marxism. However, their version of Marxism had nothing whatsoever in common with the theories originally formulated by Karl Marx: "The essence of Marxism is seeking truth from facts. That's what we should advocate, not book worship. The reform and the open policy have been successful not because we relied on books, but because we relied on practice and sought truth from facts … Practice is the sole criterion for testing truth."[84]

Increasingly, the reformers won the day. The number of private enterprises rose sharply from 237,000 in 1993 to 432,000 the next year. Capital investments in private businesses multiplied by 20 between 1992 and 1995. In 1992 alone, 120,000 civil servants quit their jobs, and 10 million took unpaid leave to set up private enterprises. Millions of university professors, engineers and graduates followed suit. Even the *People's Daily* ran an article under the headline "Want to Get Rich, Get Busy!"[85]

The official proclamation of the market economy at the Fourteenth Congress of the Chinese Communist Party in October 1992 – a step that would have been unthinkable only a few years before – proved a milestone on the road to capitalism. The reforms continued to gain momentum. Although the party stopped short of dispensing with economic planning altogether, the list of government-set prices for raw materials, transportation services and capital goods was shortened from 737 to 89, with a further reduction to only 13 to follow in 2001. The percentage of intermediate goods (i.e. products that are made during a manufacturing process but that are also used in the production of other goods) transacted at market prices rose from 0% in 1978 to 46% in 1991 and 78% in 1995.[86]

In a parallel development, attempts were made to reform state-run enterprises. Previously under public ownership, many were now part-owned by private citizens and foreign investors. Their employees lost their guarantee of lifelong employment, although they received a one-off payment by way of compensation. The government also introduced social security benefits.

The reformers initially hoped to make public enterprises more efficient by introducing performance-related payment schemes for senior executives and employees. They also brought in professionals to replace the high-ranking cadres who had been in charge of decision-making processes.[87]

These steps did achieve some progress as well as boosting morale among employees. However, they failed to address the key issue – namely, that state-owned enterprises cannot go bankrupt. In a market economy, there is a constant process of selection, which ensures the survival of well-managed companies that satisfy the demands of consumers while badly managed companies producing goods consumers don't want to buy will sooner or later go bankrupt and disappear from the market. Since public enterprises are not subject to any such selection, they were frequently in bad economic health, with less than a third of China's state-owned enterprises (SOEs) turning a profit in the mid-1990s.[88]

However, privatization continued apace during the 1990s, including with a number of companies going public. In 1978, SOEs dependent on central or local government bureaucracies still accounted for 77% of total industrial production, while collectively owned enterprises (COEs) – which, though nominally owned by the workers, were controlled by local governments or party cadres – made up the remaining 23%. By 1996, the share of SOEs had dropped to a third of total industrial production, with COEs (36%), private enterprises (19%) and foreign-financed companies (12%) accounting for the rest. With the total number of SOEs falling by 50% between 1996 and 2006, between 30 million and 40 million people employed by SOEs lost their jobs.[89]

There was strong competition between the Industrial and Special Economic Zones that sprang up across China. Foreign investors were welcomed with open arms and started to discover China both as a manufacturing base and as a new export market for consumer goods manufactured elsewhere.

How did this happen? The Chinese political leadership never pursued an official policy of privatizing public enterprises.[90] Rather, the hope was to be able to maintain public ownership by granting a sufficient level of autonomy to the enterprises in question and adequately incentivizing their management. However, this approach failed for reasons analysed by the renowned Chinese economist Zhang Weiying: from the mid-1990s onwards, many of the public enterprises, that had by then achieved a high level of autonomy, started selling their products at bargain prices, frequently below production cost. The losses incurred were absorbed by government subsidies.[91]

In a market economy based on private ownership, there are strong incentives for companies to build and maintain a good reputation. For China's SOEs, this was far less important. Their executives were more interested in raising their income in the short term. Since there is no way for consumers to sanction dishonest practices by executives of public enterprises, fraud was a frequent issue.[92] Not having the freedom to trade the firm's name – in which the value of the intangible asset of reputation is embedded – in the free market further removed the incentive to protect a company's reputation.

There was also a raft of privatizations that happened spontaneously or at the instigation of local governments. Many SOEs were not competitive enough to survive under market conditions. As Zhang demonstrates, decentralization and the introduction of economic competition unleashed a dynamic that led to the share of SOEs dropping from close to 80% of total industrial output in 1978 to just over a quarter in 1997. Once again, the market forces of economic competition had proved "far more powerful than ideology" despite the fact that privatization has never been adopted as an official government policy.[93]

To understand the dynamics of the Chinese reforms, it is crucial to note that the extent to which they were initiated 'from above' was only one part of the picture. Many contributing factors happened spontaneously – a triumph of market forces over government policy. "Key institutional innovations were instigated, not in the offices of the Politburo, but by countless anonymous agents acting on a local level, and in many cases against the rules."[94]

This is one reason why the Chinese market economy works better than the 'free markets' in Russia and other former communist Eastern Bloc countries, where reforms were frequently imposed from one day to the next, rather than allowed to evolve slowly from the bottom up. In China, this was more easily possible because, even under Mao, the government had never pursued quite as rigorous a hands-on economic policy as in the Soviet Union, for example. While economic planning is still nominally in force in China today, the Chinese economy was never subject to the same rigid controls and government-set targets as other, more traditional planned economies. "In China, political institutions acting according to plan does not necessarily constitute the normal state of affairs. Instead, their actions routinely run counter to plan, undermining or counteracting regulations. Despite the professionalization of bureaucratic processes, individuals in high office hold a great deal of authority to circumvent or interpret regulations in idiosyncratic ways."[95]

This description typifies China's transformation from socialism to capitalism. While terms such as 'socialism', 'economic planning', 'Marxism' and 'Mao Zedong thought' remain in use, they are either rendered meaningless by contemporary reinterpretations or assigned a new meaning in diametric opposition to their original content. This probably contributed greatly to the smooth transition from a socialist planned economy to free-market capitalism.

While China's ruling party continues to refer to itself as 'communist', in reality it is now communist in name only. Admittedly, China hasn't become a democracy – but that was never Deng's intention. At the same time, it would be equally wrong to deny that the political system has undergone significant change. The removal from positions of influence of those within the party who remained faithful to Mao's socialist legacy and fought the reforms, fearing – with good reason – that they would lead China into capitalism, was the prerequisite for the success of a transformation that in turn led to what was probably the largest and fastest growth in prosperity in human history.

China's development in recent decades demonstrates that rising economic growth – even when accompanied by rising inequality – benefits the majority of the population. Hundreds of millions of people in China are far better off today as a direct result of Deng's instruction "let some people get rich first". The outcomes confirm that Deng was right to make economic development his government's top priority: the regions with the fastest GDP growth also saw the most rapid drop in the poverty rate. No less remarkable is the extent to which income mobility increased across the whole country.[96] The gap between rich and poor also widened during this period, raising the national Gini coefficient, which measures the income gap, to 0.47 by 2012 (a level at which it has held steady until today). It is worth noting that income distribution is more equal in urban than in rural areas.

In this context, Zhang points out a number of seemingly paradoxical findings based on his analysis of interregional statistics. Relative income gaps are narrowest in regions with the highest per-capita GDP, while "regions with relatively low income growth have the widest relative income gaps".[97]

While regions where the remaining SOEs have a larger share of the economy might be expected to have narrower income gaps than those with larger shares of private enterprises, the statistics show that the opposite is true. Equally, income distribution might be expected to be least unequal in regions with higher government expenditures as a proportion of the GDP. Again, the opposite is true.[98] Zhang cites a number of other cliché-busting statistics, including the observation that income gaps are narrower in areas where markets are most open and companies make the highest profits.[99]

For all the positive developments China has seen in recent decades, a lot still remains to be done. Although its economic growth was accompanied by an increase in economic freedom, there are still deficits in many areas. While the 2018 Index of Economic Freedom ranks China among the countries with the strongest growth in economic freedom,[100] in the overall ranking it still languishes in 110th place.[101] In terms of the individual indicators (see Chapter 8 for more detailed information), China's scores for 'fiscal health', 'trade freedom', 'government spending', 'monetary freedom' and 'tax burden' are already within the acceptable range. Unfortunately, the same can't be said for 'investment freedom', 'financial freedom', 'property rights', 'government integrity' and 'business freedom'.

In other words, China has both a strong need for further reforms and a great potential for further improvement and growth. Zhang – who, as well as being certainly the most astute analyst of the Chinese economy, has himself contributed significantly to its development – stresses: "China's reforms started with an all-powerful government under the planned economy. The reason China was able to sustain its economic growth during the process of reform was because the government intervened less and the proportion of state-owned enterprises decreased, not the other way around. It was precisely the relaxation of government control that brought about market prices, sole proprietorships, town and village enterprises, private enterprises, foreign enterprises, and other non-state-owned entities."[102] Taken together, all of this formed the basis for China's unprecedented economic rise.

Commentators frequently cite the strong influence of the state on the country's economic transformation as evidence that China's road to capitalism was a special case. However, given the nature of this transformation from a socialist state-controlled to a capitalist economy, this is less exceptional than it may appear at first sight. In many ways, there was nothing all that special about the road China took, as Zhang points out: "In fact, China's economic development is fundamentally the same as some economic development in Western countries – such as Great Britain during the Industrial Revolution, the US in the late 19th and early 20th centuries, and some East Asian countries such as Japan and South Korea after World War II. Once market forces are introduced and the right incentives are set up for people to pursue wealth, the miracle of growth will follow sooner or later."[103]

In the final analysis, the secret to China's success was the gradual liberalization of the economy from state control and the reorientation of aspirations from government jobs towards entrepreneurship. This latter factor, in particular, is a lesson other countries embarking on the road to capitalism, economic growth and prosperity would be well advised to heed: "Thus, we may conclude that the allocation of entrepreneurial talents between government and businesses is one of the most important determinants – even if not the only determinant – of developing an economy."[104] The importance of this observation cannot be overstated: prior to the reforms, higher incomes and social status were reserved for those in government work. As Zhang points out, "Throughout the 1980s, entrepreneurship was ranked very low in social and political status, and government work was still the most attractive occupation for all Chinese people".[105]

Things finally started to change in the 1990s, when liberalization began to gain momentum in the wake of the Fourteenth Congress of the Chinese Communist Party in particular. Increasingly, the brightest talents no longer aspired to safe jobs as government employees – rather, their greatest ambition was to become entrepreneurs, which would raise their status along with their income. Rural Chinese were the first to embrace self-employment, followed by a second phase of former civil servants taking over enterprises they had previously managed as government employees. Finally, many of the tens of thousands of young Chinese who returned from their studies overseas joined the ranks of the new entrepreneurs.[106]

None of this would have been possible if it hadn't been for the legalization of the right to private ownership. This wasn't an overnight transition to full

Western-style property rights, but rather a step-by-step process that started in the early 1980s and in 2004 culminated in the introduction of a new constitution, which officially recognized private property rights.[107] There were many interim steps, including the gradual transition of public enterprises into the ownership of their management.

As Zhang emphasizes, this process of transformation is far from complete today: "Government control over large amounts of resources and excessive intervention into the economy are the direct cause of cronyism between officials and businessmen, are a breeding ground for official corruption, seriously corrupt commercial culture, and damage the market's rules of the game." Accordingly, he sees a strong need for further reforms "toward marketization, reduction of government control over resources and intervention into the economy, and the establishment of a true rule-of-law society and democratic politics".[108] Whether or not China will go down that road remains to be seen. The process of reform has never been a smooth and consistent one – rather, it has been marred by frequent setbacks, especially in recent years, when instances of governmental intervention in the economy have set back the reform process. China's positive development will continue only if it stays true to its current course of steering the economy towards the introduction of more free-market elements, which has been the basis for the country's enormous success in recent decades. "From the 1950s to 30 years ago, we believed in the planned economy," Zhang says. "The result was a tremendous disaster. If we continue to pin our hopes on the government plan and to use large, state owned enterprises to develop China's economy, we have absolutely no prospects for the future. Only if we move toward the logic of the market will China's future be bright!"[109]

In August 2018, I went on a tour of five Chinese metropolises. Standing in front of a large audience at a lecture in Shanghai, I asked everyone to put their hands up if they were better off today than their parents 30 years ago. Every single hand was raised. Then, in Beijing, I had the pleasure of meeting Professor Zhang Weiying. We spoke at length about China's economic development. He told me that the biggest misconception in China today is that some politicians and economists believe that the country's impressive growth is the result of a special "Chinese way" with a high degree of state influence. Professor Zhang Weiying stressed to me that it is important to understand that the Chinese economic miracle did not happen "because of, but in spite of" the sustained influence of the state.

CHAPTER 2

Africa: Capitalism Is *More* Effective against Poverty *than* Development Aid

In 1990, the UN made a commitment to reduce global poverty by 50% within 25 years. That this ambitious goal has been achieved is largely due to China's success. Within the same period, the percentage of the population living below the poverty line decreased from 56.8% to 42.7% across the African continent.[110] However, with 20% of Africans suffering from starvation – a higher percentage than anywhere else in the world – there is still a long way to go.[111]

The African continent has an unprecedented record of giving rise to distorted impressions. In May 2000, *The Economist* ran a cover story titled "The Hopeless Continent". The cover image showed a heavily armed African male. Almost 12 years later, in December 2011, another cover dedicated to Africa showed an African flying a kite, with the accompanying headline "Africa Rising".[112] The magazine's editor-in-chief ruefully admits: "People have gone to great pains to point out to me that if you invested in a basket of African stocks on the day we declared Africa a 'hopeless continent,' you would be doing quite well today."[113] In fact, investors who bought stocks on the NSE All Share Kenia in 2012 would have doubled their money within five years.

Western ideas of African life tend to conjure up images of a different kind – majestic animals or humans living in abject misery. "Africans who are not animals, despots, or Nelson Mandela are portrayed as suffering under the heel of poverty, war, and disease. Recall the last two movies you saw with Africans in them. You will see what I mean,"[114] says Africa expert Jonathan Berman in his book *Success in Africa*. Western pop stars putting on huge stadium concerts to raise money and awareness for the fight against poverty in Africa have done their share to popularize this image – which, though not completely wrong, is misleading because it only shows part of the picture. Their agenda echoes the demands made by left-wing critics of globalization for more financial aid for Africa. This, they believe, is the solution to the continent's problems.

Development aid has a nice moral ring to it, and in some people's view it constitutes a kind of quasi-religious atonement for the sins of colonialism and the 'exploitation of the Third World' by capitalist countries. But does it really achieve what its proponents hope it will? In 2002, the then Senegalese president Abdoulaye Wade said: "I've never seen a country develop itself through aid or credit. Countries that have developed – in Europe, America, Japan, Asian countries like Taiwan, Korea and Singapore – have all believed in free markets. There is no mystery there. Africa took the wrong road after independence."[115] The road he is referring to, taken by the majority of African countries in the wake of colonialism, was socialism in one form or another.

In Egypt, 'Nasserism' was introduced as an Arabic version of socialism. Eritrea started adopting an Albanian-style Marxism–Leninism in the early 1990s, while Ghana followed the Soviet model of a socialist planned economy and collectivization of agriculture. Congo was ruled by a unity party with a Marxist–Leninist ideology, while Madagascar adopted a socialist constitution based on the model of China and North Korea. Mozambique was ruled by a Marxist–Leninist unity party. Angola, Mali, Guinea, Uganda, Senegal, Sudan, Somalia, Zambia, Zimbabwe, Tanzania and other African countries also subscribed to socialist models. Many Africans dreamt of a distinct form of 'African socialism' that was based on indigenous values such as the notion of tribal communities and was supposed to offer an alternative to capitalism as much as to the versions of socialism practised in the Soviet Union and other Eastern Bloc countries.

The economic results were even more disastrous than in the socialist Eastern Bloc countries. A flawed economic system is only one of many factors causing poverty in Africa, where stable political institutions remain lacking in many countries, while wars and civil wars between enemy tribes or different ethnic groups continue to tear the continent apart.

DEVELOPMENT AID: AT BEST POINTLESS, AT WORST COUNTER-PRODUCTIVE

Zambia-born Dambisa Moyo, who studied at Harvard and earned a PhD from Oxford, identifies Western development aid as one of the reasons for the failure to rid Africa of poverty. "In the past fifty years, over USD 1 trillion in development-related aid has been transferred from rich countries to Africa," Moyo points out in her 2009 book *Dead Aid*. "But has more than US$1 trillion in development assistance over the last several decades made African people better off? No. In fact, across the globe the recipients of this aid are worse off; much worse off. Aid has helped make the poor poorer, and growth slower …

The notion that aid can alleviate systemic poverty, and has done so, is a myth. Millions in Africa are poorer today because of aid; misery and poverty have not ended but have increased. Aid has been, and continues to be, an unmitigated political, economic, and humanitarian disaster for most parts of the developing world."[116]

To be clear, Moyo's criticism is not directed against ad hoc famine and disaster relief but against long-term financial transfers aimed at boosting economic development. These funds have frequently ended up in the hands of corrupt despots rather than those of the poor. "Even when aid has not been stolen, it has been unproductive. The proof of the pudding is in the eating, and ever so clearly the preponderance of evidence is on this side. Given Africa's current economic state, it is hard to see how any growth registered is a direct result of aid. If anything, the evidence of the last fifty years points to the reverse – slower growth, higher poverty and Africa left off the economic ladder."[117]

A World Bank study found that as much as 85% of aid flows were used "for purposes other than that for which they were initially intended, very often diverted to unproductive, if not grotesque ventures".[118] Even where these funds are spent on projects that do achieve positive outcomes, their long-term consequences frequently outweigh any short-term gains. To illustrate this pernicious effect, Moyo tells the story of a local mosquito net maker who manufactures around 500 nets a week. His ten employees each support at least 15 relatives. Then a well-meaning Hollywood movie star persuades Western governments to collect and send 100,000 mosquito nets to the region, at a cost of a million dollars. The nets arrive, promptly putting the mosquito net maker out of business and forcing the 150 dependents of his workers to live on handouts. [119]

As Moyo points out, poverty in Africa rose from 11% to 66% between 1970 and 1998, when aid flows to Africa were at their peak.[120] Foreign aid, she goes on to argue, "props up corrupt governments – providing them with freely usable cash. These corrupt governments interfere with the rule of law, the establishment of transparent civil institutions and the protection of civil liberties, making both domestic and foreign investment in poor countries unattractive."[121] This, in turn, inhibits the development of a working capitalist economy, and thus leads to economic stagnation and a "culture of aid-dependency" that encourages "governments to support large, unwieldy and often unproductive public sectors – just another way to reward their cronies".[122]

James Shikwati, the director of the Inter Region Economic Network in Nairobi, Kenya, confirms: "If the West were to cancel these payments, normal Africans wouldn't even notice. Only the functionaries would be hard hit."[123] Shikwati explains: "Huge bureaucracies are financed, corruption and complacency are promoted,

Africans are taught to be beggars and not to be independent. In addition, development aid weakens the local markets everywhere and dampens the spirit of entrepreneurship that we so desperately need. As absurd as it may sound: Development aid is one of the reasons for Africa's problems."[124]

William Easterly, Professor of Economics and African Studies at New York University, believes that foreign aid is largely pointless and frequently counter-productive. Over two decades, "foreign aid donors spent two billion dollars in Tanzania ... building roads", he reports. "The road network did not improve. Roads deteriorated faster than donors built new ones, due to lack of maintenance." While the roads fell into disrepair, bureaucracy thrived. "Tanzania produced more than 2,400 reports a year for its aid donors, who sent the beleaguered recipient one thousand missions of donor officials per year." Foreign aid failed to supply the roads that were badly needed, although "it did supply a lot of something the poor probably had little use for".[125]

FROM STATE CONTROL TO FREE-MARKET ECONOMY?

If development aid for African countries has proved largely pointless or even counter-productive, did the turn away from state-controlled to free-market systems bring about better outcomes? In the late 1980s, when the collapse of socialism in the Soviet Union and the Eastern Bloc countries compellingly demonstrated the triumph of capitalism as the superior system, many African countries started privatizing their economies, turning their backs on state-controlled models. In 1990, 40 sub-Saharan African countries agreed to restructuring measures proposed by the International Monetary Fund (IMF). This included the privatization of public enterprises as a key component. Across all sectors – manufacturing and industry, agriculture, tourism, services, trade, transport, finance, energy, mining, water, electricity and telecommunications – "the government stake of corporate equity fell from almost 90 per cent to just 10 per cent ownership in six years".[126]

Countries such as Nigeria, which is today one of the continent's leading economic players along with South Africa, have completely deregulated all former state monopolies to establish a free-market system. With one single exception – Eritrea, which has retained a state-controlled economy – systems that are more or less free market oriented are dominant across the African continent today,[127] although they continue to be plagued by significant problems that hamper economic growth. While privatization did create an important precondition for resolving these problems, it has proved to be merely a necessary condition for more growth, though not in itself sufficient to overcome the far more complex causes of poverty across Africa. In many countries, economic development is held back by huge debts, while privatization has done little to tackle corruption and cultural mentalities that constitute obstacles to growth.

Easterly provides plenty of real-world evidence for an explanation that is crucial to understanding the evolution of capitalism: "Free markets work, but free-market reforms often don't".[128] By its nature – and in distinct contrast to socialist models of economic planning – capitalism is a social order that emerges as the result of a spontaneous development, rather than a system that relies on human invention and design. The top-down attempts by the World Bank and the IMF to impose a free-market economy on African countries in the early 1990s were doomed to fail in the same way as any attempt to enforce democracy in a country without organic democratic traditions. "Trying to change the rules all at once with the rapid introduction of free markets disrupted the old ties, while the new formal institutions were still too weak to make free markets work well. Gradual movement to freer markets would have given the participants more time to adjust their relationships and trades."[129]

Contrary to common misconceptions, there is more to capitalism and free-market economics than privatization. The Index of Economic Freedom, published annually by the Heritage Foundation, uses 12 criteria to measure economic freedom.[130] The 2018 index shows a bleak outlook for the vast majority of African countries. Apart from North Korea and Venezuela, the lowest-scoring category is largely composed of African countries, including Zimbabwe, Algeria, Guinea, Angola, Sudan and Mozambique.

A closer analysis of the factors behind the lack of economic freedom in these countries pinpoints three major issues. In the Heritage Foundation index, sub-Saharan African countries score lowest for 'property rights', 'judicial effectiveness' and 'government integrity'.[131] In other words, property rights are not guaranteed to a sufficient extent, nor is there any guarantee of judicial due process.

CORRUPTION: CAUSES AND CONSEQUENCES

Administrative and political corruption are still rife in these countries. Namibia, which achieved an overall score of 58.5 out of 100 for 'economic freedom' in the Heritage Foundation index, only scored 45.4 for 'government integrity', while Zimbabwe did even worse with a score of 18.9 out of 100[132] (compared to

71.9 for the US, 75.3 for Germany and 93.6 for Norway).[133] Analyses by the anti-corruption organization Transparency International highlight the root causes of Africa's problems. The organization has developed an index to measure and compare the perception of corruption in different countries.[134] None of the 54 African countries made it into the 20 lowest-scoring countries. On the other hand, of the 20 countries with the highest scores for perceived corruption, two thirds are in Africa. Somalia comes last among the 176 countries included in the index.

The German sociologist Jörn Sommer spent several years researching corruption in Africa, using Benin as an example. He blames the difficulties of uncovering and fighting corruption on what he calls a "repressive community of understanding", which interprets even routine company management audits – which are standard practice everywhere in the world – as a form of 'trouble-making'. Accordingly, members of the community shy away from dissent since the whistleblower who uncovers acts of corruption is more likely to be ostracized than the person committing them. Any criticism is stifled by appeals to 'harmony' and 'mutual agreement'. In the worst-case scenario, embezzled funds are 'distributed' – read: used as bribes – in order to restore peace.[135]

In African countries, men are expected to be able to feed large families of as many as 40 people. A public servant's refusal to accept bribes would be met with outrage by his family and larger community, who would interpret it as a dereliction of duty. Asked what they would think of a man who after his time in office as finance minister returned to his modest home in a small town, students at the University of Nigeria said he would be a "fool", "mentally retarded" and "incompetent".[136]

James Mworia, CEO of Centrum Investments, East Africa's largest investment company listed on the stock exchange: "Steve Jobs is not from Kenya, why? Because the Steve Jobs of this world have not been able to navigate the corruption … There were probably hundreds of such great entrepreneurs and great ideas that could not flourish for this reason."[137]

Because of the corruption and inefficient economic order, the impact of debt-relief measures for African countries along the lines of the 2005 initiative by the G8 finance ministers is limited. To be truly effective, it would need to go hand in hand with the creation of functioning institutions, efficient anti-corruption measures and systematic pro-market reforms. Otherwise, debt relief achieves very little, as several attempts in the past have shown. In fact, in some cases they even had the opposite effect and created negative incentives. Take the example of Uganda: in the year 2000, Uganda had a total debt of USD 3.2 billion and was the beneficiary of debt relief to the tune of USD 2 billion. Six years later, Uganda's debt stood at almost USD 5 billion. Meanwhile, the country's president,

Yoweri Kaguta Museveni, had treated himself to a jet worth USD 35 million and increased his staff to 109 advisers and 69 ministers.[138]

As Easterly demonstrates, debt relief and repeated IMF and World Bank lending have failed to achieve the desired outcomes. When the debt load became so extreme that the IMF and the World Bank, for the first time in their history, forgave part of their own loans, this only removed any incentive for the debtor countries to achieve the growth that would have enabled them to service their debts.[139]

One of Africa's largest problems is the lack of legal guarantees, which affects small entrepreneurs in particular. Based on his extensive research into the reasons for the economic problems of developing countries, the economist Hernando de Soto highlights the scale of the problem.[140] In these countries, informal business transactions account for the largest share of the economy. Although not strictly within the realm of legality, these provide a living for a large part of the population. Small entrepreneurs who trade goods or run small businesses without government approval assume full liability, with no legal recourse for any risks, making themselves vulnerable to extortion by corrupt officials. The lack of legal guarantees for property rights means that they are often unable to take out loans.

It is difficult to overestimate the significance of this informal economy in African countries. According to estimates published between 2000 and 2006, this sector generated 42% of the total African GDP and provided jobs for 78% of the workforce in sub-Saharan countries (except South Africa). In rural areas, as many as 90% of all non-agricultural workers made their living in the informal economy.[141] The telecommunications provider Celtel initially went into its new business venture in the Congo in 2007 with low expectations due to the country's very low per-capita GDP and was surprised when 10,000 new customers signed contracts within the first month, 2,000 of them within the first week. All of them paid in cash.[142] Accordingly, the official GDP figures quoted in this chapter do not tell the whole story.

AFRICA: A CHANGING CONTINENT

Many people are unaware of the sheer size of Africa, which is misrepresented on most commonly used maps of the world. To fly from the north to the south of the continent takes as long as flying from Los Angeles to Frankfurt. Africa is larger than the combined areas of the US, China, India, Spain, Germany, France, Italy and Eastern Europe.[143]

In the course of the past ten years, some African countries have undergone significant development. Western media primarily show images of desperate refugees coming to Europe in search of a better life, but again, this is only one side of the story. Africa is a massive continent full of contradictions and contrasts. According to the Heritage Foundation's classification of countries by the degree of economic freedom they offer, African countries are divided into four groups: Mauritius has the greatest level of economic freedom, followed by Botswana, Rwanda, South Africa, Uganda, Côte d'Ivoire, Seychelles, Burkina Faso and Cabo Verde, which are classed as 'moderately free'. All other African countries are more or less 'unfree', with Zimbabwe, Equatorial Guinea, Eritrea and the Republic of Congo bringing up the rear. Somalia is one of the few countries for which no score is available.[144] While the per-capita GDPs of over USD 27,000 in the Seychelles and USD 20,422 in Mauritius are higher than that of China (15,399 USD), and while Botswana comes close with a GDP of just over USD 17,000, Sudan's per-capita GDP of USD 4,447 shows just how large the gap is between different African countries.[145]

In a number of African countries – in particular where economic freedom is growing – there are unmissable signs of positive developments. Even in a country such as Mozambique, which is among the unfree countries with large economic problems, there is evidence that things are changing. Hans Stoisser, a business consultant with many years' experience of working in Africa, says: "When I first came to Mozambique in the early 1990s, the streets were still full of emaciated and impoverished people in threadbare clothing, women cooking outside on the street, almost everybody traveling on foot. Today, it's a completely different picture, with supermarkets, coffee shops, traffic jams, modern offices and shopping centers – the new meeting points where members of the African elite get together – and flashy night clubs. Of course, the construction boom also manifests itself in countless building sites blocking the roads and pavements. Contemporary urban Mozambique is in step with global business culture and has little in common with 1990s Mozambique."[146] These changes became possible only after the Frelimo government's severance of its ties to Marxism in 1989, the introduction of a constitution guaranteeing (in theory, if not in practice) free elections and a free-market economy in 1990, and the end of the civil war in 1992.

NATURAL RESOURCES: A BLESSING OR A CURSE?

As a consequence of the global economic boom and China's massive demand, natural resource prices rose sharply in the first decade of the 21st century, boosting economic growth in Africa. In 2010, economic growth in 22 African countries exceeded 6%. Equally, the drop in natural resource prices from 2011 onwards had a knock-on effect on economic performance in many countries across the region. In 2015, only nine countries recorded growth rates above 6%, while the number of African countries with two-digit inflation rates rose from four to ten in the same period.[147]

The following figures should suffice to show the qualitative difference between economic growth in Asia and Africa: between 2000 and 2010, both continents experienced a 500% growth in exports. However, while an increase in processed goods accounted for four fifths of the Asian growth, the same proportion of the growth across Africa was due to significant increases in commodity prices.[148]

Natural resources account for around 50% of all African exports and for only 10% of all exports from Asia, Europe and the US.[149] With 12% of all known oil deposits located in Africa and the percentage of still undiscovered deposits likely to be even higher, the continent's natural resources constitute a massive asset. According to estimates from the Energy Information Administration of the United States Department of Energy, Africa has seen its oil reserves increasing by 120% over the past 30 years to a current level of 126 billion barrels, with an estimated 100 billion barrels yet to be found. The continent also has a large share of all known gold (40%), platinum (80%) and cobalt (60%) deposits.[150]

However, equating vast reserves of natural resources with massive economic opportunity would be too simplistic. Far from automatically leading to prosperity, natural resources can even hamper development and create new issues. History is rife with examples of large-scale exporters of natural resources coming to economic grief because they relied on these assets and failed to diversify. To make matters worse, the resulting trade surpluses drove up the value of their currencies, making it harder to sell goods produced in other industries and thus exacerbating their economies' reliance on the export of natural resources.[151] Finally, large deposits of natural resources can create a strong temptation for a country's elites to make their living as rentiers whose wealth derives from the short supply of individual goods, rather than from profits generated by businesses. It is no accident that the resource-richest African countries are not the continent's greatest economic success stories.

Based on his research, the renowned economist Paul Collier lists the massive deposits of natural resources as one reason why many African countries fail to develop. The 'natural resource trap' Collier diagnoses is caused by a combination of factors including those discussed above. Fluctuating earnings are not conducive to sustainable economic success. The past 20 years have shown natural resource prices to be extremely volatile. During price booms, government ministries tend to increase spending to outrageous levels.[152] Chapter 6 will discuss the disastrous impact on Venezuela of sharp increases in commodity prices (the country with the largest oil deposits in the world), which fuelled excessive government spending.

In Ghana, too, large deposits of natural resources proved to be more of a curse than a blessing. The country was well on its way to economic success by the time vast oil deposits were discovered 40 miles off the Ghanaian coast in 2007. Commercial exploitation started three years later. Ghana's then president, John Kufuor, euphorically predicted a bright future for his country: "With oil as a shot in the arm, we're going to fly," he told the BBC at the time. Emmanuel Graham, a natural resource expert at the Africa Centre for Energy Policy, revealed that a significant share of the oil profits flowed into the president's coffers. A report in a leading Swiss newspaper quotes Graham as blaming a "kind of mental natural resource curse" for the government's loss of any budgetary restraint as soon as the extraction of the oil deposits commenced.[153] When commodity prices started dropping, the problems became obvious. In April 2015, Ghana was forced to negotiate a USD 920 million extended credit facility from the IMF.

On the other hand, recent developments in Rwanda show that a lack of natural resources doesn't necessarily hold a country back economically. In the mid-1990s, up to a million Rwandans – including almost all members of the small East African country's elite – perished during the genocide perpetrated by the Hutu against the Tutsi minority. Today, Rwanda has changed beyond recognition. "The country now has a well-developed road network, building projects are going on everywhere in the capital Kigali, and restaurants and coffee shops provide free wireless internet access as a matter of course." With school enrolment rates at nearly 100%, 91% of the country's 13 million residents covered by health insurance, and average economic growth rates of around 8% for the period between 2001 and 2015, Rwanda is way ahead of many of its African neighbours. "The government is committed to an investor-friendly free-market policy. The country has achieved a huge leap forward in the World Bank's Doing Business ranking ... To make up for its lack of natural resources, Rwanda is trying to leverage knowledge as its main source of income with the aim of becoming the regional leader in information and communication technologies."[154] The Rwandan example proves that economic freedom trumps mineral deposits when it comes to promoting economic growth. After all, Rwanda comes 39th out of a total of 180 countries – ahead of Spain and France in 60th and 71st place respectively[155] – and third out of the 48 sub-Saharan African countries in the global Index of Economic Freedom, and is on course for further growth.[156]

Kenya provides further evidence to disprove the assumption that natural resources are a prerequisite for economic growth in African countries.[157]

The former British colony has always been among the economic powerhouses in East Africa, if not the entire continent. Although bisected by the equator, Kenya benefits from a less oppressive climate than the west of Africa. Since large swathes of the country are situated at altitudes of between 6,000 and 7,000 feet, temperatures remain at pleasant levels throughout the year. Its moderate climate and high elevations make Kenya an ideal location to grow coffee and tea – a way of life memorably captured in Karen Blixen's semi-autobiographical novel *Out of Africa*. Cattle farming on the savannahs and, later on, the cultivation of colonial exports such as pineapples provided additional revenue streams.

Kenya's entrepreneurs are the country's most important asset. The country's independence in 1963 brought an end to restrictions on its citizens' freedom to travel, settle and work and was quickly followed by a strong economic upswing supported by thousands of local entrepreneurs and the influx of foreign capital. Although plagued by widespread corruption in its government and administration, Kenya has been able to sustain this positive economic trend ever since, with a solid entrepreneurial base developing despite ongoing political unrest – from small tradespeople who sometimes hire a few employees when they have a lot of work coming in to large companies whose sphere of influence goes well beyond national borders across the entire region.

In 1984, the Kenyan entrepreneur Peter Munga set up Equity Bank as a small-scale savings and loan operation to help poorer families buy modest first homes. His starting capital of 5,000 shillings was equivalent to around USD 100 at the time. After narrowly escaping bankruptcy a number of times, Munga's decision to entrust the running of the bank to 31-year-old James Mwangi in 1993 turned out to be serendipitous. Now managed by Munga and Mwangi in conjunction, Equity Bank has grown into East Africa's largest bank and one of the most important securities traded on the stock exchange in Nairobi, while staying true to its roots as a port of call for customers who would otherwise be denied access to financial services.

At the start of the new millennium, Kenya became the region's economic powerhouse due to the speed of its growth – all without oil, diamonds, gold or rare earth elements. This boom was triggered by a combination of broadband and mobile technologies and the advent of M-Pesa, a new kind of mobile banking introduced by the mobile communications provider Safaricom. Mobile banking was a game changer for the Kenyan economy because it offered a means of sending money and making cashless payments to millions of Kenyans who were too poor for the banks to bother with them.

M-Pesa is based on the recognition that a pre-paid mobile phone contract works according to the same principle as a bank account: users pay a certain amount into their account and are then able to spend that money on phoning and texting until their credit is used up. But why restrict their spending to phoning and texting only? Instead, M-Pesa allows customers to transfer their credit to other mobile phone users by text messaging.

Many Kenyan men work and live in Nairobi for weeks or even months at a time. Before M-Pesa existed, the only way for them to send money to their families in rural areas was by handing an envelope full of cash to one of the country's army of minibus drivers and paying a hefty fee to make sure it got delivered to a family member at a pre-agreed stop. Although reliable, this was an expensive and complicated system. With M-Pesa, users are now able to transfer money in less than seconds at a fraction of the cost.

Today, Kenyans use M-Pesa not just to pay their rent, utility bills and taxes but also to trade shares and even to buy insurance cover. M-Pesa has increased the population's spending power, making it possible for Kenyans to buy mobile phones, take out basic health insurance, and purchase medicine and many other everyday essentials. According to one estimate, M-Pesa has lifted 2% of the Kenyan population out of extreme poverty.[158] Today, over 40% of Kenya's total GDP passes through M-Pesa and other mobile money platforms.[159]

Above all, the combination of broadband and mobile technologies has led to an unprecedented start-up boom. Across Nairobi, in start-up hubs such as 88mph,[160] software developers are busy designing the apps of tomorrow. While European businesses are still building websites for laptop or desktop computers, their African counterparts have seen the shape of things to come and are primarily targeting mobile internet users. In Kenya, websites are yesterday's news – today it's all about apps. Nairobi's thriving start-up hubs have attracted angel investors, venture capital funds and numerous other service providers, sustaining a boom that is more stable than any economy primarily dependent on natural resources.

AFRICA'S ENTREPRENEURS AND NEW MIDDLE CLASS

Given the real-world examples discussed in the previous section, it would be wrong to assume that positive economic trends across the African continent are caused solely by rising commodity prices. The rise of broadband and mobile technologies has led to a loosening of state control across many industries and allowed entrepreneurs to thrive independent of government support and political connections. Many of this newly emerged class of self-confident young Africans have studied overseas – typically in Europe or the US, but increasingly in China or India as well. Many of them work for international corporations before they return to their native countries.

"Unnoticed by the wealthy global north, Africa is seeing the emergence of a class of entrepreneurs who are driving and shaping the economic upswing across the continent," Christian Hiller von Gaertringen comments.[161] His book – tellingly titled *Afrika ist das neue Asien* (Africa Is the New Asia) – showcases a panoply of impressive examples of the type of entrepreneurship the economist Joseph Schumpeter regarded as an essential precondition for the success of capitalism.

Among the best known of these examples is Mo Ibrahim, who has attained legendary status in Africa.[162] Born in Sudan in 1946, he was a driving force behind the development of mobile phone technologies in Africa and thus helped to bring about what was probably the most revolutionary development since the end of colonialism. He earned a PhD in mobile communications at the University of Birmingham in the UK and helped to develop British Telecom's mobile communications network. Ibrahim suggested taking the new technology to Africa, but – in what would turn out to be an extraordinary stroke of luck for Ibrahim – British Telecom failed to recognize the great potential of this unique opportunity. In 1989, the budding entrepreneur left the company to found a consultancy called MSI (Mobile Systems International), which he went on to sell for USD 900 million to UK-based Marconi Company in 2000. However, before he did so, he spun off MSI-Cellular Investments (later renamed Celtel) as a mobile phone operator, which he used to fund the development of a mobile network in Africa to the tune of several billion. Soon his company started expanding into Nigeria, Kenya, Uganda, Tanzania, Malawi, Zambia, the Democratic Republic of Congo, Congo-Brazzaville, Chad, Niger, Burkina Faso, Sierra Leone, Gabon and Madagascar as well as – trading under a different brand – into Ghana and Sudan. In 2005, Ibrahim sold his company to its Kuwaiti competitor, Zain, for USD 3.4 billion. A few years later, Zain would get a total of USD 10.7 billion for its African business.

The mobile phone market is a prime example of European and American misperceptions of economic developments in Africa. Across the continent, the penetration rate for mobile phone technology (measured as the number of mobile phone contracts per 100 residents) exploded from 15.3% to 84.9% (2015) within a decade,[163] with 14 African countries reporting penetration rates of over 100% in 2014.[164] Reflecting on these transformations, an African businessman talks about his driver, who used to have to take three to four days off work to take money home to his family. Today, he sends a single text message.[165] Likewise, mobile phones have greatly simplified the job of vegetable vendors, who, instead of having to go house to house, now take their orders by phone and get paid by phone as well.[166] This is 21st-century Africa.

Asked for their most positive images of Africa, one in three respondents to a Europe-wide TNS poll for the European Commission mentioned natural reserves, and one in four beautiful scenery. Only 1% mentioned new business models such as mobile banking, while 3% mentioned enterprise.[167] On the other hand, the Tony Elumelu Foundation Entrepreneurship Programme, set up by the eponymous Nigerian investment banker and entrepreneur, received 45,000 applications from across the continent in 2016, 1,000 of which were selected for funding and professional development.[168]

Notwithstanding the positive trends discussed above, there are still plenty of obstacles blocking further growth in Africa. According to statistics compiled by the World Bank, setting up a new company takes much longer in Angola (36 days), Nigeria (31 days) or South Africa (46 days) than in the UK (5 days) or the US (6 days). It is worth noting that Rwanda, whose economic success has already been discussed, is ahead of most Western countries in this particular statistic with a lead time of only 5.5 days. It is also worth noting that lead times for setting up a company have been slashed over the past ten years – from an unbelievable 116 days in 2006 to 19 days in contemporary Mozambique, and from 36 to 9 days in Zambia over the same period. Entrepreneurship enjoys a positive social status and a high level of acceptance among the general public across sub-Saharan Africa, and in Botswana, Ghana and Rwanda.[169]

Africa is a continent of stark contrasts. On the one hand, more people suffer from starvation in Africa than anywhere else in the world. On the other hand, more bottles of champagne were sold across Africa in 2011 than anywhere else outside of Europe and the US. Over 750,000 of the 10 million bottles exported to Africa were sold in Nigeria alone.[170] Africa reports faster growth rates in the number of ultra-high-net-worth individuals (UHNWIs, individuals with a personal wealth of at least USD 30 million) than any other continent. According to the 2016 Knight Frank Wealth Report, over half of the 20 countries with the highest growth rates in the numbers of UHNWIs over the previous ten years are in Africa. In Kenya, for example, the number of UHNWIs grew by 93% between 2006 and 2016 – globally, only Vietnam, India and China reported stronger growth rates. According to predictions by Knight Frank, over the next ten years growth rates in Africa are set to remain higher than in the US and Europe.[171]

As in China, growing numbers of UHNWIs coincide with the growth of the middle class. Some estimates now set the number of middle-class Africans as high as 350 million, around a third of the total population across the continent, and a rise of over 200% over the past 30 years. However, half of these are living barely above the poverty line.[172] In this context, it is important to be aware that the relevant studies define 'middle class' in terms that are different from those applied in industrialized countries. In emerging countries, the definition includes households whose standard of living only just exceeds the poverty line.[173]

However, even if a narrower definition is applied, the African middle class still numbers 150 million individuals whose lives are free of existential worries and who have the means to afford healthcare, holidays, property and a far better education for their children than they themselves enjoyed. The stupendous growth in the numbers of mobile phones and cars is an indicator of the growing middle class.[174] "New restaurants, nail salons, car dealerships, cinemas and night clubs are transforming the cityscape of urban centres across Africa almost from one day to the next. An increasing number of Africans wear well-known fashion brands. People are driving more expensive cars, Japanese and Korean models in particular. The signs are there for all to see: the African middle class is growing."[175]

The growth of the middle class is accelerating urbanization processes across the continent. The world's fourth-largest city, immediately behind Beijing and Shanghai, is in Africa: the Nigerian capital, Lagos, with a population of over 18 million. Kinshasa, the capital of the Democratic Republic Congo, has more than 10 million residents. At 46, the number of cities with a population of a million or more residents is twice as high as in Europe.[176]

CHINA'S ROLE IN AFRICA

Alongside the emergence and growth of an African middle class and the evolution of entrepreneurial initiative, the strong commitment invested into African economies by countries such as India, China and Brazil is another reason for the positive economic development in many African countries. Having successfully negotiated its own transformation from a poor socialist country of peasants to a capitalist economic powerhouse, China is now applying the same model to the African continent.

The evolution of Chinese business interests in Africa followed a simple four-step concept. The initial focus was on securing access to Africa's vast reserves of resources, including oil, iron ore, diamonds, cotton, wood, rice and sugar cane. In exchange, the Chinese financed huge infrastructure projects in Africa and made their technology available to their African partners. In a second step, they started exporting Chinese consumer goods to Africa to access the world's largest untapped market, with a total population of 1.2 billion, among them 250 million members of the newly emerging middle class. China was among the first to recognize the potential of this market, although initially the bulk of exports to Africa consisted of low-quality products at medium-range prices.[177]

In step three, Chinese companies outsourced some of their production to Africa in order to cut costs – African wages are lower than in newly affluent contemporary China – while at the same time raising their profile as a creator of jobs for Africans. Step four saw Chinese companies starting to manufacture goods for the African market in Africa.

A conference planned by the Chinese leader Hu Jintao in Beijing in November 2006 proved an important milestone in China's economic involvement across Africa. The Chinese hosts spared no effort to make the African delegates feel welcome. The streets of Beijing were ablaze with the flags of the 48 African nations invited to the conference. While comparable events organized in Europe tend to focus on development aid, the Beijing conference was all about the mutual benefits of economic cooperation between China and African countries. "China is executing its resource strategy with considerable aplomb, doing seemingly everything it can to make certain that commodity deals benefit both signatories to the trades. In fact, the motivation for the host countries is also not complicated: they need infrastructure, and they need to finance projects that can unlock economic growth. To achieve this, they are willing to sell their assets to the highest bidder. This is the genius of the China strategy: every country gets what it wants."[178] Between 1998 and 2012, some 2,000 Chinese companies made investments in 49 African countries.[179]

In November 2014, China signed a contract for the construction of a railway line along the coast of Nigeria. This project alone is worth USD 12 billion. The construction of the line, with a total length of around 875 miles, is set to create 200,000 temporary jobs during the construction phase and 30,000 permanent local jobs[180] – not to mention the significant long-term impact of a project of this kind on what is already Africa's largest economy. The China Railway Construction Corporation is currently committed to 112 projects with a total contract volume of USD 30 billion in Nigeria alone.[181]

It is impossible to overstate the significance of these projects on a continent where the lack of adequate infrastructure – the paucity and poor condition of roads, underdeveloped flight and rail networks, and, above all, an insufficient and unreliable power supply – is one of the main obstacles to further growth, according to studies.[182] The Chinese, of course, are well aware of this issue and are addressing it by investing massively into infrastructure projects across Africa.

Although China's African business strategy is frequently criticized for serving China's own interests, these accusations fail to convince. After all, following the opening of its markets to foreign investors, China itself profited from investments – notably by companies from Hong Kong and Europe – driven by shrewd business sense rather than pure altruism. More recently, its economic involvement across Africa has produced mutual benefits for both sides. According to China experts Andreas and Frank Sieren, "Two decades of Chinese investments in Africa have done more to help the continent than half a century of development aid from Western countries".[183]

Surveys show that it only took a few years for China's influence to be viewed far more favourably across much of Africa than that of the US.[184] More recently, however, the Chinese came close to losing the African consumers' trust due to the poor quality of goods exported to African markets and the perceived failure to create local jobs. This is one of the reasons why Chinese companies started outsourcing parts of their production to Africa. China established a large number of Special Economic Zones across Africa, thus successfully transferring a model that had contributed significantly to its own economic upswing and transition to a capitalist economy, as discussed in Chapter 1.[185]

AFRICA: A SECOND ASIA?

Will the investments made by China, India and other countries have the same impact as foreign investments did in China after the country's opening? Is Africa a second Asia, as some commentators like to claim? There are good reasons to be sceptical. Foreign investments and the creation of more market-oriented economic systems in individual countries are not the only prerequisites for growth and prosperity. The situation in Africa is replete with challenges that didn't exist in post-reform China: civil wars, tribal rivalries and insufficient levels of institutionalization. Another question is whether African populations will be able to muster or develop the strong discipline and willingness to work that distinguish many Asian populations even in comparison to European and North American competitors.

One major issue is the continuing influence of the state on private enterprise, which studies have shown to be stronger in many African countries than in other parts of the world.[186] Sam Jonah, the former CEO of AngloGold Ashanti, the first African company listed on the New York Stock Exchange, explains why the dominating role of the state in many African economies is so pernicious: "African money, like money everywhere, will flow to where there is the least risk for return. If a deal is driven primarily by political connections and you can be exposed to less risk as a result, many people will do that rather than fund a project with all the financial and operational risk of a productive enterprise."[187]

Traditionally, African governments tended to view their relationship with large enterprises as a zero-sum game. As the managing director of a Senegalese family office puts it: "If you get too big, or too powerful, someone in government would feel threatened by that, and that's a fight you could not win."[188] However, there are reasons to hope that governments may be starting to lose their fear that "the loss of control of any important element of the economy weakens the hold of the ruling party" under the weight of evidence to the contrary in China and other countries.[189]

In Chapter 1, I have already discussed the significance of Zhang Weiying's observation about the allocation of entrepreneurial talents between government and businesses being a key factor in the successful transition towards capitalism.[190] In order to properly develop entrepreneurial aspirations, gifted young people need strong role models to admire and emulate. These role models do exist in contemporary Africa, as Moky Makura has shown in an impressive volume that showcases 16 of the continent's most successful entrepreneurs.[191] They serve as role models for the next generation of entrepreneurs – young people who, instead of hoping for a lifetime of collecting bribes as public servants, harbour ambitions of making money in private enterprise.

In other words, Africa offers plenty of economic opportunities. However, some of the predictions of a massive boom across the continent currently bandied about by pundits are based on models that fall short of a realistic appreciation of the facts on the ground. Attempting to replicate Asian success stories in Africa without taking the differences between the two continents into consideration would be too simplistic. This chapter has already discussed why formulas along the lines of 'Africa has huge reserves of natural resources, therefore it's bound to achieve significant growth' amount to little more than wishful thinking: first of all, these resources have existed in Africa for aeons and have so far failed to translate into significant growth. Secondly, as we have seen, large reserves of natural resources can sometimes be more of a curse than a blessing for a country's economic development.

There is a kernel of truth in the 'demographic dividend' argument, which assumes that Africa's young population will be the motor of its growth. For the foreseeable future, the continent will benefit from an unlimited supply of labour while the proportion of the population that is either too young or too old to work will remain limited.[192] According to World Bank estimates, the positive impact of the young population on economic growth will be highest between 2025 and 2030 at approximately 0.5 percentage points, after which it is expected to decrease but remain positive in the long term.

However, there are other hypotheses based on the assumption that population growth will by far outstrip the African economy's capacity for job creation. According to UN estimates, by 2050 the population of the two neighbouring countries Niger and Nigeria alone is set to equal that of the entire European Union at today.[193] Nor do we know how population flows from Africa to Europe will develop, or what it might mean for Africa if it loses large numbers of citizens, especially as those with the financial means to leave the continent are not among the poorest.

Due to the uncertainty around all these issues, future developments in Africa are difficult to predict. However, one thing is already obvious: Africa, like the world's other regions, is more likely to experience growth and prosperity under capitalist conditions than in the state-controlled planned economies of the 'African socialism' of yore. While the introduction of capitalism may result in greater success in some countries than others, it is a catalyst for economic growth wherever it happens.

Even U2 frontman Bono, formerly the organizer of massive 'aid for Africa' festivals marked by anti-capitalist rhetoric and a seemingly unshakeable belief in foreign aid as a solution to hunger and poverty in Africa, has changed his tune under the weight of the evidence to the contrary. "Aid is just a stopgap," he said in a speech at Georgetown University in 2013. "Commerce [and] entrepreneurial capitalism take more people out of poverty than aid. We need Africa to become an economic powerhouse."[194] Likewise, Live Aid co-founder Sir Bob Geldof recently teamed up with two former senior executives to set up a private equity fund. He, too, appears to have realized that charitable donations won't be enough to solve Africa's problems.[195]

The Africa expert Vijay Mahajan predicts that "entrepreneurship and the development of consumer markets may be a more clean, stable, and powerful driver of long-term progress than political reform. Professor Pat Utomi of the Lagos Business School once suggested, only partly in jest, that if all the oil in Nigeria were given to the soldiers and politicians on condition that they would leave the nation alone, the nation would be better off."[196]

In Europe and the US, the perception of Africa is skewed towards two extremes: some only see starving children, heart-wrenching poverty, AIDS, corruption and other serious problems. Others prefer an extremely optimistic, even euphoric, view of Africa as a land of golden opportunity headed for growth on a scale to rival emerging economies in Asia. Proponents of both views are able to marshal plenty of evidence in support of their respective positions. For investors willing to take risks, the one-sided negative view of Africa is a rich source of opportunity. As Ibrahim puts it: "In business, when there is a gap between reality and perception, there is good business to be made."[197]

CHAPTER 3

Germany: You *Can't* Overtake a Mercedes in a Trabant

Germany unwittingly became the site of a large-scale experiment designed to determine whether humans are more likely to thrive under a state-controlled or free-market economy. The experiment, which took over 40 years to resolve, started with the end of World War II and the Allied powers' occupation of Germany, and ended with the collapse of the socialist regime in East Germany and German reunification in 1989–1990.

Following the end of the war, Germany was divided into four zones, each controlled by the army of one of the Allied powers. In 1947–1948, the three western zones occupied by the US, the British and the French merged to form the 'Trizone'. With only 15% of its industrial facilities destroyed by Allied bombing raids, the Soviet-controlled eastern part of Germany had suffered far less economic damage than the rest of the country.[198] However, these damages were compounded by the dismantling of factories across East Germany, which were transported to the Soviet Union by way of 'reparation' for losses sustained during the war.

Germany's decades-long partition into two states was not part of the occupying powers' original plan, but rather a consequence of the Cold War that broke out between the Soviet Union and the Western Allies in the wake of their joint victory over Germany.

THE SOCIALIST PLANNED ECONOMY
IN EAST GERMANY

The Communist Party (KPD) soon emerged as a dominant political force in the Soviet-occupied zone. Prior to its merger with the Social Democratic Party (SPD) to form the Socialist Unity Party (SED) in April 1946, the KPD issued a statement in June 1945 that, by communist standards, sounds surprisingly moderate, guaranteeing the "completely unobstructed development of free trade and private entrepreneurship on the basis of private ownership". Despite the assurance that "it would be wrong to impose the Soviet system on Germany",[199] that's exactly what would happen over the following years.

It started with an agrarian land reform that saw the expropriation without compensation of properties larger than 100 hectares (247 acres) and properties previously owned by high-ranking National Socialist leaders. The expropriated agricultural land was divided into small plots and allocated to farmers. The breaking up of large estates was justified as a 'denazification' measure with the additional benefit of providing a living for the displaced persons and refugees from the regions east of the new German border with Poland and Czechoslovakia, who were euphemistically referred to as 'resettlers' in official German Democratic Republic parlance. By 1950, two thirds of the expropriated land had been given to individual beneficiaries.

The nationalization of East German industries happened in various stages, starting in the Soviet-occupied zone as part of the 'fight against fascism'. Communist theory regarded capitalism as the root cause of fascism (the communist term for National Socialism), which needed to be eliminated in order to rid the world of fascism once and for all. Accordingly, for the SED the expropriations were an instrument of class warfare rather than a means of punishing individual landowners for collaborating with the National Socialist regime.[200]

By the end of 1948, public enterprises already generated 60% of the total production volume across the Soviet-occupied zone. By 1955, that figure had risen to 80%. The remaining private enterprises were subject to various pressures and discriminated against when it came to the allocation of production materials,[201] all of which resulted in a significant loss of entrepreneurial potential across the Soviet-occupied zone. By 1953, one in seven East German industrial enterprises – a total of over 4,000 companies – had relocated their headquarters to the west, taking with them senior executives and technical experts as well as entrepreneurial talent.[202]

True to the socialist motto of giving power to the workers, owners or managing directors in many nationalized enterprises were removed from office and replaced by workers. By mid-1948, more than half of all public enterprises in the Saxony region were run by former workers, 80% of whom had no education beyond elementary school level.[203] Massive administrative departments were set up within the companies to handle the deluge of paperwork – regulations, implementing provisions, ordinances, reports, statistics, and goals for production, finance and investment. Every state-run enterprise had to submit up to 65 complex and detailed reports per month to the economic planning authority, government departments, regional administrations, the pricing office and other public bodies.[204]

Much like in the Soviet Union itself, the economy in the Soviet-occupied zone was increasingly planned by government officials. As Fritz Selbmann, a leading communist economist, explains: "[In a] planned economy, every single detail of manufacturing is controlled by plans, every economic process from sourcing raw materials to transport, processing and sales is planned in advance."[205]

While in a free-market economy prices are determined by supply and demand, they were now set by the government. For political reasons, prices of food items and other daily essentials in particular were frequently lower than the cost of the raw materials required to produce them. 'Plan' became a magic word. As members of the Young Pioneers, children as young as six learned to sing the praise of the planned economy in a fervent paean to the "dear plan" that gave them "shoes and clothing, … homes and schools", made "trains speed back and forth", "sen[t] ships across the sea" and promised to provide "even more coal, steel and ore, and [to] gladden your hearts". [206]

On 7 October 1949, a few months after the Federal Republic of Germany was established in the western zones, the Soviet-occupied zone became the German Democratic Republic (GDR). Economic recovery was slow. Private per-capita consumption in the GDR in 1950 varied between just over a third and half of 1936 levels, and by 1952 reached between 50% and 75% of West German per-capita consumption levels.[207]

Demands made by Soviet dictator Joseph Stalin in talks with the SED leadership in April 1952 regarding the creation of "productive cooperatives" in rural areas and the country's "acquiescent" embarkation on "the route to socialism"[208] were swiftly followed by concerted efforts at collectivizing agricultural production in the GDR. The newly created agricultural collectives received preferential treatment over independent farmers – as the East German head of state, Walter Ulbricht, put it: "The production cooperative comes first and second, and only then do the small and medium-sized farms get their turn."[209] Many farmers fled to the west rather than endure the growing pressure.

The government used fiscal policy as an instrument to enforce nationalization and increase pressure on privately owned operations in trade and industry. Companies that made profits of 100,000 East German marks or more were taxed at 78.5%, a rate that rose to a full 90% for companies that made 500,000 East German marks or more.[210]

No wonder, then, that an increasing number of East Germans – farmers, tradespeople and entrepreneurs in particular – fled to the west: the monthly average of 15,000 for the period between 1950 and 1952 proved a mere trickle compared to the 37,500 a month who left during the first six months of 1953.[211] These heavy losses were a hard blow to the East German economy. The government responded by raising production targets, which – though economically necessary – led to even more discontent in the population and triggered the popular uprising of 17 June 1953, when hundreds of thousands took to the streets in protest and workers went on strike. The revolt was eventually quelled by Soviet tanks, killing between 51 and over 100 people, according to different sources.[212]

The official account published in the SED newspaper *Neues Deutschland* reframed the strikes and demonstrations as a "fascist provocation by foreign agents": "Following instructions from Washington, American agencies based in West Germany are developing plans for war and civil war."[213] Unwilling to admit that dissidents and resistance exist within their own borders, dictatorial regimes from Stalin's Soviet Union to current incarnations have always been quick to blame 'foreign spies' as the masterminds behind any uprisings.

In fact, there is plenty of documentary evidence to show that Western government and news agencies were completely unprepared for the events of 17 June. Their initial response to reports of the uprising was disbelief, which in some cases gave rise to the absurd notion that the demonstrations might have been a Russian-led attempt to put Ulbricht under pressure.[214]

The trauma of the uprising would continue to haunt the communist rulers for decades to come. Their determination to avoid another uprising at any cost made them more reluctant to step up pressure on workers. Thanks to the reports compiled by the national security agency, the notorious Stasi, the party was intimately aware of the popular mood. Detailed information on popular discontent and criticism of the regime also fed into the East German government's dealings with the Soviet Union, prompting requests for financial and material support to prevent the economic situation in East Germany from escalating.

While all this was going on, the restructuring of East German agriculture in accordance with socialist dogma wreaked havoc on the country's food supplies. Between 1952 and 1961, the proportion of agricultural collectives where – in addition to collective management of fields – all equipment, animals and pastures were under collective ownership rose from just over one in ten to just under two thirds. Farmers continued to leave in growing numbers.

Between 1952 and 1956 alone, a total of 70,000 agricultural operations – 30% of them 'large farms' of 20 to 100 hectares – were dissolved because their owners had fled the country.[215]

The East German regime zigged and zagged a fair bit in its efforts to collectivize agricultural production. An initial hardline period of stepping up pressure on farmers was followed by a U-turn in June 1953, with a promise that farmers who had left would be able to return and get their land back. Of the 11,000 farmers who had left in the first six months of 1953, only 10% took up the offer. On the positive side, 2,500 court verdicts against farmers who had failed to deliver their target quotas were reversed, and a significant number of farmers serving prison sentences were released.[216]

Though aware of the huge cost of collectivization, the East German regime was able to take solace from knowing that other socialist countries had borne a similar burden. As Erich Mückenberger, the Central Committee secretariat member in charge of agriculture, put it: "Creating a socialist society in rural areas always costs money and no country has ever succeeded in doing it on the cheap."[217]

Contrary to the regime's proclaimed intention to overtake the West German economy, in the late 1950s per-capita consumption in the GDR was still 12% below pre-war levels and 50% below West Germany's per-capita consumption.[218] This was before the Berlin Wall was built, when East Germans were still able to cross over into West Berlin and marvel at the better quality, the lower prices (by 20% to 30%) and the more reliable supply of goods on offer in the shops.[219]

While essential food items were sold below cost in the GDR's planned economy, prices for 'luxury foods' and clothes were significantly higher. Coffee beans cost 19.40 Deutschmarks per kilo in the west and 80 East German marks in the east. A pair of men's shoes would set a person back 32 Deutschmarks in the west on average and over 73 marks in the east.[220] Bread and bread rolls, on the other hand, were almost ridiculously cheap. The leading North Korea expert Rüdiger Frank, who grew up in East Germany, remembers some of his fellow citizens abusing the pricing system: "Government planners in the GDR must almost have felt despair at the sales figures reported to Berlin by bakeries across East Germany, which showed that all GDR citizens seemed to eat vast quantities of bread. What they didn't know, or couldn't do anything about if they did know, was that some farmers bought fresh bread to feed to their pigs, since it was far cheaper than actual pig feed. They were then able to sell their meat at a large profit because prices were subsidized by the government."[221]

The East German communists themselves were unwavering in their belief in socialism as the superior system. At the 1958 SED party conference, Ulbricht defined the regime's most important economic policy task: to bring the per-capita consumption of the "working population" for "all essential food items and consumer goods" up to and above the level of "the entire population of West Germany" by 1961.[222]

Among the actions Ulbricht's government took to achieve this ambitious target, accelerated collectivization once again became a priority. July 1958 marked the end of the regime's more conciliatory approach and the beginning of a new attack on private ownership of agricultural operations – an absurd and self-defeating, purely ideology-driven measure given that independent farmers achieved better yields than the existing collectives. Farmers who ran successful medium-sized operations were still holding out against joining a collective.[223]

In December 1959, the SED launched a national programme of compulsory collectivization, pitching local party leaders in competition with each other to achieve complete collectivization first. Agitation brigades were deployed to the villages to win the locals over with loud music and propagandistic slogans. Anyone not swayed by the propaganda was threatened or simply arrested.[224] A refusal to join the local collective 'voluntarily' was considered 'counter-revolutionary' – a dangerous accusation that could land the accused in prison for years.[225]

By April 1960, all districts across East Germany had reported complete collectivization, although around 15,000 farmers fled to the west in the course of this campaign, which the party celebrated as their 'socialist spring'.[226] With only very few independent farms remaining, the "revolution had been victorious across rural areas, the ideologues were triumphant, and there were long queues outside butchers' and greengrocers' shops all over the country".[227] Without the help of additional food imports from the Soviet Union, East Germany's food supply system would have collapsed entirely.

The situation continued to escalate. In order to bring in the harvest, additional workers had to be seconded from their regular jobs for municipal enterprises. Due to the lack of suitable equipment and facilities required for large-scale farming, the degree of mechanization deployed in the grain harvest dropped from 68% to just 39%. From late 1960 onwards, an increasing number of farmers attempted to leave the collectives, some of which even came close to being shut down. According to estimates by the National Planning Committee, collectivization cost the GDR a total of 1 billion marks, a staggering amount at the time.[228]

At the same time, the supply of goods available to the general population deteriorated progressively. From meat and dairy products to shoes, all kinds of textiles and laundry detergent, everything was in short supply. Shelves were often empty and the overall situation appeared worse than in the late 1950s.[229] The GDR's economy seemed further away than ever from achieving Ulbricht's express goal to overtake standards of living in the capitalist West.

In early 1961, Ulbricht reported to the Soviet leaders: "The gap between us and West Germany has not narrowed in 1960. On the contrary, internal difficulties increased due to non-compliance with deadlines as well as material and technical supply shortages. A state in which continuity of production processes can no longer be guaranteed in many companies has caused strong discontent among workers and the intelligentsia." Among his inner circle, Ulbricht voiced fears that the situation would deteriorate further and that the mass exodus of East Germans leaving for the west would continue unabated.[230]

"The rash attempt at achieving collectivization by force had created a vicious circle in the GDR," Stefan Wolle says in his account of everyday life and government power in East Germany prior to the building of the Berlin Wall. "The compulsory measures had led to a deterioration of living standards that prompted a growing number of people to leave the country. Their mass exodus in turn created more economic difficulties, which led to a further deterioration in living standards."[231]

It also became increasingly clear that the principle of a planned economy as such – i.e. a system in which the allocation of resources is controlled by a governmental planning department, rather than by prices reflecting shortages in the relationship between supply and demand – was causing significant issues. As the historian André Steiner explains: "Companies would make a start on any project that had been included (i.e. budgeted for) in the plan, whether or not the equipment required was available; they were afraid of having the money taken away again if they didn't. That's why many projects were started without ever being completed or yielding any output. The funds tied up in these uncompleted projects across the manufacturing industry in 1960/61 roughly equaled, and in subsequent years exceeded, the annual investment volume."[232] In 1961, investment had fallen to a quarter of the 1959 level.[233] The rising numbers of people leaving the country only aggravated the situation.

In August 1961, the East German leadership took the desperate step of building a wall to stop more people from joining the 2.74 million who had already left since 1949. According to figures by the National Planning Committee, the East German economy had lost a total of 963,000 workers, 13% of the entire workforce.[234]

In official parlance, the Berlin Wall was an 'antifascist defence' designed to prevent fascists and Western agents from infiltrating the country. Everybody knew this was as much of a lie as Ulbricht's famous denial of any intent to build a wall in June 1961, two months before construction started. In truth, the wall was already an admission of defeat. By fleeing the country in droves, the people had made their will abundantly clear and left no doubt as to their opinion on the relative merits of East German socialism and the free-market economy in the western part of the country.

Of course, this was not a conclusion the East German leadership was willing to draw. Once it became clear that the construction of the wall had done little to resolve the crisis, the government launched a 'New Economic System' that transferred more independence to individual enterprises. "Basically, the reformers were attempting to simulate the mechanisms of a free-market economy without laying the foundations for a free-market economy."[235] The reforms failed to achieve any significant impact and were subject to a number of amendments and modifications. After all, the regime remained intent on achieving its stated targets, which in 1969 were defined as a "jump in the development of technology and the production base". According to internal documents, the assumption was that the East German economy would be able to overtake and exceed West German levels of production and standards of living by or before 1980.[236]

Standards of living across East Germany did rise to some extent. Between 1960 and 1970, the percentage of households owning a car multiplied from only 3.2% to 15.6%, while the number of households with washing machines and refrigerators saw an even steeper rise from 6% to 50%. These items were considered luxury commodities, with 40% of their sales price used to subsidize prices for essential items. At 1,350 and 1,200 East German marks respectively, in 1965 refrigerators and washing machines cost more than twice the average worker's monthly take-home pay of 491 East German marks.[237] Despite growth rates of around 2% a year during the 1960s, real wages in East Germany lagged further and further behind West German growth rates of 5% to 6% a year.[238] The problem was compounded by shortages and/or long queues for specific items, including warm underwear, children's clothing and sportswear, winter shoes, batteries, irons, modular furniture, toothbrushes and spark plugs.[239]

In order to afford the facilities and equipment required to modernize the manufacturing industry, the GDR started borrowing money from West Germany and other capitalist countries. "We're borrowing as much as we possibly can from the capitalists just to ensure our basic survival," Ulbricht told his Soviet counterpart Leonid Brezhnev in May 1970.[240] He was forced to resign a year later, his attempts to push through a moderate programme of reforms having met with resistance from the Soviet Union as well as in his own party.

Ulbricht's successor, Erich Honecker, pursued a new line, which he defined as "merging economic and social policy". Rather than first attempting to lay the economic foundations for improving standards of living, his idea was to start by implementing social policies that would have a direct impact on people's lives and thus eventually raise productivity.

In part, this change in direction was motivated by the fear of seeing events similar to the demonstrations, strikes and workers' protests that had swept Poland in December 1970 repeated in East Germany. As part of the new policy, minimum wages, annual leave allowances and pension rates were raised repeatedly, while mothers of several children had their mandatory working hours reduced. The ambitious housing development programme launched in 1973 was another cornerstone of Honecker's new policy.[241]

Warnings by the National Planning Committee that the economy was not growing fast enough to finance these comprehensive measures were ignored; the head of government, Willi Stoph, said in spring 1972: "The National Planning Committee's current calculations have not taken into account the growth in productivity that will result from our appeal to the workers by announcing these social policy measures."[242] Statements of this kind were an expression of the self-delusions of an economically inefficient regime.

Even the modest attempts at reform of the Ulbricht era came to an end. The performance of individual enterprises was now measured by production volume rather than profit. The more a company produced – regardless of efficiency – the better its reported performance.[243] This made no economic sense and created misdirected incentives.

At the same time, the communist regime further increased pressure on the remaining small and medium-sized enterprises. Honecker stirred up feelings of envy against erstwhile "petty capitalists" who had "turned into millionaires". In 1971, the owners of the last remaining private or partly-state-owned enterprises made around three and a half times as much after taxes as the average blue- or white-collar worker. The year 1972 saw the launch of a massive nationalization programme that affected around 11,000 businesses – trade cooperatives engaged in industrial production, partly state-owned enterprises and private enterprises. This too was irrational and motivated purely by ideology since it ran counter to the stated goal of improving the supply situation. Instead, even more consumer goods became unavailable, creating new shortages.[244]

The 15,000 letters of complaint Honecker received every year were filed under 'submissions' and analysed by statisticians. Housing issues, travel to West Germany and everyday supply shortages emerged as primary concerns in these letters.[245] One husband and father sent Honecker a desiccated orange accompanied by a note that said: "When my wife was at our local sales point this week, she was lucky enough to receive an orange for our daughter because the delivery had been so 'large' as to include exactly one orange for every child in the town. Today we were going to give the orange to our daughter but were dismayed to notice that it was almost completely desiccated and inedible ... Every day, like many workers in our country, we work for the common good of the people and deliver a high standard of quality. In exchange, we would really appreciate being able to buy QUALITY for once!!!"[246]

Others took more drastic measures to express their discontent, as illustrated by a report submitted by the district administration in Halle concerning events that took place during the night from 18 to 19 May 1961, when "provocative messages" appeared on a number of shop windows. Among other things, the pointed messages left by the "hitherto unidentified perpetrators included "no bread on Saturdays", "fresh cream" painted on the window of a self-service shop, "bananas – tomatoes – cucumbers" and similar. These scrawls were found in a total of twelve locations across the city. The perpetrators used white oil paint. "The security forces have opened investigative procedures as required."[247]

Honecker's social policy led to a situation in which the country increasingly lived off its assets. Urgently needed investments failed to materialize, factory equipment fell behind the current state of the art, and there was not enough money to advance development in science and technology. Productivity in the GDR lagged further behind West German levels than ever, doubling the gap from a third in the early 1950s to two thirds in the 1980s.[248]

In the short run, however, the new political direction did achieve the intended outcomes. Increased production of consumer goods, in combination with a cutback in exports and a rise in import volumes, meant that by the mid-1970s the government succeeded in improving the supply of items to meet the demand for greater choice and quality and more competitive pricing. However, the goods available to consumers in East Germany still didn't come anywhere close to West German standards. The quality of premium goods, such as cars and colour TVs, was far below that of similar items available in the capitalist West.

Honecker only managed to achieve his most important goal of raising standards of living by borrowing even more money from capitalist countries. By 1982, the amount East Germany owed to capitalist countries – which had stood at around 2 billion Valuta marks (a currency unit used in East Germany to denominate foreign trade prices, equivalent to 0.95 Deutschmarks) when Honecker took office in the early 1970s – exceeded 25 billion Valuta marks.[249] GDR economists warned that the country's debts were no longer sustainable: the international consensus was that no more than 25% of a country's foreign currency revenue should be spent on debt repayments and interest payments. In the GDR, this figure had risen to 115%, while a staggering 168% of the country's all-important convertible foreign currency income went to its creditors.[250] A refusal by Western countries to extend new loans to socialist countries brought the GDR to the brink of insolvency, which was averted only by the West German government stepping in to guarantee two loans to the tune of a billion West German marks each.[251]

The widening technological gap between the GDR and the Western world became evident in Honecker's ambitious micro-electronics programme, which guzzled up 14 billion East German marks in investments between 1986 and 1989 alone. Another 14 billion East German marks were invested in research and development in this field, not to mention the 4 billion Valuta marks spent on imports from Western countries.[252] Despite this massive expenditure, the outcome was depressing: the production cost for a 256-kilobit memory chip in the GDR was 534 East German marks, while the same component was available for four to five Valuta marks in the global market. The GDR lagged eight years behind the international state of the art and achieved only 10% of the average quantities manufacturers in the West were able to produce.[253]

The automotive industry was another area in which the gap between the GDR and West Germany was particularly obvious. When the Berlin Wall fell in 1989, only just over half of all East German households owned a car, and more than half of these were Trabants – the notorious East German make with a two-stroke engine and a maximum of 26 horsepower – while only 0.1% were Western imports. Private citizens had to wait between 12.5 and 17 years for a new car. Almost everybody applied for a car, and applications were sold on to those impatient to jump the queue for anything between 2,000 and 40,000 East German marks. At the same time, used cars were sold for two or three times the price of a new car on the thriving black market.[254]

During the late 1980s, the difference between their own standard of living and that of the 'capitalist West' became abundantly clear to the increasing number of

East Germans who were given permission to travel to West Germany. Although watching Western TV channels was illegal in East Germany, the majority of the population did, and many received parcels from relatives and friends in West Germany. Western goods were also on display in state-run Intershop outlets, although they were available to buy only for those lucky enough to have foreign currency. These constant reminders of a better life on the other side of the inner German border did nothing to quell the growing discontent.

Not only had the GDR failed to achieve its stated goal to catch up to and then overtake West Germany – the gap between both systems had widened even more. Hampered by the systemic failings of its planned economy, East Germany never stood a chance of catching up to its western neighbour, whose very different model of a 'social market economy' proved far superior at ensuring prosperity.

WEST GERMANY'S 'SOCIAL MARKET ECONOMY'

Germany's three western zones had been hit even harder than the east by wartime devastation. On the other hand, it was to their advantage that the dismantling of infrastructure never reached the same levels as in the Soviet-controlled east.

In the immediate aftermath of the war, many Germans in both parts of the country suffered from hunger. In late 1945, the average daily food intake in the UK of 2,800 calories was double that of the daily intake in West Germany. It took until the second half of 1948 to get back to acceptable levels. To make matters worse, wartime bombing had rendered between 22% and 25% of West German housing stock uninhabitable.[255]

With regard to the political situation, however, the West Germans were in a far better position than their compatriots in the Soviet-occupied zone, with none of the Western Allies insisting on the adoption of a planned economy. Nonetheless, anti-capitalist sentiment was rife across post-war Europe. In 1945, a Labour government headed by the left-wing union leader Clement Attlee came to power in the UK, while the Communist Party won 28.6% of the votes in the 1946 French elections and was a core component of the tripartite alliances that governed the country from 1944 to 1947.

This strong anti-capitalist sentiment was reflected across both parts of Germany as well. Then as now, West German politics was dominated by two major parties – the Social Democrats (SPD) and the Christian Democratic Union (CDU), which was founded in the immediate aftermath of World War II. The SPD was even more committed to socialist dogma than it is today. It took the party until 1959 to adopt free-market principles in its 'Godesberg Manifesto'.

Anti-capitalist sentiment in the CDU was reflected in the 1947 'Ahlen Manifesto', adopted by the party's regional section in North Rhine-Westphalia. Published with the tagline "CDU transcends Capitalism and Marxism", the manifesto was hailed by its supporters as the articulation of Christian Socialist principles. Its opening lines leave little doubt as to its priorities: "The capitalist economic system has failed to meet the national and social interests of the German people. After the terrible political, economic and social collapse as a result of a criminal power politics, a comprehensive restructuring has become necessary. The content and objective of this new social and economic order can no longer be the capitalist quest for profit and power, but only the well-being of our people." The manifesto goes on to demand partial nationalization of major industries and extensive workers' participation in management. After Konrad Adenauer's election to the office of Federal Chancellor in September 1949, the CDU started adopting more market-oriented economic policies.

That West Germany bucked the trend by adopting a free-market economy at a time when state-controlled economic planning prevailed elsewhere across Europe was largely due to one man's efforts. That man was Ludwig Erhard, who came from a family of entrepreneurs and in 1942 founded the Institute for Industry Research to identify strategies for establishing a market-oriented economic order in post-war Germany. Although the National Socialists had stopped short of abolishing private ownership of the means of production, they did increasingly interfere in economic matters and impose party-political and ideological constraints on companies. Erhard's distinctly market-oriented model was an explicit rejection of Third Reich economic policy.

Erhard, who was not a member of any party, became Minister for Economic Affairs in Bavaria after the war and director of the Special Money and Credit Department set up by the Americans to prepare for currency reform. As early as October 1946, he laid out his arguments against a state-controlled planned economy and in favour of a market economy with free competition and free pricing in a newspaper article under the headline "Free-Market or State-Controlled Economy".[256]

Coined by the economist Alfred Müller-Armack in 1947, the term 'social market economy' is still used today to describe Germany's economic system, although its current usage has little in common with Erhard's understanding of the concept. Far from designating a 'golden mean' between free-market competition and social policy, Erhard saw the social market economy as a chance to overcome traditional approaches to social policy by way of an economic order that promoted the creation of wealth.[257] He firmly believed that more economic freedom was the route to greater social welfare.[258] The economic historians Mark Spoerer and Jochen Streb are probably right to point out that in the late 1940s the social market economy formula was primarily designed to "make the return to a capitalist economic system – which was far from an inevitable given at the time – palatable to a materially impoverished and profoundly ideologically unsettled population".[259] After all, Germans had grown accustomed to the National Socialists' explicitly anti-capitalist rhetoric, while notions of 'social welfare' have long been a staple of political discourse in Germany.

Contrary to current interpretations, Erhard regarded the free-market economy as a driver of social welfare in and of itself – irrespective of any subsequent attempts at redistribution, of which he was rather sceptical. As he said, it is far easier to "grant every individual a larger piece of a growing pie than to keep fighting to the point of exhaustion about distributing the earnings whilst drifting off the only course to success, which is to increase the gross national product".[260] Accordingly, a successful economic policy would over time obviate the need for social welfare policies in the traditional sense.[261]

Erhard was able to put his vision of economic policy into practice. In his capacity as the director of the Bizone economic administration, which had been established during the combination of the American and the British occupation zones on 1 January 1947 during the occupation of Germany after World War II, Erhard made a radio announcement the day before the currency reform on 20 June 1948 – without first consulting the Allied powers – to declare an end to production and price controls for many essential foodstuffs. Germany was still an occupied country, and Erhard later claimed that he was called to account by the military governor, Lucius D. Clay, who objected to his unilateral decision to relax Allied regulations. "I have not relaxed them. I have abolished them," Erhard replied, to which Clay countered: "My advisors are telling me you've made a terrible mistake." Erhard responded: "My advisors are telling me the same thing."[262] Whether or not this conversation really happened, Erhard's initiative definitely raised a lot of eyebrows at the time.

Marion von Dönhoff, a journalist who would later become one of the leading lights of Germany's left-wing intelligentsia, poured scorn on Erhard's proposals: "Even if Germany hadn't already been ruined, that man would definitely get us there with his absurd plan to abolish all production controls. May God protect us from what would be a third disaster after Hitler and the dismemberment of Germany."[263]

Erhard's abolition of production and price controls was a courageous step and a key condition for the subsequent economic upswing. The National Socialists had created a dense network of price and wage regulations, which the Allied administrations initially retained. "This network made it difficult for companies to obtain important intermediate products by offering high prices. Conversely, the price caps made it impossible for companies to benefit from customers' high willingness to pay. Prices and wages had lost their key function in the context of a market economy – reflecting relative scarcity – and were no longer able to balance supply and demand on the goods and labour markets."[264]

On Sunday 20 June 1948, every West German citizen received 40 D-Mark in exchange for 40 Reichsmark, and another 20 D-Mark were paid out within the following two months. The rate for amounts in excess of these limits was set at 6.50 D-Mark for 100 Reichsmark, to be exchanged once the initial two-month period had passed.

After the currency had been floated and controls on prices relaxed, the shop windows quickly filled with goods that had previously been stockpiled. At the same time, however, prices rose sharply, triggering vociferous protests. The unions called for the only general strike in German post-war history. They roamed the streets with banners demanding "Erhard to the gallows".[265] As the economist Karen Horn comments: "The social market economy was not widely accepted at the time."[266] Since unemployment also rose at first and there were strong reservations about Erhard's market-economy orientation among both the Western Allies and the political parties in Germany, it was by no means a foregone conclusion that this course would prevail.

In view of rising prices and unemployment, plans to return to production and price controls had already been drafted and were ready for implementation in the drawers of the economic administration.[267] "The free-market experiment was almost allowed to fail before it ever had a chance to properly demonstrate its capabilities."[268] Criticism from the political left notwithstanding, Erhard was the most popular politician in the western zones at the time, and in 1949 the CDU entered the election campaign with the slogan "Planned Economy or Market Economy" – and won, albeit by a slim margin, with 31% compared to 29.2% for the SPD.

There can be no question that the economic policy course set by Erhard's market-economy initiative was more instrumental in fostering the Federal

Republic's 'economic miracle' than the Marshall Plan (named after the then US Secretary of State, George C. Marshall), which provided aid for the suffering and in some cases starving population of Europe after the war. Of the programme's total volume of USD 13.1 billion, about 25% went to the UK, another 20% to France and 10% each to Western Germany and Italy. The rest was distributed among a dozen other countries. According to calculations by the economic historian Barry Eichengreen, these funds increased the GDP of the beneficiaries by an average of 0.5% between 1948 and 1951.[269]

The period that now started in West Germany has frequently been referred to as the 'German economic miracle'. Between 1948 and 1960, GDP per capita grew by an average of 9.3%, and it continued to grow by 3.5% in the period between 1961 and 1973.[270] Although a recession hit in 1967 with a 0.5% drop in GDP, the West German economy soon picked up speed again. Unemployment, which had been very high after the war, was reduced within a few years and gave way to full employment. Despite several further recessions – including one after the global oil price shock at the end of 1973 – it was obvious that economic conditions in West Germany were improving much more rapidly than in the east.

The race between the two systems was won, not by the socialist east, as had been Ulbricht's and Honecker's very public ambition, but by market-oriented West Germany. The conclusive evidence provided by all available economic data only confirms what ordinary German citizens already knew. When the time came in 1989 to take stock,[271] 67.8% of West Germans owned a car, compared to only 54.3% of East Germans. West German cars – BMW, Mercedes, Volkswagen, etc. – were of a significantly higher quality than the East German makes Trabant and Wartburg. And, while West Germans were able to visit a car dealership at any time to buy a car produced at home or abroad, GDR citizens had to wait at least a decade for their vehicle.

In 1989, 12% of East Germans owned a computer, while the percentage was three times higher in West Germany (37.4%). In the GDR, only the homes of the privileged few – 16% of the total population, most of them public servants and senior employees – boasted telephones. Across West Germany, coverage stood at 99.3%. Following the introduction of a free-market system in the former East Germany, the gap closed quickly. By 2006, differences in ownership rates of cars (72.9% in the former East Germany vs. 78% in the former West Germany), computers (66.6% vs. 69%) and landlines (99.8% vs. 99.2%) had shrunk to near-negligible levels.

Although Honecker's regime had made housing a priority, the difference between the two economic systems was nowhere more visible than in the housing market. While rents were controlled at extremely affordable levels, East Germans had to wait for years for a much-coveted apartment in one of the new buildings constructed from pre-fabricated concrete slabs. Existing pre-war multi-family buildings in Leipzig, Dresden, East Berlin, Erfurt and other East German cities were so dilapidated that it took a massive tax-funded refurbishment scheme to the tune of several billion euros to bring them up to scratch after German reunification. By that time, the pre-fabricated apartment buildings dating back to the post-war era also required large-scale renovation in addition to the extensive new building activity required to solve the housing shortage in eastern parts of Germany.

With the help of tax incentives, a total of 838,638 homes were completed in the former GDR during the 1990s at a cost of 84 billion euros.[272] This is all the more remarkable considering that housing was a key policy during the Honecker era. Germany's chancellor, Helmut Kohl, was mocked for his promise to create 'flourishing landscapes' – but a comparison between the cities in eastern Germany during the era of the GDR planned economy and today compellingly demonstrates the superiority of the market economy.

For all the impressive achievements of the German market economy, there is little cause for complacency. Erhard's model of a social market economy, which almost all current German parties have incorporated into their manifestos – some more explicitly than others – has been subject to gradual reinterpretation over the years. Today, it is frequently misunderstood to mean large-scale redistribution of wealth by an all-encompassing welfare state. Erhard himself warned against this tendency in a book published in 1957 under the title *Wohlstand für alle* (Prosperity for All): "The ideal I have in mind is based on the individual's strength to say 'I want to prove myself by my own devices, I want to bear the risks of life myself, I want to be responsible for my own fate. It's up to you, state, to ensure that I'm able to do so.' The individual's appeal to the state must not be 'Come to my aid, protect me and help me', but the opposite: 'Stay out of my affairs, but give me so much freedom and leave me enough of my earnings that I am able to shape my own existence, my fate and that of my family.'"[273]

Subsequent German governments increasingly turned their backs on these principles. In the early 2000s, the excessive expansion of the welfare state led to an explosion in public spending and significantly compromised economic performance. Spending on social welfare skyrocketed from 15.5% of GDP in 1970 to 27.2% in 2005 – compared to 20.6% in the UK and 15.8% in the US.[274]

From being Europe's economic powerhouse, Germany had been reduced to bringing up the rear and hampering growth. Rising unemployment figures accentuated the need for an urgent response to a problem the then chancellor, the Social Democrat Gerhard Schröder, had long been aware of. In a statement written for the German newspaper *Handelsblatt* in December 2002, Schröder said: "It's no longer a question of distributing a surplus. Additional expectations can no longer be satisfied. Instead, if we want to preserve solid prosperity, sustainable development and new fairness, we will need to lower some current expectations and cut back or even abolish welfare benefits that may have been justified half a century ago, but which have today lost their urgency and thus their rationale."[275]

Over four years of 'fireside chats', Schröder attempted to sell his proposals for reform to employers and trade unions. However, the unions remained stubbornly recalcitrant. Sick of the incessant demands for higher taxes for high earners, increased public borrowing and a billion-euro investment scheme, Schröder lost his patience and responded harshly to criticism by union leader Frank Bsirske during a final talk on 3 March 2003: "That's the stupidest blather I've ever heard."[276]

Less than two weeks later, on 14 March 2003, he presented his Agenda 2010 proposals in a 90-minute speech to the German parliament: "We will have to cut back welfare benefits, reward initiative and expect every individual to contribute more." Schröder's tough and uncompromising reform package included merging jobseekers' allowance and social security benefits at the level of the latter to ensure that in future nobody "will be able to sit back and let others do the work. Anybody who turns down a reasonable job offer – we will amend the criteria for what counts as reasonable – will face penalties."[277]

Schröder's Agenda 2010 was designed to redress the balance between social welfare and the free-market economy by loosening regulations on protection against unfair dismissal and other workers' benefits. Unemployment benefit was limited to 12 months, and stricter guidelines applied to determine whether a job offer was reasonable. Over the previous years, Schröder's government had already cut taxes for private individuals and businesses. Between 1999 and 2005, the rate for the top income bracket was gradually reduced from 53% to 42%.

As with similar attempts at reforming a bloated welfare system in other countries, Agenda 2010 met with strong resistance from the public, not least from Schröder's own party and the unions, who saw the reforms as an attack against workers' rights driven by the forces of 'neoliberalism' and 'market radicalism'.

However, in the medium term they proved extremely effective and helped to slash unemployment across Germany by 50% from 11.6% in 2003 to 5.6% in 2017. In part, this was achieved by greatly improving Germany's ability to maintain its competitive edge in the global market, which translated into a GDP increase from 2,130 billion euros in 2003 to 3,263 billion euros in 2017. Meanwhile, other European countries that had failed to impose similar reforms – France and Italy, to name just two – have watched Germany's economic performance with envy.

CHAPTER 4

North and South Korea: Kim Il-sung *versus* the Wisdom of the Market

Like Germany, Korea emerged from World War II as a country divided by two competing economic systems. Prior to its partition into a capitalist south and a communist north in 1948, Korea was one of the poorest countries worldwide, on a par with sub-Saharan Africa. This only started changing in the early 1960s. Today, capitalist South Korea is the eighth-largest export nation worldwide, whose per-capita GDP of USD 27,539 puts it ahead of countries such as Spain (26,609), Russia (8,929), Brazil (8,727) and China (8,113).[278] Samsung, Hyundai and LG are among the most successful and popular Korean brands.

Vague estimates – there are no exact figures available – put North Korea's per-capita GDP at roughly 583 USD.[279] The country is frequently ravaged by famines that kill thousands of its inhabitants. More compelling proof of the advantages of a capitalist over a communist economic order would be hard to imagine. It seems that the market is able to outsmart even Kim Il-sung, the country's founder, whom North Koreans worship as a god.

Anybody brave – or foolhardy – enough to voice this thought in North Korea would be liable to arrest and imprisonment. North Korea proscribes any suggestion that the 'eternal president', his son Kim Jong-il and his grandson Kim Jong-un might not be the wisest men on earth. The preamble to the constitution of the 'Democratic People's Republic of Korea' states: "The Socialist Constitution of the Democratic People's Republic of Korea shall, as the codification of the Juche-oriented ideas of the Supreme Leaders Comrade Kim Il Sung and Comrade Kim Jong Il on State building and their exploits in it, be called the Kim Il Sung and Kim Jong Il Constitution."[280]

The cult surrounding the North Korean leaders is without precedent anywhere else in the world – even Stalin and Mao did not enjoy this level of devotion among their compatriots. Kim Il-sung's birthday (19 April) is celebrated annually as the 'Day of the Sun', the most important public holiday in the national calendar.

Furthermore, the North Korean calendar, which was introduced in the late 1990s, counts time from the year of Kim Il-sung's birth in 1912. Accordingly, as of this writing, North Koreans are living in 107 rather than 2018.[281] Any items Kim Il-sung ever laid his hands or eyes on are worshipped as sacred relics, with a red plaque or an inscription in gold commemorating this momentous event and more often than not declaring the sacred site or item off limits for ordinary mortals. This is why nobody is allowed inside the central elevator in a bank of three in the Kim Il-sung University high-rise in the North Korean capital Pyongyang, which was once used by the Supreme Leader. Rocks that served as resting places for Kim Il-sung during one of his hikes are fenced in for protection, while the most beautiful spots in the North Korean mountain ranges are adorned with the Supreme Leader's quotes and slogans carved deeply into the rock face.[282]

There are strict regulations governing the compulsory display of photos of Kim Il-sung and his son Kim Jong-il in every North Korean home. North Korean literature is full of accounts of the heroic deeds of devoted men and women who risk their own lives in order to save these pictures during disasters such as fires or shipwrecks.[283] According to official propaganda, Kim Il-sung and his successors have the ability to heal others and the auspicious occasion of Kim Jong-il's birth was marked by the appearance of an unusually bright star. When he died, cranes supposedly took to the air everywhere across the country.[284]

In the West, the North Korean leader is the object of fear or ridicule, while North Koreans are convinced that the entire world envies them their Supreme Leaders. As the introduction to a biography of Kim Jong-il has it: "His love is truly great; it cures the sick and brings forth new life, like the spring rain the sacred country drinks ... All of this arouses admiration in the peoples of the world, causing them to envy us."[285] For all his wonderful qualities, the author goes on to say, the Supreme Leader remained a modest man who chose to have the larger-than-life statues of himself dotted across the country plated with simple bronze rather than gold.[286]

There is a company with over 4,000 employees who are primarily engaged in manufacturing monuments, statues and paintings glorifying the Supreme Leader. Production continues even during times when many North Koreans suffer from starvation. The company does have a lucrative sideline in responding to demand for similar works from dictators in other parts of the world, Zimbabwe's erstwhile ruler Robert Mugabe among them.[287]

The cult of personality surrounding Kim Il-sung dates back to the war of liberation from Japanese occupation, the creation of North Korea and the Korean

War between 1950 and 1953. Just as Germany was occupied by the Western Allies and the Soviet Union at the end of World War II, Korea was split between a Soviet-occupied and a US-occupied zone in 1945. And, just as Germany was split in two, with the Federal Republic in the west and the German Democratic Republic in the east, Korea was divided to form the Democratic People's Republic in the north and the Republic of Korea in the south.

In June 1950, North Korean troops attacked South Korea, starting the Korean War, which pitched China and the Soviet Union against a US-led coalition of UN members. The war ended with an armistice agreement in 1953 after killing 940,000 soldiers and around 3 million civilians, and almost destroying the country's entire industry. Kim Il-sung remained in power until his death in 1994. He was succeeded by his son, Kim Jong-il, who died in 2011 and was himself succeeded by his own son, Kim Jong-un.

NORTH KOREA AND THE KIM IL-SUNG AND KIM JONG-IL DOCTRINE

North Korea initially adhered to Marxist–Leninist doctrine and aligned itself closely with China and the Soviet Union. After occupying the northern part of the country, the Soviet Union started restructuring the local economy along the lines of its own system, much as it had done in East Germany and other Eastern European countries. Specifically, this meant compulsory nationalization of industrial operations – the majority of which had previously been Japanese-owned – and land reform.

From the early 1960s onwards, however, North Korea's leaders – intent on proving their independence – started propagating an alternative route to socialism, which was informed by the dogmas of Kim Il-sung and Kim Jong-il and has become known as the 'Kim Il-sung and Kim Jong-il Doctrine'. North Koreans use the term *juche* to refer to an idiosyncratic ideology that combines key elements of socialism with an extreme form of nationalism and a cult of personality.[288] The large portraits of Marx and Lenin displayed on Kim Il-sung Square in Pyongyang were taken down in 2012 – probably to ensure that North Koreans worship no other god but their own Supreme Leader, who alone decides on the right way forward towards socialism.

North Korea's constitution defines socialism as the country's prescribed economic order, with Article 20 stipulating that the means of production are owned by the state or – in agricultural production – by collectives, and Article 34 stipulating that North Korea's economy is a planned economy.[289] As long as the Soviet Union and China kept providing economic support, North Korea was able to meet its targets according to plan. By playing both communist powers off against each other and using the offers made by one party to obtain similar concessions from the other, it even profited from the rivalry between them.

From the early 1960s onwards, North Korea started emancipating itself from the influence of the two larger communist powers. Without their financial aid, however, it was no longer able to meet its planning targets. The three-year extension of North Korea's first seven-year plan for the period from 1961 to 1967 set the pattern for the decades to follow: the six-year plan for 1971 to 1976 was extended by two years, as was the second seven-year plan (for 1978 to 1984). After the third seven-year-plan (for 1987 to 1993), the regime put a temporary stop to the publication of detailed economic plans.[290] The wording of the strategic ten-year plan proclaimed in 2011 was vague and general and even the five-year plan adopted at the 2016 party conference contained few figures.[291] After all, not making its targets public was the safest way for the North Korean regime to make sure it didn't miss them.

As with other planned economies, North Korea has always been plagued by across-the-board shortages. Rüdiger Frank, who is one of the foremost experts on North Korea, recalls travelling to Pyongyang in 1991 for a study visit that was to last several months. In order not to exceed his baggage allowance of 20 kilograms, he didn't bring a coffee mug. "One thing I thought I knew: if you're not too particular about aesthetics, you should be able to find this kind of thing even in a shortage economy. On the first day after I got there, I went to the 'Department Store No. 1', the best department store in town at the time. It didn't take me long to find an entire pyramid of *very* ornate coffee cups on the second floor. The comrade in charge of the department gave me an uncertain smile and I put on my best Korean accent to ask for one of the miniature works of art displayed right in front of me. Her reply was immediate and surprising: 'We don't have any.' Assuming there had been some kind of misunderstanding, I rephrased my question and used sign language for additional emphasis, which caused the woman's carefully maintained facade of composure to crumble while the smile on her face was replaced by an expression of utter panic. She ran off without saying another word, and I went back to my dormitory with many questions in my head, but without a coffee cup."[292]

Frank later found out a likely explanation for this curious event. During one of his 'on-site instructions' some years earlier, Kim Il-sung had noted how much the sight of so many gaps on the shelves of his beautiful country pained him.

Presumably, this was merely intended as a reminder to the people of North Korea to step up production. However, the entourage crowding around him at all times – who wrote down his every word and turned them into instructions, which were then displayed on banners and proclaimed over loudspeakers in public announcements all across the country – took it literally: the Supreme Leader did not want to see any more gaps on the shelves of his beautiful country's shops. "And so, from then on, the shelves of the public sales facilities were always full. No leader and no foreign visitor was able to tell whether a specific item was available or not. Unfortunately, neither were the North Koreans – at least not by looking at the shelves, which were well-stocked at all times. When an actual delivery came in, the goods would end up in bundles on the floor, or they were quickly piled up on the counter and sold off immediately."[293]

However, as Frank says, a lot has changed since his failed attempt to purchase a coffee cup. Increasing awareness of the weaknesses of economic planning led to tentative attempts at economic 'mini-reforms' from 2002 onwards. Similar attempts to instigate reforms simulating the mechanisms of a functioning market economy in the GDR are discussed in Chapter 3. However, as in the GDR – and unlike in China, whose current economic system is 'socialist' in name only – these efforts had a limited effect at best due to the North Korean regime's refusal to radically reconsider its commitment to a socialist system and initiate a transition to capitalism.

The minor reforms the regime did bring in included a slight shift towards more incentives to improve the performance of individual workers. Previously, the regime had primarily relied on propaganda in its efforts to boost productivity. Every year, Kim Il-sung's birthday served as an occasion to urge workers to increase their efforts. Loudspeakers proclaiming the latest motivational slogans are a ubiquitous feature of North Korean workplaces in any case. On building sites, loudspeakers mounted on top of vans provide a constant soundtrack of recitals of official documents alternating with revolutionary songs to keep the workers motivated.[294]

One of the measures adopted during the short-lived tentative attempt at reforming the North Korean economy was a price reform in 2002, which did result in more realistic pricing. However, like its East German counterpart, the North Korean political leadership shied away from taking the next step and allowing prices to be determined by the interplay between demand and supply – which is the prerequisite for a functioning economic system because fluctuations in price are the most reliable indicator of surpluses and shortages in production.

North Korea's rulers seem to live in persistent fear of their power slipping away, as it did from the Soviet leaders and their communist comrades in other Eastern European countries who instigated extensive economic reforms in the late 1980s and early 1990s. When the North Korean price reform brought to light the actual scale of inflation, which had previously been hidden and suppressed, the rulers understandably became frightened and their willingness to reform the economy soon reached its limits.

Frank's book contains an account of a lecture on fighting inflation he gave in Pyongyang in 2005. In subsequent conversations with North Korean experts, he realized that they were very well informed on Western economic concepts, but completely lacking in the awareness that it would take a different economic system – specifically, a free-market economy – to make these concepts work. The experts sought his advice on specific action points while refusing to listen to lectures on the mechanisms that drive a free-market economy.[295]

The regime's commitment to reforming the economy, which had at best been hesitant in any case, soon died down and the state-controlled press started publishing frequent warnings about the risks of succumbing to the "sweet poison of capitalism".[296] In November 2009, the currency was devalued with the exchange rate set at 100:1. Although prices, incomes and savings were all subject to the same depreciation factor, North Koreans were only allowed to exchange savings up to the equivalent of around USD 100. In other words, the currency reform amounted to an expropriation of those who had savings in excess of this amount and had not exchanged them for foreign currency.[297]

This caused a lot of anger in the population, as those affected included ordinary families who had, for example, been saving for their daughter's wedding as well as those who were genuinely rich by North Korean standards. Any confidence the population had previously had in their currency was lost completely thanks to this ill-considered reform. In order to safeguard their savings, North Koreans started investing their money in material assets such as rice and gold, or tried to get hold of foreign currencies. The government responded by banning all foreign-currency transactions, but de facto two-currency systems co-exist alongside each other in contemporary North Korea: the official currency, which is used to pay for goods in accordance with allocation quotas, and foreign currencies, which buy their lucky owners various minor luxuries. Taxis, restaurants and swimming pools are all happy to accept dollars.[298]

While even the tiny steps taken towards reforming the economy came to nothing in the end, North Korea's Special Economic Zones have survived. As discussed in Chapter 1, when introduced in China, these testing grounds for economic reform played an important role in easing the transition from socialism to capitalism by providing a space for small-scale experiments with private ownership, free-market economics and international collaboration within a geographically defined territory. North Korea also set up several Special Economic Zones – however, compared to their Chinese counterparts, their contribution to the economy has so far been insignificant. Some of them existed for decades without achieving any noticeable results, while others have already been shut down. Frank, who is otherwise quite optimistic with regard to North Korea's economic development, is less sanguine about the prospects of the Rason Special Economic Zone: "North Korea is opening a door, and nobody enters, except for a few Chinese speculators … The investments made so far into this 'Golden Triangle of the Northeast' wouldn't even match the standard of a small Chinese city." Another Special Economic Zone, the Kaesong Industrial Zone, was aborted in 2016 after South Korea cancelled a trade agreement following a North Korean rocket test.[299]

Apart from the planned economy, North Korea's massive military spending is another contributing factor in the country's dire economic situation. The regime has only been able to stay in power by instituting a permanent state of siege and emergency across the country. North Koreans are constantly braced for an attack from the 'imperialist powers', the US in particular. North Korea maintains one of the largest armies in the world and, depending on which source you take, the period of compulsory military service varies between three and ten years.[300] North Korean society is comprehensively militarized: instead of *walking* to work or school, North Koreans *march*. Uniforms are everywhere, military drills a frequent occurrence in companies, schools and government agencies. Funding the country's ambitious nuclear programme puts a significant strain on the economy.

That North Korea has such a low standard of living despite its exceptionally large reserves of mineral deposits is primarily due to the political leadership's insistence on retaining a socialist economic system. North Korea takes great pride in having stayed true to its socialist principles, with only temporary and rather marginal attempts at reform, while Russia, China and other former socialist nations have been lured by the 'temptations' of capitalism.

Although North Korea's agricultural sector employs around six times as many people as its South Korean counterpart, the country's agricultural production barely meets demand even in good years.[301] When crops fail because of droughts or other natural disasters, food shortages and frequent famines of a similar magnitude as those sustained in pre-capitalist China are the result.

The worst of these famines happened in 1996, when the combined effects of a mismanagement of resources, drought and flooding left 200,000 North Koreans dead from starvation, according to official figures. The actual death toll is hard to verify – estimates by foreign agencies set the total at up to 3 million, or one in eight North Koreans. Just as China's communist leadership once blamed millions of deaths from starvation on natural disasters (see Chapter 1), the North Korean regime does the same, shifting the blame for any food shortages and other economic troubles onto either Western sanctions or natural events.

However, as China's example shows, bad crop seasons – which can happen in any political or economic system, e.g. due to extended periods of drought – don't necessarily have to lead to its inhabitants dying of starvation. It is not droughts as such that cause thousands of deaths, but the deficits of a planned-economy system whose agricultural production barely meets demand even under normal conditions, which means that fluctuating crop yields caused by changes in weather patterns can have fatal consequences.

SOUTH KOREA

The contrast between North and South Korea could hardly be starker. According to the 2018 Index of Economic Freedom, the latter ranks 27th among the freest countries in the world, just behind Germany in 25th and ahead of Japan in 30th place and with a score of 90.7 out of 100 possible points in the 'business freedom' category.[302] North Korea, by comparison, brings up the rear in 180th place and scores only 5.0 out of 100 points in the 'business freedom' category.[303]

In the wake of World War II, South Korea found itself in a difficult starting position with no financial aid coming from the US, while North Korea received considerable support from the Soviet Union and China. South Korea was an agricultural country without any significant mineral deposits – almost all of the Korean peninsula's reserves of natural resources, which include iron ore, gold, copper, lead, zinc, graphite, molybdenum, limestone and marble, are located in North Korea.[304] South Korea's population grew very quickly – from 16 million to 21 million between 1945 and 1947 alone – due to the influx of refugees from the communist north. Many people lived at or below subsistence level.[305]

In July 1961, the Japanese government listed seven reasons why economic independence would be impossible for South Korea: over-population, lack of resources, lack of industrialization, massive military obligations, lack of political skills, lack of capital and lack of administrative skills.[306] South Korea's failure to achieve any meaningful economic progress in the 1950s, immediately after the Korean War, initially appeared to confirm this view. At USD 79, South Korea had one of the lowest per-capita incomes in the world.

The country's prospects finally started to improve with Park Chung-hee's rise to power in 1961. By the time the autocratic ruler was assassinated by the director of the Korean Central Intelligence Agency in 1979, he had become the founding father of South Korea's economic miracle. Park initially favoured a centralized state-controlled economic system but was persuaded otherwise by Samsung founder Lee Byung-chull, who is reported to have advised him "that only a relatively liberal market economy would be able to release the entrepreneurial initiative and creative thinking required to compete in the global market and ensure the availability of state-of-the-art products".[307] The Korean term for conglomerates such as Samsung is *chaebol*, which translates as 'business family'. These powerful family-owned enterprises have made a crucial contribution to South Korea's rise to economic prosperity. It is no coincidence that the founder of one of them should have had a decisive influence on Park's economic policy.

The close relationship between the government and these large family-owned enterprises was a defining feature of the South Korean economy at this time. Although the government issued plans to set development and production targets, these were completely different from the economic planning in socialist systems. Rather than the government telling companies what to do, as would be the case in a planned economy, the companies themselves had a significant influence on government policy. Corruption was rife in this system. In building his own power base, Park relied on the support of the powerful *chaebol* companies, which preceded his regime – 27 of today's top 30 *chaebol* conglomerates date back to before 1961.[308]

Unlike the privately owned enterprises in North Korea, which were nationalized, their South Korean counterparts were compensated for their wartime losses. This was achieved by privatizing Japanese assets, which were then sold to a few owners of family-run enterprises. Almost half of the new owners came from families of medium-size or large landowners. "This is where the roots of the rapid advance of the model of hierarchically organized, family-coordinated corporations lie and the corporate structure shaped by family clans able to leverage borrowed capital to flexibly expand into different industries to meet industrial policy targets was established."[309]

Today, the large Korean *chaebol* brands are – literally – household names for consumers all over the world: Samsung is Apple's main competitor, while TV sets and home electronics made by LG are popular worldwide. These family-owned groups are more diversified than most US corporations, excepting a few outliers such as General Electric. Many *chaebol* conglomerates consist of dozens of individual companies that operate across a range of different industries. In the mid-1990s, the largest five were active in an average of 142 markets each (calculated by product category), while the 6th to 10th and 11th to 15th largest served averages of 63 and 39 markets respectively.[310]

Small and medium-sized enterprises, on the other hand, were struggling to compete and did not play a significant role in South Korea until the 1980s and 1990s. The percentage of the total workforce who were employed in small and medium-sized enterprises (up to 100 employees) grew from 35% in 1970 to around 58% in 1998.[311] Today, the large *chaebol* brands are still crucial to the Korean economy. They have always had a very strong focus on research and development. Both Hyundai and Samsung grew their research departments exponentially between 1980 and 1994, with a sixfold increase from 616 to 3,890 employees and a staggering 13-fold increase from 690 to 8,919 employees respectively.[312]

Of the many disruptions that threatened to derail the development of the South Korean economy, the 1997–1998 financial crisis was the most severe. Korea was hit hard by the crisis, with a 25% loss in the average total income from 1996/97 to 1997/98, rising unemployment and a drop in real wages resulting in negative welfare effects of 45% during this period according to estimates by economists.[313] Critics of capitalism like to cite crises of this kind as proof of the weakness of the capitalist system, when in fact they are a necessary part of the cycle and often have a cleansing effect by ensuring that companies which are no longer profitable disappear from the market.

The collapse of the Daewoo Group is a prime example. Founded by Kim Woo-choong, a hugely successful entrepreneur who started in the textile industry and subsequently entered the heavy metal, automotive and electronics industries, the company went bankrupt in 1999 in the wake of the 1997–1998 financial crisis.[314] Today, the companies that came out of the breakup of South Korea's fourth-largest group operate as independent enterprises, some of them very successfully.

As a result of the severe crisis in 1997–1998, South Korea was temporarily placed under monitoring by the International Monetary Fund (IMF). Although the restructuring reforms imposed by the IMF garnered a lot of criticism, they quickly produced positive results, which enabled the country to overcome the crisis in a surprisingly short period of time. Even more importantly, the reforms generated long-term positive effects by adding momentum to the liberalization of the South Korean economy that had started in the 1980s.

Many *chaebol* groups were dismantled or stripped down to their core operations, while the South Korean economy was opened to foreign investors to a previously unprecedented degree. The year 1998 also saw the complete liberalization of the financial market and the legalization of mergers and takeovers – including hostile ones – involving foreign companies.[315]

Samsung sold dozens of divisions that were not part of the corporation's core operations and let go around a third of its remaining employees during this period. These measures would pay off, making Samsung one of the fastest-growing South Korean brands after the crisis.[316] Today, it is one of the world's 20 largest companies by market capitalization, ranking immediately behind the US giant Walmart and ahead of AT&T.[317]

While South Korea's economic rise was driven by economic liberalization, at least initially this didn't coincide with the country's transition to a democracy, which didn't happen until 1987. Free-market reform and political liberalization may coincide in some cases but, as the examples of China and Chile (see Chapters 1 and 6) confirm, it is sometimes possible for the former to happen without the latter. From the early 1980s onwards, the South Korean government started to gradually relinquish its strong influence on the economy. The privatization of the banks was an important step in this direction. The percentage of loans managed by the country's National Investment Fund went down from 25% in 1979 to 5% in 1991. In 1980, the Korea Fair Trade Commission was set up under a new anti-trust law. Continuing liberalization during the 1990s made it possible for South Korea to join the Organisation for Economic Co-operation and Development (OECD) in 1996.[318]

In his standard reference work on the Korean economy, published in 2013, the German economist Dieter Schneidewind reports: "The government is increasingly withdrawing from managing day-to-day economic activity but continues to set targets and grant loans and tax incentives to support promising developments. With free rein given to the domestic free-market economy, regulations that previously controlled and restricted international exchange are to a large extent being relaxed, allowing entrepreneurship and creativity to develop powerfully to their full potential."[319] Werner Pascha, who is less impressed by the country's record of economic liberalization, argues that South Korea's most recent presidents all actively instituted industrial policy agendas – including Park Chung-hee's daughter Park Geun-hye, who held the office between 2013 and 2017. While nowhere near as interventional as her father's economic policy, her government influenced industrial development by promoting a 'creative economy' and giving financial support to IT businesses.[320]

The example of South Korea – especially when held up for comparison with its communist neighbour – demonstrates the superior strength of capitalism. By the same token, it also shows that the economic system is only one of several preconditions for a country's rise to economic success. Although the restructuring of the economy in the capitalist mould laid the foundations for success, cultural factors have always contributed significantly to the magnitude of that success. Specifically, I am referring here to the South Koreans' legendary willingness to work and study hard. I remember one of my previous bosses, Professor Jürgen Falter, returning from a trip to South Korea when I was working as a research assistant at the Free University of Berlin. The large numbers of students who were still in the library at midnight – at a time when the library at our university closed at 6.30pm – had made a huge impression on him.

Education is taken more seriously in South Korea than almost anywhere else in the world. With a 20% share – a number that has remained more or less constant over the past 30 years – education is the largest item in the public budget.[321] Add to this government spending the significant private investment in education, which amounts to around 3% of GDP, and South Korea spends more on education than any other country. With around 80% of higher-education institutions in private ownership, the South Korean education system has a far stronger free-market focus than most other countries. The quality of its institutions is excellent. Eight Korean universities are ranked among the world's 100 most innovative universities, with the Korea Advanced Institute of Science and Technology the only university outside the US to make it into the top ten.[322]

For all their top-rate quality, these universities are no match for the zeal of Korean students. Wealthy families in particular frequently send their sons and daughters overseas, preferably to US universities, to finish their education. With almost all leading positions in politics and business currently held by individuals with a PhD from a US university, a degree from a South Korean elite university followed by postgraduate studies in the US has become virtually de rigueur for any South Korean aspiring to a successful career.[323]

At primary and secondary levels, private schools also play an important role. On top of their regular lessons, 77% of schoolchildren spend an extra 10.2 hours a week on average at one of the almost 100,000 *hagwon* or private tuition schools. The average South Korean family spends USD 800 a month on private tuition,[324] although the country's public schools are among the best-equipped and most progressive in the world. As early as 2001, all primary and secondary schools were connected to the internet and South Korea's 340,000 teachers all had their own computers. By 2003, 14 'cyber universities' had gone online.[325]

The positive outcomes of this educational zeal are reflected in international rankings. In the OECD's 2015 Programme for International Student Assessment, the performance of South Korean students was ranked 11th out of 70 countries in science (ahead of the UK in 15th place, Germany in 16th and the US in 25th) and 7th in mathematics. Perhaps even more impressive is the country's high share of top performers in at least one subject, which at 25.6% far exceeds the OECD average of 15.3%. Conversely, at 7.7%, South Korea's share of low achievers in all three subjects is far below the average of 13%.[326]

These outcomes are a reflection of the tremendous propensity for hard work typical of Korean students. *Sadang orak* (literally: 'four rise, five fall') is a slogan drummed into students preparing to sit their university entrance exams: anybody who spends more than four hours a day sleeping rather than studying will fail the exams.[327] School starts at 9 am and finishes at 5 pm, after which students do their homework and spend time on the internet. Between the ages of 10 and 12 and again between 16 and 18, the vast majority attend *hagwon* schools to help them get into the best secondary schools and universities.[328]

Adults work equally long hours. "Koreans are expected to keep hard at it until the job at hand is finished," Schneidewind says. "Many Koreans work as long as they still can, and many elderly people keep working pretty much until they die, with barely a glance at the clock or the day of the week, let alone their annual leave." Those who have more spare time – the employees of large corporations, for example – rarely fritter it away on leisure activities. Instead, they attend professional development courses or take on a second job.[329]

Although these cultural dispositions have played a key role in the economic success of South Korea and other Asian nations, that success was only possible in combination with a capitalist system. After all, North and South Korea share the same centuries-old traditions. However, in an economic system as inefficient as the North Korean one, their positive impact on economic development is hampered or channelled into ideological ceremonies, military drills and arms production.

CHAPTER 5

Chancing More Capitalism: Thatcher's *and* Reagan's Pro-market Reforms in the UK *and* the US

Every once in a while, capitalist systems require comprehensive reforms because people have lost sight of the foundations of their success. In democratic countries, politicians often win elections with promises of free gifts for their voters. Their attempts to address supposed 'social injustices' usually involve borrowing ever larger amounts of money to spend on social welfare schemes. Politicians and civil servants also have a tendency to interfere in the economy in the misguided belief that they can steer the economy better than the market – a belief they share with the adherents of the socialist planned economy.

THATCHER'S PRO-MARKET REFORMS IN THE UK

In 1966, the Beatles released a track called 'Taxman,' which starts with the lines:

Let me tell you how it will be
That's one for you, 19 for me...
Should 5 percent appear too small,
Be thankful I don't take it all.

The lyrics were written in protest against the excessive taxation in the UK, which up until the 1970s was tantamount to expropriating high-earning individuals, with an income tax rate of 83% for those in the highest bracket, while capital gains were taxed at up to 98%.

After World War II, the UK had taken a path that was very different from West Germany's introduction of the 'social market economy' under Ludwig Erhard, which laid the foundations for the 'economic miracle' of the 1950s and 1960s (see Chapter 3). In the UK, the victory of the left-wing Labour Party in the 1945 general elections had led to the implementation of a form of democratic socialism under the then prime minister Clement Attlee, at the core of which was a massive programme of nationalization. Once banks, civil aviation, and the mining and telecommunications industries had been nationalized, the railways, shipping canals, road freight transport, power and gas soon followed, as did manufacturing industries including iron and steel. In total, about a fifth of the UK economy was nationalized. In many cases, senior executives stayed in their jobs, although they were now working as civil servants.

The government also tried to take control of what remained of the private sector. In her memoirs, Conservative prime minister Margaret Thatcher quotes the liberal economist Arthur Shenfield, who quipped that "the difference between the public and private sectors was that the private sector was controlled by government, and the public sector wasn't controlled by anyone".[330] If Labour had its way, the UK was to become a textbook example of democratic socialism as a third way between communism and capitalism.

Even after the Conservative Party (known as the Tories) returned to power after the general elections in October 1951, the new government under Winston Churchill retained the majority of the socialist policies implemented by its Labour predecessor. This post-war consensus lasted until the 1970s, with many Conservative politicians sharing the belief that the economy should be controlled by the state.

During the 1950s and 1960s, the UK enjoyed an improved standard of living, low unemployment and increased consumption, but lagged behind other European countries – West Germany in particular – in terms of the number of telephones, refrigerators, TV sets and washing machines per 100 residents. The gap continued to grow because productivity was too low in the UK.

During the 1970s, the UK's weaknesses became painfully obvious. The unions were very strong, and the country was riven by frequent strikes. A report published in the German news magazine *Der Spiegel* in January 1974 depicts a country with millions of un- or underemployed and a capital plunged into darkness at night:[331] "For what seem quite minor reasons, a row about wages between miners and nationalized collieries turned into a showdown between the government and the unions, which has plunged the country into a 'new dark age' (*Newsweek*). Last week saw a 40-percent drop in coal production and a 50-percent drop in steel production. Over a million people are already unemployed, over two million only in part-time employment, with a further ten million plus – almost half of the British workforce – likely to suffer the same fate in the next few weeks. Every short working week costs the British people the equivalent of 2.5 billion Deutschmarks." In an attempt to save coal, the government had introduced three-day weeks.

"The swinging London of the 1960s", the report went on, "has become as bleak as in Dickensian times, its imperial avenues more sparsely lit than the streets in the urban slums of the UK's former colonies. Candles flicker in the offices of the financial district, while hurricane lamps provide emergency lighting in department stores, and warehouses are illuminated by the headlights of lorries. Only one in four radiators is turned on inside the prime minister's residence at 10, Downing Street, and signs at underground stations advise passengers to take the stairs as escalators have been taken out of service to save power."

These strikes and emergencies made the deep-rooted problems of the British welfare state blatantly obvious. Even *Der Spiegel*, a left-leaning magazine not known for its pro-capitalist sympathies, had to concede: "No other nation in history has allowed trade unions to grow as rampantly as they have done in [Britain] since the early years of the industrial age. Class warfare was invented in this country, and so was strike action as one of its most effective weapons. A power that had once been at the forefront of industrialization became an industrial invalid ... The shop stewards – the unions' spokesmen within the companies – were able to call a strike and to break collective agreements whenever they wanted to, without the need to hold a strike ballot. Neither the unions nor their officials could be held accountable for any damages caused by these wild strikes. The shop stewards took advantage of the licence they were given to occupy positions of unprecedented power within the companies. For some union officials, their own interest and envy of their co-workers mattered more than their fight against the company owners. In many cases, the shop stewards' behaviour on the factory floor was every bit as imperious as that of the company bosses in their offices ... For several months, the rivalry between two steelworkers' unions, both of which were trying to secure well-paid jobs as operators of the new equipment, prevented testing of a new manufacturing process. The dockworkers' union protested against the construction of state-of-the-art container terminals, where loading tasks were to be done by workers from a different sector of the transport industry. England's most advanced high-speed train stood idle on an unused track for almost half a year because the railroad workers' union insisted on two drivers, although there was only room enough for one in the operator's cabin."

The UK was notorious for the power of the unions – 466 in total – and their members' predilection for strike action. Throughout the 1970s, the country saw over 2,000 strikes a year with an average loss of almost 13 million working days.[332] In 1972 alone, almost 24 million working days were lost, a level the country had last experienced during the General Strike in 1926. The British unions were dominated by communists and other left-wing militants who were far less interested in improving their members' living and working conditions than in destroying what was left of the free-market economy. Their workers' poor standard of living led them to agree with their demands.

The economically deprived regions within the UK – Northern England, Scotland and Wales – were home to Western Europe's lowest-paid workers, who were earning 25% less than their peers in other European Community (EC) member states. "With London and South East England the only parts of the country where incomes are above the community-wide average, among the nine member EC states only the Italians and the Irish are worse off than the British," *Der Spiegel* reported. "While the worst-paid miners [in the German coal industry] earn a basic salary of around 220 Deutschmarks a week, their British counterparts make only [the equivalent of] around 170 Deutschmarks. With a GDP of 9,240 Deutschmarks per capita, [the UK] ranked in seventh place among EC members in 1972 (with 13,345 Deutschmarks, the Federal Republic of Germany came second behind Denmark). The pay rises British workers have fought so hard for over the past years have been consumed by rising prices to a higher extent than in other countries. Between 1968 and mid-1972, the buying power of their wages rose by a meagre 8 percent, while West-German workers recorded a plus of 26 percent in real terms, and the French and the Dutch were better off by 17 percent."

While paying lip service to the idea of reducing government influence in the economic sphere and restricting the power of the unions, the Tory government under Edward Heath failed to make any meaningful changes to the status quo. With inflation on the rise in 1972, the Heath government resorted to stopgap measures in the time-honoured socialist mould. In Thatcher's words: "After a reforming start, Ted Heath's Government [of which she was a member] proposed and almost implemented the most radical form of socialism ever contemplated by an elected British Government. It offered state control of prices and dividends, and the joint oversight of economic policy by a tripartite body representing the Trades Union Congress, the Confederation of British Industry and the Government, in return for trade union acquiescence in an incomes policy. We were saved from this abomination by the conservatism and suspicion of the [Trades Union Congress], which perhaps could not believe that their 'class enemy' was prepared to surrender without a fight."[333]

Thatcher didn't reserve her criticism for the unions and Labour alone – she also castigated her own party for having done nothing to reverse the UK's transition to a socialist welfare state. "We boasted of spending more money than Labour, not of restoring people to independence and self-reliance."[334] Her verdict was scathing: "No theory of government was ever given a fairer test or a more prolonged experiment in a democratic country than democratic socialism received in Britain. Yet it was a miserable failure in every respect. Far from reversing the slow relative decline of Britain vis-à-vis its main industrial competitors, it accelerated it. We fell further behind them, until by 1979 we were widely dismissed as 'the sick man of Europe.'"[335]

The German economist Holger Schmieding, who first visited the UK in the late 1970s as a young man, remembers feeling shocked "by the terrible standard of living across the country. Many households lacked the appliances we had in our kitchen, utilities room and living room at home. Large parts of the country looked picturesquely dilapidated. The antiquated transport system and the abominable quality of many goods and services made matters worse. At the time, the UK was miles away from the standards I was used to from home or those I had been privileged to experience a few years earlier as a high-school student in the US. If it hadn't been for the memory of the many British soldiers stationed close to my parents' house near Osnabrück at the time, my first visit to the UK might have made me wonder which country had actually won the war."[336]

Conditions escalated during the winter of 1978–1979, when the country was paralysed by yet another round of strikes by public service and transport workers. The public transport system broke down in many places, while rotting garbage piled up on the pavements and the National Health Service was on the brink of collapse. "The country appeared to descend into chaos, and the Labour government's inability to restrain the unions lent credibility to Thatcher's urgent appeals for a change of direction."[337]

On 3 May 1979, the Conservatives won the general election with a majority of 339 out of 635 seats. Thatcher's economic vision had crystallized during the 1970s. While in the 1960s her criticism of the welfare state had stopped short of proposing to dismantle it altogether, she had already raised strong concerns about "scroungers" exploiting the system and the dangers of exploding expenditure.[338] In the meantime, she had studied the writings of liberal thinkers – those of Friedrich August von Hayek in particular – as well as the Austrian-born philosopher Karl Popper's trenchant critique of socialist ideas, and had been impressed by their radical critique of socialism and the welfare state. She now had the opportunity to put these ideas into practice, although she was well aware of the massive resistance she was likely to encounter from socialists and unions.

The challenges seemed so huge that a successful outcome was by no means a foregone conclusion. Thatcher's cabinet included a number of traditional Conservatives who weren't willing to support radical reforms – "wets", as Thatcher liked to call them – "political calculators who see the task of Conservatives as one of retreating gracefully before the Left's inevitable advance".[339]

Inflation stood at 10% by the time she took office and was bound to keep rising. Resisting the temptation to stick to price controls and other conventional measures, as her predecessors had done, Thatcher used the debate following her government's first Queen's Speech (the Queen's formal statement to open Parliament and outline the government's policy priorities) to announce her intention to abolish price controls: "Perhaps the first time our opponents truly realized that the Government's rhetorical commitment to the market would be matched by practical action was the day we announced abolition [of the Price Commission]."[340]

Thatcher's reforms initially focused on fighting inflation, which predictably led to a sharp rise in unemployment from 1.3 million in 1979 to 3 million in 1983 – caused partly by global economic upheavals and partly by her government's pro-market reforms, as Thatcher herself admitted. "The paradox which neither British trade unions nor the socialists were prepared to accept was that an increase of productivity is likely, initially, to reduce the number of jobs before creating the wealth that sustains new ones."[341] Inflation did fall to below 10% in the short term, accompanied by a significant improvement in the sluggish productivity rates that Thatcher considered the root cause of all other problems plaguing the UK economy.

One of her first steps towards a more business-friendly economy was to cut marginal tax rates from 33% to 30% in the lowest brackets and from 83% to 60% in the highest brackets (followed by further cuts to 25% and 40% respectively in 1988). Faced with a disastrous budgetary situation, she was forced to raise VAT from 12.5% to 15% while retaining existing exemptions for food items and other essentials. She also took steps to reduce bureaucracy by expediting planning permissions for industrial and office developments and simplifying or abolishing a range of planning controls.[342]

Thatcher saw her greatest challenge in restricting the power of the unions – an issue that would plague her throughout her time in office and constitute one of the defining conflicts of her premiership. Much to the disgust of Labour and the unions, Thatcher used her government's first Queen's Speech to announce proposals for a three-pronged legislative attack against traditional cornerstones of union power: secondary picketing, the closed shop and secret ballots. Firstly, by outlawing secondary picketing, she proposed to restrict the right to picket to "those in dispute with their employer at their own place of work". Secondly, her government was "committed to changing the law on the closed shop, under which employees had effectively been compelled to join a union if they wished to obtain or keep a job, and which at that time covered some five million workers". Thirdly, Thatcher proposed to introduce legislation to make public funds "available to finance postal ballots for union elections and other important union decisions".[343] The first steps towards implementing these changes were adopted as early as 1980.

Subsequent measures included restrictions of the right to carry out sympathy strikes. In 1984–1985, Arthur Scargill – a prominent union leader and outspoken critic of Thatcher's policies who refused to "accept that we are landed for the next four years with this Government"[344] – led the miners into a large-scale strike against planned pit closures and privatizations. Although three in four pits were operating at a loss and "the industry was receiving £1.3 billion of subsidies from the taxpayer in 1983–84",[345] the union fought bitterly against closing a single pit.

Since many miners didn't support the strike, Scargill had decided against holding a strike ballot. The situation escalated when violent means were used to prevent those miners who wanted to work from crossing the picket lines. Attacks on police officers by striking workers or sympathizers resulted in serious injuries in many cases. The families of miners who didn't take part in the strike were threatened and bullied. There were frequent escalations of violence, including the killing of a Welsh taxi driver by two striking miners who dropped a concrete block from a footbridge onto his taxi while he was driving a strike-breaking miner to work.

Support for the striking miners in the general population was undermined by allegations of secret slush funds flowing from Libyan dictator Muammar al-Gaddafi and bogus unions in Soviet-occupied Afghanistan. Nevertheless, the strike went on for almost a year. On both sides, there was far more at stake than pit closures. On the part of the unions, the strikes were a display of power and an attempt to cut Thatcher down to size. When she refused to give in, the unions eventually had to abandon the strike when they ran out of money.

Their defeat had a symbolic impact – Thatcher's uncompromising stance broke the power of the unions, who had lost a third of their members and much of their political influence by the time she left office. During the final year of her premiership, there were fewer strikes than in any other year since 1935. At less than 2 million, the number of working days lost to strike action was significantly lower than the 1970s average of nearly 13 million.

No other European politician has ever implemented a pro-market-reform programme as uncompromisingly as Thatcher did. During her second term in office, she pushed the privatization of state-owned enterprises. Thatcher saw privatization as "one of the central means of reversing the corrosive and corrupting effects of socialism". Far from putting the people in control, public ownership was simply "ownership by an impersonal legal entity: it amounts to control by politicians and civil servants", she argued. "But through privatization – particularly the kind of privatization which leads to the widest possible share ownership by members of the public – the state's power is reduced and the power of the people enhanced."[346]

From being a marginal aspect, privatization grew to become the mainstay of Thatcher's political agenda and legacy. British Telecom, which employed a staff of 250,000, was the first service provider to undergo privatization. Of the 2 million Britons who bought shares in what was then the largest initial public offering (IPO) in economic history, around half had never owned shares before. During Thatcher's time in office, the percentage of Britons who owned shares rose from 7% to 25%.[347]

The privatization of British Airways, BP (British Petroleum), automotive companies including Rolls Royce and Jaguar, shipbuilding companies and a number of local utilities resulted in the state losing its dominant influence on the British economy. Under the right-to-buy scheme, local councils sold off much of their housing stock to tenants to create a million new homeowners.[348] However, in this instance it might well have made more sense to sell the publicly owned properties to professional property management companies, or to float them on the stock market, as was done with other privatized assets.

Productivity increased considerably in privatized businesses. Ten years after privatization, telecommunications prices had fallen by 50%, while prices for the products and services of other privatized companies also dropped. Studies have shown improvements in service quality in privatized businesses across the board. "Before privatization, it had taken months and sometimes a bribe to get a new telephone line," Chris Edwards claims in an article on "Thatcher's Privatization Legacy". Over the decade following privatization, the share of service calls completed within eight days rose from 59% to 97%.[349]

So successful was the British model that it triggered an "ongoing privatization revolution that has swept the world since the 1980s", with governments in over a hundred countries following the UK's lead and privatizing formerly state-owned businesses valued at over USD 3.3 trillion in total.[350]

Although Thatcher confides in her Downing Street memoirs that there "was still much I would have liked to do", her overall assessment of her time in office is a positive one: "Britain under my premiership was the first country to reverse the onward march of socialism. By the time I left office, the state-owned sector of industry had been reduced by some 60 percent. Around one in four of the population owned shares. Over six hundred thousand jobs had passed from the public to the private sector."[351] Her policies had resulted in a rise of profitability and productivity that in due course enabled the creation of 3.32 million jobs between March 1983 and March 1990.[352]

Thatcher largely deregulated the financial sector, making the UK one of the first countries to abolish currency and capital controls. Over the course of a few short years, the City of London firmly established its reputation as a global magnet for asset management companies. The 1986 Financial Services Act liberalized the rules of the London Stock Exchange, abolished the separation between those who traded stocks and shares and those who advised investors, and eliminated restrictions on foreign banks. These changes were so comprehensive and transformative as to be dubbed a 'Big Bang' by the media. They made London the world's leading financial centre – rivalled only by New York – and created hundreds of thousands of new jobs, many of them with the rapidly growing branches established by foreign banks.

Thanks to the tax revenue generated by these increases in productivity, the UK was able to significantly reduce its public debt. In 1976, the country had been close to sovereign default and had been forced to borrow USD 3.9 billion from the International Monetary Fund.[353] In 1978, the deficit stood at 4.4% of GDP (compared to 2.4% in Germany). A decade later, in 1989, the UK economy generated a surplus of 1.6%. Public debt fell from 54.6% of GDP in 1980 to 40.1% in 1989.[354]

Pre-Thatcher Britain had been the country with the highest marginal tax rate in Europe (up to 98%). By the time she left office, the UK's maximum tax rate of 40% was lower than that of any other European country except for tax havens such as Liechtenstein and Monaco. The stuffy socialist culture of envy was replaced by a pro-market and pro-business environment where ambition was richly rewarded, which in turn led to a sharp increase in the number of private businesses and self-employment. From 1.89 million in 1979, the total number of businesses registered in the UK rose to over 3 million by 1989, while the number of people registered as self-employed grew from 1.9 million to 3.5 million during the same period.[355]

Thatcher has been criticized for widening the income gap. But she at no time promised voters greater equality – she was voted into office on a mandate to liberate the economy from the shackles of state control. And, as a result of these reforms, the production workers experienced 25.8% growth in real take-home pay between 1979 and 1994.[356] During the same period, net wages in Germany and France rose by only 2.5% and 1.8% respectively. The British voters honoured Thatcher's success by re-electing her – not just once, but twice. She stayed in office for a total of 11 years, longer than any other 20th-century British prime minister.

For many on the left, Thatcher may have been a figure of hate for her anti-socialist policies. However, many outcomes of her reforms were so successful that the new government under Tony Blair made no attempt to reverse the reforms when Labour eventually came back into power in 1997. Much like Germany's Social Democratic chancellor at the time (Gerhard Schröder, initially a close ally of Blair), Blair broke with his party's tradition of supporting a state-controlled economy and instead positioned himself as a staunch proponent of free-market capitalism.

RONALD REAGAN'S PRO-MARKET REFORMS IN THE US

Fans and critics alike tend to mention Margaret Thatcher and Ronald Reagan in the same breath – rightly so, since the two politicians shared an agenda best summarized as 'chancing more capitalism'. In the 1970s, the US was plagued by an ever-growing array of problems, most of which were the result of excessive government intervention in the economy and the proliferation of welfare programmes, belying the popular European image of the US as a textbook example of a free-market economy unburdened by any welfare programmes and institutions.

Welfare spending in fact increased from USD 3.57 billion to USD 66.7 billion between 1940 and 1970 – and more than quadrupled to USD 292 billion by 1980. Adjusted for inflation and population growth, per-capita federal spending on welfare programmes almost doubled from USD 1,293 in 1970 to USD 2,555 in 1980.[357]

Annual growth in per-capita welfare expenditure stood at 12.5% a year under the Johnson administration (1963–1969), 8.3% a year during Richard Nixon's and Gerald Ford's presidencies (1969 to 1977), and 3.2% a year during Jimmy Carter's term in office (1977–1981).[358]

Many US citizens' economic situation had deteriorated prior to Reagan's arrival in the White House, although the economic decline had been nowhere near as drastic as in pre-Thatcher Britain.[359] In real terms, white Americans' household incomes dropped by 2.2% between 1973 and 1981, while African Americans saw their household incomes shrink by 4.4.%. Worst off were the poorest 25% of the overall population, whose incomes dropped by 5%. At the other end of the income spectrum, high earners were squeezed with tax rates of up to 70%.

Unemployment had risen to 7.6% when Reagan took office, while inflation stood at over 10% for three consecutive years, climbing to 13.5% – the highest level since 1947 – in 1980. Homeowners and property investors were hit especially hard when already-high interest rates of 15% in 1980 soared to a record level of 18.9% in the following year.[360]

In other words, Reagan took office at a time when the economic outlook was bleak. Having grown up in a modest home, he started his career as a radio announcer before moving on to film with acting roles in over 50 Hollywood films. Between 1967 and 1975, he served two terms as governor of California, where he successfully balanced the budget and achieved a significant economic recovery.

Reagan won 44 states, a large majority of the electoral vote (489 to 49) and 50.7% of the popular vote in his landslide victory over the incumbent president, Jimmy Carter, on 4 November 1980. Rather than basing his election campaign on conservative values, he "simply asked voters if they were better or worse off in 1980 than they had been four years ago".[361] His inaugural address on 20 January 1981 conveyed a simple message, which he would repeat many times over the coming years: "In this present crisis, government is not the solution to our problem, government *is* the problem."[362] Some years later, in a news conference in August 1986, he would famously say: "The most terrifying words in the English language are: 'I'm from the government and I'm here to help.'"[363] Reagan's political agenda was a simple one: restricting the influence of the state in the economic sphere and increasing the role of the free market. In order to restore a more robust version of capitalism, he reduced bureaucracy, abolished unnecessary restrictions and slashed taxes.

In 1981, around 60 Democrats voted with the Republican minority in Congress to pass Reagan's Economic Recovery Tax Act, which phased in a 25% cut in marginal individual tax rates over three years along with introducing incentives for small businesses and personal savings. The bill also included a provision to index tax rates from 1985 onwards to avoid bracket creep (the process by which inflation pushes income into higher tax brackets, resulting in higher taxation but no increase in real purchasing power). Democrats had also proposed tax cuts of their own, spread over four years instead of three, but experts calculated that if inflation remained at 8% over the four-year period, 98% of the 25% cut would be lost to bracket creep unless tax rates were adjusted in response to inflation.[364]

These were the most drastic tax cuts in American history to date, and they would save American taxpayers a total of USD 718 billion between 1981 and 1986 according to a prognosis by the US Treasury. However, Reagan hoped that they would in fact help him to keep his election promise of raising tax revenue by stimulating growth. At a press conference in October 1981, he quoted the 14th-century Muslim philosopher Ibn Khaldūn's foreshadowing of the Laffer Curve theory, as this effect is called in economic jargon: "In the beginning of the dynasty, great tax revenues were gained from small assessments. At the end of the dynasty, small tax revenues were gained from large assessments." Reagan added: "And we're trying to get down to the small assessments and the great revenues." And that's exactly what he did.[365]

The economists William A. Niskanen and Stephen Moore have analysed ten key supply-side indicators to compare the economic record of the Reagan years with the periods immediately preceding (1974 to 1981) and following (1989 to 1995) his two terms in the White House.[366] Following are their conclusions.

Economic growth during the Reagan years was 3.2% per year, compared to 2.8% during the Carter–Ford years and 2.1% during the Bush–Clinton years. Niskanen and Moore emphasize that the growth rate for the Reagan years includes the recession of the early 1980s, a side effect of reversing Carter's high-inflation policies. From 1983 to 1989, GDP grew by 3.8% a year, and by the end of Reagan's second term the US economy was almost one third larger than when he first took office.[367]

This growth was a direct consequence of Reagan's deregulation and tax reform policies in conjunction with falling oil prices. The growth rate in the 1980s was higher than in the 1950s and 1970s, though substantially below the growth rate of 5% following John F. Kennedy's 1964 tax rate cuts of 30%.

Median household incomes grew by USD 4,000 from USD 37,868 in 1981 to USD 42,049 in 1989 after having stagnated during the preceding eight-year period. Under Reagan's successor, George W. Bush Sr., they fell by USD 1,438.

Unemployment stood at 7.6% when Reagan took office, rising to almost 10% during the 1981–1982 recession. It then continued to fall to 5.5% by the end of his second term. Between 1981 and 1989, 17 million new jobs – roughly 2 million a year – were created.

Inflation was in double digits when Reagan arrived at the White House. By his second year in office, it had fallen by more than half, to 6.2%. By the end of his second term, it stood at only 4.1%, largely due to the prudent monetary policy of Paul Volcker, who was chairman of the Federal Reserve from 1979 and 1987. Although well aware that it would cause a temporary recession, Reagan explicitly supported Volcker's strategy. Contrary to the dire predictions of many of his critics, his drastic tax cuts did not lead to further increases in inflation.

As a November 1981 article in the *Wall Street Journal* explained, this combination of fiscal restraint and drastic tax cuts was precisely the secret to Reagan's later successes: "You fight inflation with a tight monetary policy. And you offset the possible recessionary impact of tight monetary policy with the incentive effects of reductions in marginal tax rates. Since we are now having a recession, you could claim the formula has failed, except for one detail: We've had tight money all right, but dear friends, we haven't had any tax cut."[368] The tax cuts took effect on 1 January 1983, marking the beginning of an era now remembered as the 'Seven Fat Years'.

Interest rates fell sharply during the Reagan years. Interest rates on a 30-year mortgage fell from 18.9% in 1981 to 8.2% in 1987, while the Treasury Bill rate fell from 14% in 1981 to 7% in 1988.

These achievements are only slightly overshadowed by less positive figures in three areas of analysis. *Productivity* grew by only 1.5% a year, which was lower than in the three decades preceding Reagan's presidency, though significantly higher than the 0.3% annual growth achieved under Bill Clinton. The *personal savings rate* fell from 8% to 6.5% during the 1980s.

Reagan's critics like to point to one statistic in particular to show what was wrong with his economic policy: the *budget deficit*, which in 1981 stood at USD 101 billion[369] and 2.7% of GDP, rose to USD 236 billion and 6.3% of the GDP by 1983. When Reagan left the White House, he left a USD 141 billion deficit (2.9% of the GDP). National debt doubled from USD 1,004 to USD 2,026 billion during his presidency – a dramatic growth rate compared to the previous years, though relatively modest in comparison to the growth rates under Bush Sr. and Barack Obama.

Reagan had campaigned on a platform that included the promise to create new jobs, fight inflation, lower taxes and promote economic growth, while increasing military spending and reducing the budget deficit. Achieving all of this at the same time proved impossible even for him – not least because his administration had promised to protect 'core safety net programs' including social security, unemployment benefits, cash benefits for the elderly poor and the veterans programme, which accounted for two thirds of federal transfer payments.[370] Along with the cost of his ambitious plans to accelerate defence spending, these expenses added up to 70% of the total budget for 1981, which left him very little room for manoeuvre to reduce the level of spending.[371]

The attempt to establish a direct link between the growing debt and Reagan's tax cuts flies in the face of the facts. Despite – or rather because of – the lower tax rates, tax revenue grew by 58% from USD 347 billion in 1981 to USD 549 billion in 1989. The growth in tax revenue during his time in office was only slightly below that achieved by his successors Bush Sr. and Clinton, who both raised taxes whereas Reagan cut them.

The growing accumulation of debt was caused by Reagan's large military expenditures, which saw the defence budget almost double from USD 158 billion in 1981 to USD 304 billion in 1989. Niskanen and Moore show that the cumulative increase in defence spending even outpaced the cumulative increase in the budget deficit. If not for this massive increase in military expenditure, Reagan would have succeeded in cutting taxes and debt while creating jobs and getting inflation under control.[372]

However, the second key issue confronting the Reagan administration – the Cold War, which the president proposed to end by massively escalating the arms race – made this impossible to achieve. The NATO 'Double-Track' Decision in December 1979 (parallel courses of nuclear forces modernization and arms control) immediately preceded the Soviet invasion of Afghanistan. With the Soviet Union already experiencing serious economic troubles during the 1980s, Reagan was determined to bring about the collapse of the communist superpower he liked to call the 'Evil Empire'. As Niskanen and Moore point out, this raises a key policy question: "If the entire accumulation of debt in the 1980s went to finance the Reagan defense build-up, the key policy question would shift to whether it was appropriate to borrow for those large military expenditures. Was the Reagan administration justified in paying for this one-time increase in 'public investment' spending through debt rather than taxes?

Or, put another way, was it appropriate to have asked our children and grandchildren to help defray the cost of defeating the Soviet menace?"[373]

Equally unsubstantiated by evidence is the assumption that the economic upswing during the Reagan years was achieved by means of brutal welfare cuts. In fact, total federal spending on welfare programmes rose from USD 339 billion in 1981 to USD 539 billion in 1989.[374] Adjusted by population growth and inflation, this represents an annual growth rate of 0.9% – lower than in any other period in post-war American history.[375] Incomes rose for every income quartile, from the richest to the poorest, during Reagan's time in office.[376]

The American Dream of income mobility, which for many today has turned into a nightmare of discontent, was alive and well in the 1980s: 86% of households that were in the poorest income quintile in 1981 were able to move up the economic ladder into a higher quintile by 1990. The percentage of poor households that moved all the way up to the richest income quintile between 1981 and 1990 was even slightly higher than the percentage of those who remained in the poorest quintile. The number of Americans earning less than USD 10,000 a year fell by 5% during the 1980s, while the number of those earning more than USD 50,000 rose by 60% and the number of those whose annual income exceeded USD 75,000 rose by a staggering 83%. Among the fables Niskanen and Moore debunk, the claim that wealthy whites were the sole beneficiaries of Reagan's policies at the expense of poorer African Americans is one of the most persistent and pernicious. In fact, African American households saw even stronger growth in real take-home pay between 1981 and 1988 than their white peers.[377]

Among the most striking achievements of the Reagan administration is the fact that he successfully implemented these sweeping pro-market reforms in the face of the Democratic majority that dominated Congress for most of his two terms in office. That he was able to do so was largely due to two key factors: first of all – as is often the case – the political changes had been preceded by changes in the cultural and intellectual climate that were reflected in the public discourse on economics. Proponents of the once dominant Keynesian views (even Nixon was a self-confessed Keynesian) found themselves at a loss to explain the simultaneous rise in inflation and unemployment. In January 1977, the *Wall Street Journal* ran an editorial titled "Keynes is Dead".[378] By contrast, uncompromising pro-market thinking – as espoused by Milton Friedman's Chicago School in particular – was in the ascendancy.[379]

The public mood had changed, and even Democrats were now in favour of tax cuts. As alluded to above, their main initiative in 1981 was a bill to reduce marginal tax rates for those in the highest tax bracket by 25% over four years.[380] This was the second reason for Reagan's success: he was able to achieve bipartisan support for many of his reform proposals.

After a decade of price controls and government intervention in the 1970s, Americans now started to put their faith in the market again. The optimistic mood helped to boost the economy, and the economic upswing helped to boost optimism. The 1980s witnessed a revolution in communications technology. From only 1% in 1980, the proportion of American households that owned a VCR skyrocketed to 58% by the end of the decade.[381] The 1980s also saw the number of personal computers explode from just over 2 million in 1981 to 45 million in 1988, around half of them in private homes. The 1980s' greatest economic success stories included Microsoft (which issued its first public stock in 1986), Apple and Sun Microsystems. Young, innovative companies raised capital from venture capitalists or IPOs. At the same time, a fitness revolution swept the country, with health clubs springing up everywhere and Arnold Schwarzenegger – himself a great admirer of Friedman and Reagan – kicking off a craze for physical exercise.

Poll data from 1977 show that 53% of respondents ranked inflation as the most important problem facing the US, followed by recession or unemployment at 39%. In 1981, a staggering 70% of Americans were most concerned about inflation. By 1987, that number had fallen to 13%, with 11% citing the deficit as their largest concern.[382]

Reagan's economic advisers during his two terms in the White House included Friedman, who in his memoirs gives a very positive overall assessment of Reagan's political legacy, praising him for his unprecedented "adherence to clearly specified principles dedicated to promoting and maintaining a free society".[383] However, Friedman does take Reagan's administration to task for deviating from pro-market principles by negotiating a protectionist agreement with Japan to impose a 'voluntary' quota on exporting cars to the US.[384] Reagan's second term in office, Friedman goes on to say, was "much less productive than the first" because his second presidential campaign in 1984 lacked any "specific commitments for action".[385]

Despite these minor reservations, Reagan's reforms proved compellingly that a return to its traditional capitalist free-market values was the way to make America strong again. Unfortunately, his successors failed to adhere to this lesson and persevere with his reforms. Instead, the reforms were little more than a short hiatus on the road towards increasing government intervention and a burgeoning welfare state. Samuel Gregg's *Becoming Europe* describes the likely outcomes of the progressive 'Europeanization' of the US economy in drastic terms,[386] while William Voegeli's *Never Enough* warns that, for all he accomplished, not even Reagan was able to reverse the disastrous slide towards a welfare-state system – although he did succeed in keeping the growth in inflation-adjusted federal welfare spending below 1%.

Reagan, Thatcher and Erhard were the most significant and most adamant proponents of free-market capitalism among the 20th century's Western political leaders. All three rejected the social democratic welfare state along with socialism in its undiluted Marxist form. And all three made significant contributions to a growth in prosperity for the nations they governed.

CHAPTER 6

South America: Why Are Chileans *Better* Off *than* Venezuelans?

The contrast between these two Latin American countries could hardly be starker: Chile ranks 20th out of 180 countries in the 2018 Index of Economic Freedom, while Venezuela is at the very bottom, even behind Cuba and beaten to last place only by North Korea.[387] While Chileans are better off today than ever before, Venezuelans are suffering from inflation, economic decline and growing political oppression. In the course of the 20th century, Venezuela went from being one of the poorest countries in Latin America to becoming the richest. In 1970, it ranked among the 20 richest countries in the world with a higher per-capita GDP than Spain, Greece and Israel, and only 13% lower than the UK.[388]

VENEZUELA: '21ST-CENTURY SOCIALISM'

Venezuela's reversal of economic fortune started in the 1970s. The reasons why this happened are subject to an intense and ongoing debate between academic experts.[389] Venezuela's strong dependency on oil is a prime suspect, along with a number of other reasons, first and foremost the unusually high degree of government regulation of the labour market. From 1974 onwards, the applicable rules were tightened even further to a level that was unprecedented almost anywhere else in the world – let alone Latin America. From adding the equivalent of 5.35 months' wages to the cost of employing someone in 1972, non-wage labour costs soared to add the equivalent of 8.98 months' wages in 1992.[390]

These factors exacerbated the problems frequently facing countries whose economies are largely dependent on exports of natural resources (see the discussion of African economies in Chapter 2). Many Venezuelans put their faith in the charismatic socialist leader Hugo Chávez as the saviour who would deliver their country from corruption, poverty and economic decline. Following a failed attempt to seize power in 1992,[391] Chávez was elected president in 1998.

A year later, the Republic of Venezuela was renamed the Bolivarian Republic of Venezuela (República Bolivariana de Venezuela) at his behest. A beacon of hope for many of Venezuela's poor, Chávez's talk of a new kind of '21st-century socialism' also reawakened dreams of a utopian paradise among members of the European and North American left.

After the collapse of the socialist economies in the Soviet Union and the Eastern Bloc in the late 1980s and China's transition to capitalism, leftists in the West needed a new real-world example to stoke their utopian longings. North Korea and Cuba, the only two remaining communist states, didn't quite fill that gap. Then along came Chávez, who was hailed by many as a new messiah. Prominent members of the Left Party in Germany saw him as a role model whose "fight for justice and dignity" – evidence that "an alternative economic model is possible" – was showing them "the way to resolve Germany's economic problems".[392]

Chávez had plenty of admirers among left-wing intellectuals in the US as well, with the late Tom Hayden enthusing: "As time passes, I predict, the name of Hugo Chávez will be revered by millions."[393] Cornel West, too, declared himself a fan: "I love that Hugo Chávez has made poverty a major priority. I wish America would make poverty a priority."[394] The influential broadcast journalist and talk-show host Barbara Walters concurred: "He cares very much about poverty, he is a socialist. What he's trying to do for all of Latin America, they have been trying to do for years, eliminate poverty. But he is not the crazy man we've heard … This is a very intelligent man."[395]

Thanks to the Venezuelan oil deposits – the largest in the world – and the oil price explosion that coincided with Chávez's presidency, filling his government's coffers to the brim, his large-scale experiment in 21st-century socialism got off to a promising start, although it would eventually descend into economic disaster, hyperinflation, hunger and dictatorship.

In the early days, Chávez employed a surprisingly conciliatory rhetoric, casting himself as a great admirer of Western values who welcomed foreign investors, a "Tony Blair of the Caribbean".[396] Much as the Communist Party in East Germany had promised in 1945 to uphold property rights and entrepreneurial initiative and refrain from imposing a Soviet-style system (see discussion in Chapter 3), Chávez initially vowed that he would never "expropriate anything from anyone". This didn't stop him from denouncing "savage neo-liberal capitalism" and celebrating Cuban socialism as a "sea of happiness".[397]

The oil industry, by far Venezuela's most important source of revenue, had already been nationalized in 1976 with the creation of the oil and natural gas company Petróleos de Venezuela, SA (PDVSA), which employed a workforce of 140,000 in 2014. Although state owned, PDVSA was run like a for-profit enterprise and "recognized as one of the best-run oil giants in the world". Thanks to the company's strong links with private enterprises overseas, Venezuela was able to increase its oil production to 3 million barrels a day during the 1990s.[398]

PDVSA was far too independent for Chávez's liking. In 2002, he stuffed the board with political allies and generals without any business experience. In protest against Chávez's meddling, thousands of PDVSA employees declared a two-month strike that paralysed Venezuela's oil industry. Chávez responded by having 19,000 striking workers fired and denounced as 'enemies of the people'.

However, the conflict between workers and the socialist government didn't stop there. In 2006, energy minister Rafael Ramírez, who also happened to be the head of PDVSA, threatened workers that they would lose their jobs unless they backed Chávez in the upcoming elections: "PDVSA is red, red from top to bottom." Chávez himself affirmed: "PDVSA's workers are with this revolution, and those who aren't should go somewhere else. Go to Miami."[399] The company's profits were used to fund social welfare programmes, keep failing companies afloat and build homes for the poor at a cost of billions of dollars a year.[400]

PDVSA was even enlisted to pay for welfare programmes in the US. In November 2005, Chávez ordered the company to supply heating oil to low-income households in Boston at 40% below market price via its subsidiary Citgo. Similar deals were struck with other cities and communities across the northeastern US. According to Citgo's own figures, between 2005 and 2014 the programme supplied a total of 235 million gallons of heating oil to 1.8 million people. Socialist Cuba and other allies also received heating oil donations.[401]

In 2007, in an attempt to secure a controlling interest of at least 60% in Venezuelan oil ventures for PDVSA, the Chávez government forced foreign oil companies to accept minority stakes or face nationalization.[402] ExxonMobil refused and filed an arbitration request with the World Bank's arbitration tribunal, the International Centre for Settlement of Investment Disputes (ICSID), while simultaneously taking legal action in courts in the US and the UK. After a British court froze PDVSA assets worth USD 12 billion, the state-owned company stopped selling oil to ExxonMobil in 2008 and suspended business relations. In 2014, the ICSID ordered Venezuela to pay ExxonMobil USD 1.6 billion in compensation.[403] When Chávez first came to power, over 50% of the oil production profits went to the government. By the time of his death in 2013, the government take of over 90% was one of the highest in the world.[404]

Chávez hugely benefited from the oil price explosion during his time in office. By the time of his death in 2013, the oil price had skyrocketed to

USD 111 per barrel – more than ten times as much as the historic low of USD 10.53 in 1998 when he took office. As discussed in Chapter 2, rising natural resource prices have a tendency to seduce governments into handing out their bounty right, left and centre, rather than creating cash reserves to safeguard against future slumps in the natural resource markets.

This proved particularly risky in a country largely dependent on oil exports whose socialist president was busy lavishly bestowing benefits handing out benefits right, left and centre and restructuring the economy in accordance with socialist principles. Chávez made barely any effort to diversify production. As the German Latin America expert Hans-Jürgen Burchardt reported in 2009, rather than Chávez reducing his country's dependence on exporting oil and importing essential goods, "the opposite has happened over the past ten years: the country's agrarian and industrial production has decreased further, the latter recording the worst performance in four decades. Some commentators are already raising the spectre of deindustrialization ... With the Bolivarian revolution now in its tenth year, 85 percent of export volume and 60 percent of government revenue is generated in the crude oil sector, which only employs one percent of the workforce. Venezuela's oil dependency has not decreased but grown since Hugo Chávez took office."[405]

Following his re-election in 2006, Chávez nationalized an increasing number of industrial enterprises, starting with the iron and steel industries. Government takeovers of the cement and food sectors, power utilities and ports soon followed. Between 2007 and 2010 alone, around 350 businesses were moved from the private to the public sector. In many cases, executive positions in the newly nationalized enterprises were awarded to loyal party members.[406] With one in three workers employed in the public sector by 2008, the government payroll ballooned.[407]

When his government offered massive tax and financing incentives to companies run by workers' cooperatives, their number increased from 820 in 1999 to 280,000 in 2009. The majority of these were unproductive shell companies that only existed so their owners were able to access subsidies and cheap cash loans.[408]

Chávez's interference in economic affairs became increasingly heavy handed. The 'immunity decree' in Venezuela's Organic Labor Law for Workers, which prohibited mass dismissals for operational reasons, proved calamitous for some companies. The government also set very cheap fixed prices, in many cases below production cost, for meat and other basic food items. Companies that refused to sell at these prices were denounced as speculators and threatened with prison sentences.[409]

While the oil price was high, there appeared to be no limits to the boundless generosity of Venezuela's 21st-century socialism. Critics of capitalism around the world admired Chávez for the social welfare programmes he funded with free-flowing oil revenue: cash transfers to the poor, and government subsidies for food, housing, water, power and phone services. Filling up with petrol cost next to nothing – tipping the attendant would often cost more than the actual fuel. US dollars, which were in plentiful supply thanks to the oil revenues, were exchanged at preferential exchange rates.

Badly managed public enterprises received generous subsidies, which enabled them to retain more employees than they needed. The payment of oil revenues into a rainy-day fund had already been stopped in 2001, and investment in the oil industry – the very basis of the country's livelihood – was also sacrificed in favour of ever more ambitious social spending plans.[410]

Chávez's admirers thought they were witnessing a socialist miracle – after all, his social policies succeeded in reducing extreme poverty by 50%, according to official figures. Whether these figures can be trusted is another question. For example, Chávez's claim to have improved the literacy rate by 1.5 million is a "gross exaggeration", with the real figure closer to 140,000 according to calculations by the Venezuela expert A. C. Clark.[411] Likewise, the homicide statistics published by Chávez's regime exclude victims of gang-related violence as well as those killed "resisting authority". According to data compiled by the Venezuelan human rights organization PROVEA, the total number of crime-related deaths averaged 15,000 a year between 2000 and 2005.[412]

Even some left-leaning academics began to criticize Chávez's welfare programmes for "catering to special interests" while doing little to ensure robust and sustainable outcomes in the fight against poverty: "In boom times, a consumption-oriented way of life alters the shape of social polarization, using social and economic policies of redistribution to alleviate the worst social excesses of a dependent economy … without, however, effecting any major structural changes to the conditions in which the poor live."[413] Accordingly, rather than eliminating poverty, Chávez's reforms had created a "quasi-'state socialist' caste of bureaucrats … whose rapid advance through the social hierarchy is enabled by top salaries and corrupt practices".[414]

After Chávez's death in 2013, his successor and former second-in-command Nicolás Maduro accelerated the nationalization of dairies, coffee producers, supermarkets, manufacturers of fertilizers and shoe factories. Production buckled or stopped entirely.[415] Then the oil prices plummeted, losing almost 50% of their value within a single year from USD 111 per barrel in late 2013 to USD 57.60, then dropping to USD 37.60 another year later and fluctuating between USD 27.10 and USD 57.30 in 2016.

While this would have caused a predicament for any oil-producing nation, these problems were amplified in a country with an extremely inefficient socialist economy and strict price controls. Now the fatal effects of Chávez's socialist policies became obvious once and for all. The entire system fell apart. As in other countries, it became apparent that, far from being an efficient means to fight inflation, price controls only make it worse. Inflation reached 225% in 2016, higher than anywhere else in the world except for South Sudan. It was probably close to 800%, accompanied by a 19% drop in economic output in 2016, according to an internal report by the Governor of the National Bank.[416] In May 2018, the rate of inflation ballooned to nearly 14,000%.

Although Venezuela owned state-of-the-art money presses, including a German-made Super Simultan IV, these were no longer up to the task of printing the huge numbers of bills required. Venezuela was forced to outsource a large share of this work to companies based in the UK and Germany and the central banks of some friendly nations. Boeing 747 planes carrying between 150 and 200 tons of bills landed in Venezuela every two weeks.[417]

In January 2017, the cost of the basic food basket had gone up by 481% compared to the previous year, to a value of 15.3 times the minimum wage.[418] To fully understand what this means, it is important to know that teachers were making twice the minimum wage, while taxi drivers were soon earning more than doctors or architects. According to estimates, 1.2 million of the country's best-trained professionals had left for the US or Europe by 2014.[419]

Because many goods were subject to price controls, while raw materials and production goods had to be paid for in US dollars, the decline of the currency led to increasingly dramatic shortages in supply. People started hoarding all sorts of things that were sold very cheaply and would frequently queue for hours to buy something they would then sell on at a much higher price on the black market.

This is what happened with toilet paper, which was hardly ever available in the shops any more. The companies making it were forced to sell it at a fixed price far below production cost, which was driven up by inflation. And when production was suspended due to the lack of raw materials, the workers still had to be paid because companies were not allowed to reduce their workforce without government approval.[420] However, the head of the National Statistics Institute managed to turn the toilet paper shortage into a good-news story, hailing it as proof of the plentiful national diet.[421]

On the rare occasions when toilet paper was available at fixed government prices, it sold out rapidly. Many Venezuelans gave up their jobs because, with wages failing to keep up with soaring prices, selling shortage goods – including toilet paper – on the black market was a far more lucrative option. Feminine hygiene products also disappeared from the shops. Instead, Venezuelan women were urged to watch a tutorial aired on the state television channel on how to make their own washable and reusable sanitary pads. The demonstrator in the video even put an anti-capitalist spin on the situation, enthusing: "We avoid becoming a part of the commercial cycle of savage capitalism. We are more conscious and in harmony with the environment."[422]

In July 2016, 500 Venezuelan women took the extraordinary step of crossing into neighbouring Columbia via a closed border crossing to buy food. "We are starving, we are desperate," one of the women told the Colombian station Caracol Radio. There was nothing left to eat in her country, she said.[423]

A care worker in a retirement home told reporters from a German radio station about her own desperate situation. Only 9 of the 24 residents were left. The others had either died or been sent away because there wasn't enough to eat and their supplies of essential medication for patients suffering from diabetes or hypertension had run out. Subverting a ban on visits from journalists, a doctor showed the reporters around a public hospital where the only X-ray machine had been broken for a long time, the lab was unable to process any urine or blood samples, there was no running water in the toilets and the lifts were out of order.[424] Hospital patients had to supply their own medication because stocks of everything from painkillers to drugs for cancer treatment had run out.[425]

Within a single year, between 2015 and 2016, child mortality rose by 33%, while the rate of women dying in childbirth grew by 66%. The health minister who published these statistics was sacked by Maduro, who prohibited the release of any social or economic indicators in a bid to prevent "political interpretations".[426] After an initial drop from 20.3% to 12.9% over 13 years under Chávez,[427] infant mortality reached levels above UNICEF estimates for war-damaged Syria in 2016.[428]

A 2016 survey by the Central University of Venezuela found that four out of five Venezuelan households lived in poverty.[429] Some 73% of the population experienced weight loss, with the amount lost averaging 8.7 kilograms (20 pounds) in 2016.[430] In a hearing before the US House of Representatives Subcommittee on the Western Hemisphere in March 2017, Hector E. Schamis, adjunct professor at Georgetown University, reported record poverty rates of 82%, with 52% living in extreme poverty.[431]

In the face of continued popular protests and an opposition victory in parliamentary elections, Maduro dissolved the National Assembly and abolished freedom of the press along with all other remnants of democracy. By October 2017, the death toll of those killed during anti-government demonstrations and protests had risen to over 120 – testament to the failure of yet another socialist experiment.

CHILE: FROM SOCIALISM TO FREE-MARKET CAPITALISM

Much as with Hugo Chávez's ascent to power 28 years later, left-wing intellectuals all over the world drew fascination and pride from Salvador Allende's election as Chilean president in September 1970. The Unidad Popular candidate was the first hardline Marxist ever to come to power as the result of a democratic election – albeit with a slim majority of 36.5% of the vote – rather than a violent revolution or a lost war, as was the case with the Soviet-imposed regimes in East Germany and North Korea after World War II.

The Unidad Popular was assisted in its ascent to power by the oligarchic nature of the Chilean economy and the huge income gap between the 1.5% share of total income that went to the poorest 10% and the 40.2% share for the richest 10%,[432] while inflation stood at 36.1% in 1970.[433]

In his first official act as president, Allende nationalized the copper mines that were Chile's most important source of income. Rather than paying compensation to the multinational corporations that had previously run the mines as part of the "negotiated nationalization" agreement signed with Allende's predecessor, Eduardo Frei Montalva, in 1969, Allende's government presented them with deductions for "excessive profits" beyond "normal business practice" that exceeded the sale value of most of their holdings.[434] Banks and other companies were also nationalized in quick succession. By the time Allende was ousted in 1973, 80% of the country's industrial production had been moved to the public sector.[435] Rents and prices of basic food items were fixed by the government, which also provided free healthcare.

The socialist government's use of public spending to bolster its popularity saw social expenditure rise by almost 60% in real terms in a period of only two years. Between 1970 and 1973, employment in central government and public-sector firms expanded by 50% and 35% respectively.[436] These measures were paid for, not from increases in tax revenue but by increasing public debt and expanding the money supply. The budget deficit grew from 3.5% of GDP in 1970 to 9.8% in 1971. A 10.3% increase in public-sector investment was counterbalanced by a 16.8% drop in private-sector investment[437] – which is not surprising given the rate of expropriation of private business owners: 377 productive firms were nationalized between 1970 and 1973.[438]

Economically, nationalization was a failure. Highly skilled workers and experienced executives left the country in droves and were replaced by loyal party members. "Many nationalized businesses also recorded frequent incidents of undisciplined behavior and absenteeism. In companies that hadn't been moved into state ownership yet, the workers themselves took initiative by occupying production facilities."[439]

In addition, almost 16 million acres of land were expropriated. In some instances, collectives were set up in accordance with the familiar socialist model. Farmers made landowners by the 1960s reforms now had to work in agricultural collectives as public-sector employees.[440] Expropriations or occupations happened at a rate of 5.5 agricultural estates per day; "every other day a productive firm was nationalized or taken over".[441] Productivity took a dip, and by 1972 Chile had to spend a large share of its export revenue on food imports.[442] The attempt to restructure the agricultural sector in accordance with socialist principles was as much a failure in Chile as it had been in China, East Germany and North Korea. "Overall, the Unidad Popular's economic policy was a failure. This is true in the fiscal arena even more so than in the agricultural and industrial sectors. The government was no more able to control inflation than its predecessor had been – in fact, generous public spending only made it worse."[443] Inflation, which had stood at 36% in 1970, skyrocketed to 605% in 1973, a pattern that would repeat itself in Venezuela three decades later[444] – as would the protests that started breaking out in Chile. During a three-week state visit by the Cuban leader Fidel Castro in late 1971, thousands of Chilean women joined a 'March of the Empty Pots and Pans' on the presidential palace. They were attacked by Marxist activists and dispersed with tear-gas grenades by the police, resulting in dozens of injuries. In October 1972, half a million small business owners, farmers and self-employed professionals took part in anti-government protests.[445]

In September 1973, the Chilean army, led by Allende's appointed army chief Augusto Pinochet, overthrew the socialist government. Allende killed himself shortly before the leaders of the coup d'état stormed the presidential palace. General Pinochet established a military dictatorship. Freedom of the press and other democratic rights were abolished; those who opposed the regime were arrested and tortured. In stark contrast to the authoritarian and anti-liberal thrust of his domestic policy, Pinochet's economic orientation was, for the most part, liberal and pro-market.

Chile's transformation into a free-market economy under Pinochet was masterminded by a group of economists who subsequently became known as the 'Chicago Boys'. They were admirers and former students of Milton Friedman, the Nobel Prize-winning economist and fervent proponent of free-market capitalism, at the University of Chicago. On their return to Chile, they drafted 189 pages of economic analysis and reform proposals for the attention of the generals, who initially "did little with the proposals". It was only when the military's own efforts failed to stem inflation that Pinochet appointed several of the Chicago Boys to positions of power.[446]

Friedman himself gave a number of seminars and public talks in Chile during a six-day stint in March 1975. His perceived role as Pinochet's adviser has given rise to a lot of harsh criticism. In truth, Friedman only met the Chilean dictator once, and subsequently wrote him a letter in which he recommended a programme for fighting hyperinflation and liberalizing the economy.[447] He gave similar advice to communist rulers in the Soviet Union, China and Yugoslavia.[448] But, while his supposed involvement with the Chilean regime triggered a global campaign against him, nobody seemed too bothered about his role in advising communist regimes.

On the whole, Friedman was impressed by the economic policies implemented by the Chilean economists he had inspired – among them Sergio de Castro Spikula, who was Pinochet's minister of economic affairs and later became finance minister – although he was critical of Castro's decision to peg the Chilean currency to the US dollar. Castro and his followers started to instigate an economic agenda centred on reducing public spending, deregulating the finance and economic sector, privatizing state-owned enterprises (except for the copper industry) and opening the economy to foreign investors, and generally reversing the policies of the Allende government: "The state and everything linked to the public sector was turned into the central cause of all the problems; the less it interfered in the economy, the greater and faster would be the growth of social welfare. This formed the background to the numerous economic reforms introduced during the military regime: privatizations and reprivatizations, reform of the state and fiscal reform, liberalization, deregulation, opening up the economy and Central Bank autonomy."[449]

From 400 state-controlled enterprises and banks in 1973, the number dropped to around 45 firms (including one bank) in 1980.[450] Fiscal and tax reforms and deregulation measures introduced in the mid-1970s minimized government influence across the board by abolishing price controls, wealth and capital gains taxes and cutting income tax. VAT, set at a standard rate of 20% charged on all goods and services, became the government's main source of tax revenue. This resulted in an 'economic miracle' of a similar magnitude to those achieved by Margaret Thatcher and Ronald Reagan: lower tax rates led to a growth in revenue from 22% of GDP in 1973–1974 to 27% in 1975–1977, and the transformation of the chronic fiscal deficit into a surplus in the period from 1979 to 1981.[451]

A comparison between key indicators for 1973 and 1981 clearly shows just how successful these policies were. Inflation, which had stood at above 600% in 1973, had dropped to only 9.5% by 1981, although progress had been slow. During the same period, Chile had seen its economic growth rate recover from −4.3% to a healthy 5.5%, while exports almost tripled from USD 1.3 billion to USD 3.8 billion. More impressive still was the growth of non-traditional exports (excluding copper and other natural resources) from USD 104 million to USD 1.4 billion. Real wages, which had dropped by over 25% in 1973, grew by 9% in 1981.[452]

The fiscal and economic policies introduced by the Chicago Boys were key to Chile's long-term recovery and its current economic stability. In the short term, however, their outcomes were less straightforward: as with Thatcher's and Reagan's reforms, positive long-term effects came at the price of an initial rise in unemployment.

With foreign investors increasingly putting their faith in the Chilean economy, exports started rising while the deficit decreased and the economy grew by a total of 32% over four years. Chile's economic miracle was hailed in the world of global finance and celebrated in the business press. Mass consumption increased as standards of living improved across the population, as reflected in the dramatic rise in the number of cars registered between 1976 and 1981.[453]

In the early 1980s, a massive debt crisis swept across Latin America. In 1982, Mexico defaulted on its sovereign debt. In the same year, Chile – along with other Latin American countries – was plunged into recession by a drastic decline in capital inflow. In 1982–1983, Chile experienced its worst recession since the 1930s, with GDP plummeting by 15% and unemployment rising to 30% in real terms.[454] The root causes of the 1982–1983 crisis are the subject of an ongoing debate. What is clear, though, is that Chile was able to get over the crisis much faster than its Latin American neighbours: "Chile led the continent in climbing out of this recession. It was the only debt-crisis country that got back to the pre-crisis levels of GDP before the end of the decade of the 80s, so for most of the countries, it was the full decade that they called the 'lost decade.'[455]

Once the crisis was over, the government carried on with more reforms. The second round of reprivatizations took into account the lessons learned from the first, which had largely been a debt-based privatization process. This time, companies were transacted on the stock exchange, giving them a debt-free start. The privatization of the largest firms in public ownership – excluding the state-owned General Minerals Corporation – started in 1986, generating a total asset value of USD 3.6 billion.[456]

The political system started changing following Pinochet's 1988 defeat in a plebiscite on the extension of his rule for another eight years. The 1989 general elections were won by a democratic alliance led by the Christian Democrat Patricio Aylwin Azócar, who ruled as president from 1990 to 1994. Friedman emphasizes the role that economic liberalization, which in turn led to political liberalization, played in the transition from dictatorship to democracy: "The Chilean economy did very well, but more importantly, in the end the central government, the military junta, was replaced by a democratic society. So the really important thing about Chilean business is that free markets did work their way in bringing about a free society."[457]

Although the liberalization of the economy was clearly a contributing factor in ending the dictatorship by strengthening Chilean civil society, Friedman's claim that the victory of democracy was a direct and inevitable consequence of the economic reforms is an unsubstantiated exaggeration. The fact that in other countries – including China, as discussed in Chapter 1 – economic liberalization has so far failed to produce a transition to democracy makes his contention difficult to uphold.

Nonetheless, there is no denying the long-term positive effects of the economic reforms instigated by the Chicago Boys. Although watered down somewhat by subsequent governments, these reforms laid the foundations for Chile's current economic success and led to the country's high ranking in the Index of Economic Freedom. Even the socialist incumbents Ricardo Lagos Escobar (2000–2006) and Michelle Bachelet (2006–2010 and 2014–2018) did not fundamentally alter Chile's orientation as a free-market economy. In 2010, Chile became the first South American nation to join the Organisation for Economic Co-operation and Development – a clear sign that, unlike most other countries in the region, Chile is part of the 'First World' of developed countries. This is all the more remarkable given that, prior to the reforms, Chile was among the most protectionist economies in the world.

The fact that neither the Christian Democrats who governed Chile during the 1990s nor the socialist governments elected in the 2000s made significant changes to the reforms introduced under Pinochet has to count as one of the strongest arguments in favour of their efficacy. As shown in Chapter 5, a similar observation holds true for the UK and the US, where neither Tony Blair's Labour government nor Bill Clinton's White House meddled with the substance of the reforms introduced by Thatcher and Reagan.

Critics of Pinochet's Chicago Boys reforms like to point to the rising social inequality that accompanied their undeniable economic success – to which Chile's former economy and finance minister Sergio de Castro responds: "In 1970, for instance, infant mortality was 80 to 1,000. By 1990, at the end of the military regime, it had dropped to 20 to 1,000. That is due to the economic health of the country and the fact that the government was able to spend more money on the poor."[458]

However, other economic and social indicators do show a high degree of inequality in Chilean society persisting into the present. The Gini Index, which measures the income distribution among residents, ranks Chile among the 20 most unequal countries in the world.[459] The majority of Chileans seem to value the economic progress achieved in their country more highly than the 'social equality' bemoaned by critics – as evidenced by the successive socialist governments that largely adhered to a free-market course and by the 2010 election of Sebastián Piñera for president. A former close ally of the Pinochet government whose brother had been instrumental in rolling out a privatized social security system, Piñera was a staunch believer in the free market. His election victory, the German newspaper *Handelsblatt* commented at the time, "might herald the beginning of a new era of pure capitalism in Latin America".[460] Piñera lost the 2013 presidential elections against Michelle Bachelet, who in turn was voted out of office in 2017 to make way for Piñera's second term, which started in March 2018.

In late June 2017, the leftist German weekly newspaper *Die Zeit* ran a feature on Chile that runs the gamut from dismay to grudging admiration: "Capitalism has an unusually powerful hold here, and the impact on social cohesion and the weaker members of society is equally strong. If you can't keep up, you don't belong: this mindset is part of the legacy bequeathed on Chile by the military dictatorship of Augusto Pinochet, who ruled the slim country on the edge of South America between 1973 and 1990. Long after Pinochet's death, his Chicago Boys live on … So far, his democratic successors in government have continued his policy of very little market regulation."[461]

On the other hand, even the *Die Zeit* journalist is forced to concede: "At six per cent, unemployment is about as low as in Germany, and inflation is almost non-existent too. Chilean government bonds have a good rating. Compared to their Latin American neighbors' reputation for economic chaos, Chileans are considered good business partners. They also have a functioning infrastructure, solid rates of construction and investment and well-organized transport networks. Improvements in the standard of living over recent years have benefited even the poor."[462]

It's true: with a population of just under 18 million, Chile has a per-capita income almost twice as high as Brazil, while the percentage of the population living below the poverty line dropped from 20% in 2003 to 7% in 2014. During the same period, the poorest 40% saw their incomes rise more steeply than the national average. In 2017, Chile was the top-ranking Latin American country in the *Global Competitiveness Report* compiled by the World Economic Forum. It has the most stable banking system in the region and some of the best conditions for private enterprises worldwide. The most open economy in Latin America, it has signed free-trade agreements with countries that together produce 75% of the global economic output. Over the past 30 years, Chile's economy has achieved annual growth rates of around 5%.[463]

In the period between 1990 and 2005, Chile recorded one of the highest economic growth rates in the world – far higher than any other Latin American country and on a par with South Korea. In conjunction with the consistent privatization of infrastructure assets from public transport over hospitals, prison and telecommunications to water and sewage management, low corporate tax rates and deregulated capital markets created incentives for investors.[464]

On the negative side, Chile's economy continues to depend to a very large extent on copper. The country has the largest copper deposits in the world and around a 30% share of global copper production. The price of copper has hardly been stable over the past 20 years, soaring from a record low of USD 1,438 per ton in 1998 to a record high of USD 8,982 in 2008 before plummeting to USD 2,767 later the same year, followed by a 150% increase over the next year and a period of extreme fluctuations ever since.

These trends are obviously problematic for a country whose economy is largely dependent on copper. But unlike Venezuela, where the fluctuating oil price that initially triggered the economic boom and allowed Chávez to give away social benefits with both hands was subsequently blamed for the country's dramatic economic downturn, Chile's free-market economy was much better equipped to cope with the drops and fluctuations in the price of copper. Venezuela, too, might have thrived in spite of its high degree of dependency on oil – if it hadn't been for its state-controlled socialist economy.

Chile's development over recent decades does not only demonstrate that capitalism is superior to socialism. Crucially, the Chicago Boys' attempt to roll out a capitalist system overnight in the 1970s also highlights a key difference between the two. Unlike socialism, capitalism is not a system invented by intellectuals – and, thus, its sudden imposition from one day to the next is doomed to fail even under a dictatorship.

Rather, capitalism grows organically and spontaneously. As discussed in Chapter 1, China's successful transition from socialism to capitalism took many years of spontaneous bottom-up initiatives supported by changes in policy instigated by Deng Xiaoping and others. While the Chicago Boys' reforms constituted an important change of direction that marked the beginning of Chile's road to economic success, it took the country several decades to transition to a full-blown capitalist free-market economy.

CHAPTER 7

Sweden: *The* Myth *of* Nordic Socialism

I spent two months in New York during the 2016 presidential election campaign. I remember seeing a young man raving about the benefits of socialism on television – an image that stuck in my mind because it didn't really fit with my idea of the US. The young man was talking about 'Scandinavian socialism'. He was a fan of Bernie Sanders, the self-confessed socialist whose own interpretation of that ideology has little to do with a Soviet or German Democratic Republic-style system. Rather, the socialist paradise Sanders would like to implement in his native US is modelled on one that he believes exists in Scandinavia, in Denmark and Sweden in particular.

Sweden stopped being a socialist country several decades ago – if it ever was one in the first place. But, just as individuals frequently find it hard to change the image that stubbornly adheres to them in the minds of others, the same is true of nations. On the whole, we are very reluctant to change long-held beliefs about other countries.

Spoiler alert: contemporary Sweden is not a socialist country. According to the Heritage Foundation's 2018 Index of Economic Freedom ranking, Sweden is among the most market-oriented economies worldwide. Overall, it ranks in 15th place, ahead of South Korea (27th) and Germany (25th) and behind Denmark – another supposedly socialist country – in 12th place.[465] What is most remarkable is the extent to which Sweden has changed over the past two decades, increasing its overall score by 14.9 points (from 61.4 to 76.3 points) between 1995 and 2018. China, which underwent its economic transformation during the same period, only added 5.8 points to its score, while Chancellor Gerhard Schröder's pro-market reforms increased Germany's score by a paltry four points, and France (−0.5) and the US (−1.0) recorded very little change. From trailing behind by more than 15 points in 1995, Sweden now has the same level of economic freedom as the US.

However, Sweden's scores in other categories paint a slightly different picture.[466] Public spending is still high at 51.1% of GDP for the period between 2014 and 2016, landing Sweden in 170th place out of 180. While income tax rates have come down considerably from their peak in the 1970s and 1980s, at 42.7% of total domestic income (179th place), they are still higher than almost anywhere else in the world. However, what many don't realize is that taxes on inheritance, accession, wealth and capital gains have all been abolished. On the other hand, the Swedish labour market is still heavily regulated (126th place).

In other words, despite the ascendance of capitalist elements, Sweden is not entirely free of socialist influences. However, the image of Sweden and other Scandinavian countries as strongholds of socialism harks back to the 1970s and 1980s. The economist Nima Sanandaji offers the following description of their economic trajectory during the period since 1870: "These countries had a phenomenal economic growth when they had small governments and free markets. As they moved towards socialism, entrepreneurship, growing prosperity and new jobs all came to a halt. A shift back to free markets brought back growth."[467]

The foundations for Sweden's burgeoning economic strength were laid prior to the social democratic era, between 1870 and 1936. During this period, when Sweden still had a free-market economy and low taxes, its economic growth significantly exceeded that of other European countries such as Germany, Italy or France, with annual growth rates that were twice as high as in the UK.[468]

The Social Democrats' ascent to power in 1936 was followed by a 'pragmatic' period of moderate first steps towards introducing welfare-state policies, which came to an end in the late 1960s and early 1970s. Between 1936 and 1970, Sweden fell behind countries such as Italy and France with annual growth rates that were only slightly higher than Germany's.[469]

During the period of socialist welfare-state expansion from 1970 to 1991, Sweden dropped far behind many of its European competitors. Economic growth was lower than in a number of other countries, including Italy, France, Germany, the UK, the Netherlands and Austria, the last of which recorded a growth rate twice as high as Sweden's.[470] From fourth place in the Organisation for Economic Co-operation and Development (OECD) per-capita GDP ranking in 1970, socialist-era Sweden had dropped to 16th place by 1995.[471]

During the market-reform era from 1991 to 2014, Sweden was again ahead of Germany, France and Italy in terms of economic growth.[472] By 2016, Sweden had the 12th highest GDP per capita in the OECD ranking – which is remarkable given the significant progress achieved in a number of other countries since 1995, when Sweden recorded its poorest performance in 16th place.

Of course, there are complex reasons for the rise and fall of economic growth from one period to the next, which cannot be reduced to the degree of socialist or capitalist orientation at any given time. Global economic trends, which affect any nation with a strong focus on export, are a contributing factor, as are structural weaknesses of the economic system. But it is worth noting that the period in which Sweden fell behind other European countries coincided with the implementation of socialist, welfare-state policies.

However, the Swedish example also illustrates that, while the economic system does play an important role, cultural factors are also significant in determining a country's economic success, as the example of South Korea (discussed in Chapter 4) has shown. In South Korea's case, work ethos, educational aspirations and a high degree of motivation and diligence all played important roles. Are there any factors that are of similar significance for Sweden's economic success?

Compared to other European countries, Sweden's population is remarkably homogenous. Economists believe that its relatively low degree of ethnic, denomi-national, cultural and linguistic diversity promotes consensus-building and reduces the potential for conflict.[473] Social scientists consider the Swedish mentality to be a key reason for the comparatively narrow income gap, which was already in evidence in the 1920s and thus precedes the introduction of welfare-state policies and tax-based income redistribution in the 1960s and 1970s.[474]

A strong work ethos, ambition and honesty are characteristic of Sweden and other Nordic countries. It is these factors, rather than the Swedish welfare state, that have brought about the high standard of living and high levels of income in Scandinavian countries. Studies comparing data for Americans of Scandinavian descent (a total population of 11 million) with data for the US population as a whole and data for Scandinavian countries confirm this. For example, per-capita GDP in 2013 stood at USD 68,897 for Swedish Americans, significantly higher than the national average of USD 52,592 and also higher than the Swedish average of USD 45,067.[475]

Likewise, the rate of high school graduation is much higher among Swedish Americans (at 96.6%) than the rate of 86.3% among the population at large. Swedish Americans also record lower unemployment (3.9%) and poverty (5.1%) rates than the national averages of 5.9% and 11.7% respectively.[476] These numbers show that, contrary to common misconceptions, the Swedish welfare state isn't the reason for the high standard of living in Sweden. In turn, this is reinforced by the observation that Sweden was economically successful long before introducing welfare-state policies. To be more precise, the country was particularly successful before embarking on this path. Although the Social Democrats were in power between 1932 and 2006 with only three short interruptions, they did not initially pursue any ambitious nationalization schemes. Swedish trade unions, too, were less pugnaciously inclined than in other countries, demanding the abolition of government subsidies and protective tariffs in order to facilitate expansion into new export markets.[477]

SWEDEN'S SOCIALIST PHASE

Until the mid-1960s, there were no significant differences between Sweden and other European countries and nothing that could be defined as a distinct 'Swedish model'. In the late 1960s, government spending was still in the same ballpark as average levels across the OECD states.[478] However, this would change during the late 1960s, the 1970s and the 1980s. In the period between 1965 and 1975, the number of civil servants grew from 700,000 to 1.2 million, alongside increasing government intervention in economic affairs and the creation of a number of new regulatory authorities. Between 1970 and 1984, the public sector absorbed the entire growth of the Swedish workforce, with the largest number of new jobs created in social services.[479]

It is well worth taking a closer look at the development of two key groups over time. In 1960, for every 100 'market-financed' Swedes (i.e. those who derived their income predominantly from private enterprise), there were 38 who were 'tax-financed' (i.e. dependent on the public sector for their income, whether as civil servants or as recipients of payments from the state). Thirty years later, that number had risen to 151. During the same period, the total number of those employed or self-employed in the market sector fell from just under 3 million to just under 2.6 million, while the total number of tax-financed individuals grew from 1.1 million to 3.9 million.[480] These figures reflect Sweden's move away from a capitalist free-market economy to a socialist model during that period.

When Sweden was hit by the global recession during the mid-1970s, the Social Democrats stuck to their guns, extending their welfare-state policies, further increasing social benefits and introducing stricter regulations to protect workers against dismissal. In 1973, unemployment benefit was extended from 30 to 60 days, while the statutory pension age was lowered from 67 to 65 years in 1975. The government kept borrowing more and more money to finance the extension of its welfare-state policies.[481] The unions, which were allied closely with the Social Democratic Party, made matters worse by attempting to enforce socialist notions of equality via irresponsible demands aimed at levelling salaries. In some cases, salaries were increased by as much as 35% over three years.[482]

Unions grew even more powerful than in the UK prior to Margaret Thatcher's first term in office (see Chapter 5). During the 1970s, new laws significantly expanded the influence of unions at the workplace. Designated health and safety representatives had the power to suspend any workflow processes they deemed unsafe pending further review by public officials. Protection against dismissal was extended for older workers and union members, and the burden of proof was reversed in any legal dispute between employers and unions, which meant that companies accused of wrongdoing were now presumed guilty until they were able to prove otherwise in a court of law.

The Co-Determination at the Workplace Act of 1977 stipulated that employee representatives must be appointed to the supervisory boards of all companies with 25 or more employees. In this way, the unions gained influence at every level from day-to-day operational matters to the recruitment or dismissal of employees and overall corporate strategy.[483]

The socialist agenda damaged the Swedish economy and resulted in prominent entrepreneurs leaving the country in frustration. Ikea founder Ingvar Kamprad was one of them. The marginal income tax rate of 85% was supplemented by a wealth tax on his personal assets, which forced him to borrow money from his own company in order to pay his taxes.[484]

To pay back his debt to Ikea, Kamprad wanted to sell one of the small companies he owned to Ikea at a profit – at the time a common practice among Swedish entrepreneurs attempting to reduce their wealth tax burden. As Kamprad was preparing the sale, the government made retroactive changes to tax legislation.[485] He was stuck with the costs and furious at his country's unfair treatment of entrepreneurs. In 1974, he moved to Denmark and later to Switzerland, where he spent the next few decades – for a time as the wealthiest man in Europe. Kamprad didn't return to Sweden to live and pay taxes until 2013 – a textbook example of how countries cut their own throat by taxing the rich excessively.

The German writer Hans Magnus Enzensberger expressed his support for Sweden's beleaguered rich: "It seems that life is not a bed of roses for the rich in a society such as this. Would that it were only a matter of taxes! Though reluctantly, they do want to pay them on time – they're upstanding citizens, after all. Far more hurtful is the fact that nobody has any sympathy for their predicament." Sweden had become a country where the rich felt "superfluous, ignored and ostracized", Enzensberger added.[486] The fact that any Swedish resident earning more than 50,000 crowns had their income listed in a publicly accessible 'tax list' only compounded the pressure on public figures.[487]

These radical socialist policies alienated even those who were sympathetic to the Social Democrats' project. Astrid Lindgren, the world-famous author of a raft of children's classics including the *Pippi Longstocking* series, is just one example. Her long-standing commitment to the social democratic beliefs espoused by the likeable newspaper editor with a strong sense of justice who is a central character in her *Madicken* series didn't stop her from feeling outraged by the 102% marginal tax rate levied on her earnings in 1976.

Lindgren vented her anger in a satire on the Swedish tax system titled "Pomperipossa i Monismanien" published in a leading newspaper. In response, Sweden's minister of finance, Gunnar Sträng, arrogantly added insult to injury during a session in parliament, saying: "The article is an interesting combination of stimulating literary ability and deep ignorance of the maze of fiscal policy. But we don't expect Astrid Lindgren to manage that."[488] He suggested that Lindgren must have added up her numbers incorrectly. Undaunted, the writer retorted: "Gunnar Sträng seems to have learned to tell stories, but he sure can't count! It would be better if we exchanged jobs."[489] The public was on Lindgren's side. If an election had been called at that time, the Social Democrats would have won only 38% against 53% for the centrist opposition. Eventually, Swedish prime minister Olof Palme took care of the matter himself and admitted on television that Lindgren did have her numbers right.

A month after Lindgren's "Pomperipossa" article was published, the renowned film director Ingmar Bergman, winner of the Cannes Film Festival's Palm of Palms award, announced his intention to leave the country following a dispute with the tax authorities.[490] In late January, two plainclothes police officers had shown up at the Royal Dramatic Theatre in Stockholm to interview him. "I hope he shows up, otherwise things will get serious for him," one of the policemen told the receptionist. Bergman was taken to the police precinct, where he was interviewed for several hours; simultaneously, his home and office were searched and his passport confiscated. The arrest made headlines around the world.[491]

Lindgren went on record to support the film director, who – like her – had fallen foul of Sweden's excessive marginal tax rates. The minister of finance remained unrepentant, insisting that 'cultural workers' were subject to the same laws as everyone else. The allegations against Bergman were subsequently dropped due to lack of evidence. The public prosecutor who had initiated the proceedings received a disciplinary warning, and Bergman was cleared of any wrongdoing. He fell into a severe depression and had to be hospitalized.

His subsequent decision to leave Sweden was partly motivated by insinuations that the tax authorities hadn't finished with him. Bergman and his wife fled to Paris, where they were welcomed by a large crowd of journalists. "Sweden had succeeded in driving the man who was probably the country's best-known living artist into exile," Olof Palme's biographer Henrik Berggren comments.[492]

These examples go to show the extent to which even intellectuals tend to forego their lofty anti-capitalist sentiments (discussed in more depth in Chapter 10) and their professed sympathies for Scandinavian-style socialism as soon as their own assets are under threat. Lindgren and Bergman responded true to type. In 1975, the Swedish government unleashed a storm of protest by reclassifying 'cultural workers' as entrepreneurs. "Unlike the meek members of the business community, the 'cultural workers' had always had a strong voice in the Swedish mass media. They were able to give eloquent expression to the discrimination they were subjected to, the injustice they were suffering and the ignorance they were confronted with. They shed light on problems that had been concealed for as long as they only affected the business community."[493]

Their new status as entrepreneurs obliged cultural workers to keep accounts and files for tax audits and pay an advance corporate tax unrelated to their actual earnings as well as stultifying social benefits for non-existent employees. "I've repeatedly had tax inspectors – whose profession doesn't exactly involve wide reading and a good knowledge of the literary world – telling me which books to buy to advance my literary work," the writer Per Erik Wahlund complained.[494]

The most sympathetic attitude writers could hope to encounter in their dealings with the Swedish tax authorities was encapsulated in these instructions from the head of the new Budget Department: "Of course, writers should always be able to travel if that enhances the value of their books. As for myself, the book I wrote at home turned out every bit as good as it would have if I'd travelled to London or Paris." The book in question was a work of sociology. In response, the writer Anderz Harning retorted: "The Fiscal Courts are by no means inspired by a great love of justice, as you assume. On the contrary, when it comes to travel expenses for the purpose of generating income, the courts and the auditors are influenced by purely emotional thinking." Accordingly, travels to tropical destinations were classified as non-deductible junkets as a matter of principle, while a trip to Afghanistan in deepest mid-winter would always be classified as deductible. Harning added that – in accordance with the requirement to take the cheapest form of transport for any business trip – he had been advised by the tax authorities to travel from Cyprus to Beirut by train rather than flying.[495]

By drawing public attention to the ways in which the Swedish tax regime sought to control all aspects of their working lives, and publicly denouncing the tax bureaucracy, the writers' vociferous protests finally succeeded in doing what the business community had failed to achieve. This was the prevailing mood in the Swedish model of socialism so admired by the left around the world during the 1970s.

As Assar Lindbeck emphasizes in an article on "The Swedish Experiment", this 'Swedish model' of very high taxes, extensive redistribution, massive government intervention in economic affairs, a high degree of regulation and the dominant position of the unions, which were closely affiliated with the Social Democrats, wasn't planned in accordance with some grand design, but rather the "ex-post outcome of hundreds of separate decisions". Lindbeck adds: "Behind many of these decisions, however, it is possible to detect a specific view of the world, such as a firm belief in the importance of returns to scale, the usefulness of centralized political intervention in the economic life of firms and families, and strong suspicion of markets, economic incentives and private entrepreneurship not embodied in large firms."[496]

In the September 1976 elections, Swedish voters penalized the Social Democrats for taking their socialist agenda too far, ousting them from power for the first time in over 40 years. Unfortunately, the new centrist government lacked the courage for a radical turnaround, given that the specific view of the world cited by Lindbeck was by now deeply entrenched in Swedish society far beyond the political left. The new government continued to increase public debt for job-creation schemes in the public sector and generously granted subsidies in the private sector. However, this only concealed the problem of unemployment while failing to address its underlying causes. Key industries were nationalized and entire swathes of the economy bailed out with taxpayers' money.

In some areas, the absurdities reached almost farcical proportions. Super-tankers that were no longer economically viable were built and stockpiled with government subsidies, only to be scrapped with more taxpayers' money. Finally, the entire shipbuilding industry was nationalized. All in all, bailing out the shipbuilding industry cost Swedish taxpayers the equivalent of around USD 12 billion.[497] "Even when Sweden was hit by the worst economic crisis since World War II, the generous welfare state and full employment policy were not called into question but pursued more tenaciously than ever before."[498]

Many excesses of the welfare state were equally absurd, including the generous sick pay. As well as statutory payments, most employees in Sweden received additional sickness benefit under company agreements and their collective agreements, which meant that those who took sick leave ended up with a larger paycheck than a healthy person who came to work every day. Unsurprisingly, Sweden held on to the OECD record for the highest rate of non-working adults in the labour force for several decades.[499] Also unsurprisingly, spikes in the rate of absence due to sickness frequently coincided with major sporting events. Even during the 2002 soccer World Cup – by which time reforms had already reversed the very worst excesses – the number of sick days increased by 41% among male workers.[500]

The Social Democrats' return to power in 1982 marked the beginning of a slow change in thinking. The errors of the Swedish way of expanding the welfare state and strangling the market with more and more regulation had become glaringly obvious. With national debt reaching such high levels that the time-honoured policy of incurring more debt in order to create new jobs in the civil service simply became untenable, the Social Democratic Party's new policy of 'growth before redistribution' focused on strengthening export capacity rather than socialist experiments.

The refusal of many Social Democrats to let go of their ideology led to pro-tests, from within the party as well as from the unions, against finance minister Kjell-Olof Feldt's more pragmatic policies. His government attempted to secure consent for the necessary cuts to social welfare spending by raising taxes for high earners at the same time. But, while government policies were aimed at ridding the country of the worst excesses of the welfare state, the unions attempted to enforce the introduction of 'workers' funds', which would make it mandatory for companies to put a large share of their profits at the disposal of the unions. "The instigators of these workers' funds were aware and didn't bother to deny that they constituted an assault against the basic principles of capitalism."[501]

The intention behind the funds was to progressively expropriate Swedish companies from their private owners and move them into the unions' control. According to calculations, after 20 years one in three companies would be owned by the funds, paving the way for the eventual disappearance of private enterprise from the Swedish economy.[502]

However, polls show that the majority of the population opposed these funds. One of the largest demonstrations in the country's history took place in protest against their introduction shortly before the vote in the Swedish parliament in October 1983. Although the form in which they were passed into law in 1984 was moderate compared to the original concept, by 1992 the workers' funds already held 7% of Sweden's total market capitalization. After the election victory of the centrist parties, however, the existing funds were dissolved and the Social Democrats later made no attempt to reintroduce funds of this kind.

POST-SOCIALIST SWEDEN

Pushback against the proponents of socialist ideas increasingly gathered momentum, and by the 1990s there was a comprehensive counter-movement that – without fundamentally questioning the Swedish model of high taxes and comprehensive welfare benefits – nevertheless eliminated many of its excesses. A major tax reform in 1990/91 slashed corporate taxes from 57% (including payments into workers' funds) to 30%.[503] Income from shares was exempted from taxation, while capital gains from shares were taxed at only 12.5%.[504]

The top marginal income tax rate was set at around 50%, a reduction by 24 to 27 percentage points for the majority of the workforce. The proportion of earners taxed at a marginal rate of over 50% dropped from over half to only 17% paying income tax to the central government, while the majority of earners were only paying municipal income tax. The wealth tax was cut from 2% to 1.5%. The reforms also included the introduction of indexing to prevent bracket creep due to inflation.[505]

These tax cuts were accompanied by the abolition of special exceptions and amortization rates that had led to misdirection of resources. The government also raised indirect taxes to offset the direct tax cuts. The reforms continued over the following years: in 2004, the estate and accession tax of up to 30% was scrapped. The abolition of the wealth tax, which had already been cut, came into effect retroactively as of 1 January 2007. The corporate tax rate of 30% was cut to 26.3% in 2009 and to 22% in 2013. Property tax rates were also cut substantially.[506] Subsequent reforms gave business owners and self-employed professionals the option to significantly reduce their tax burden by declaring a part of their earnings as capital gains rather than income.[507]

The abolition of a number of exemptions has simplified the Swedish tax system to a point where the majority of taxpayers now file their own income tax returns without the assistance of an accountant. In 2013, 750,000 Swedish residents used the government's text-message service to review and confirm a pre-printed income tax return. A large majority of the population filed their tax returns online, with only one in three residents sending postal returns.[508]

In 1992, the Swedish government appointed a commission of independent academics chaired by Lindbeck to analyse, and propose solutions for, the country's economic crisis. Their findings were unequivocal: attempts by previous governments to alleviate the crisis had only resulted in aggravating it and delaying necessary adjustments. In September 1993, unemployment reached unprecedented levels of around 14% (including the official figure of 9% as well as the 5% of the labour force "engaged in various types of active labor market programs").[509] The economists proceed to demonstrate that the dramatic rise in public-sector spending (from 25% of GDP in 1950 to 70% in 1992) had contributed to a number of serious issues including "the overheating of the economy during boom periods and … recurring budget deficits".[510] Specifically, the attempts by Swedish policymakers in the 1970s and 1980s to avoid high unemployment by increasing employment in the public sector had contributed to "a steep inflationary trend".[511]

To remedy the situation, the commission gave a clear recommendation in favour of strengthening the market and reducing the public sector. "What the commission would like to see regarding the market system is nothing less than the restoration of those freedoms of entry, occupation, and profession that new legislations in 1846 and 1864 established in Sweden. Those liberal reforms preceded a period of unprecedented growth. But during the last century these freedoms have been more and more diluted by regulations and barriers to competition, largely due to the influence of different short-run special interests."[512]

The swingeing reforms implemented during the 1990s did provide correctives to quite a few harmful developments, including cuts to unemployment benefit from 90% to 80% and the introduction of a five-day waiting period.[513] Between 1993 and 2000, social spending dropped from 22.2% to 16.9% of GDP, economic subsidies from 8.7% to 1.8% and public-sector payroll costs from 18.2% to 15.6%.[514]

One of the most admirable aspects of these reforms was Sweden's adherence to a strict budgetary discipline even during the difficult years of the financial crisis, when public debt ballooned everywhere else.[515] Between 1990 and 2012, government spending fell from 61.3% to 52.0% of GDP, second only to Norway, which recorded an even more impressive drop from 54.0% to 43.2% of GDP in the same period. The Swedish achievement is all the more remarkable in comparison to the OECD-wide 2.5% *increase* in government spending relative to GDP (3.2% in the US and a whopping 11.3% in Japan).[516]

The Swedish population seemed willing to accept that the stripping back of the welfare system resulted in a more drastic decline in equality than almost anywhere else in the world. The Gini coefficient, which measures income distribution, grew by around 30% between the mid-1980s and the late 2000s.

Only New Zealand recorded a similar growth in inequality during the same period.[517] Sweden has long lost its ranking as the world's most egalitarian country – it currently sits in 12th place, just behind Belarus.

While Swedish society may have become slightly less egalitarian, this ranking also proves that the Swedish welfare state is still alive and kicking. The data cited by the French economist Thomas Piketty as evidence of his contention that inequality has risen drastically[518] are based on a distortion of the actual figures. Simply put, he selectively analysed data points for the years that best suited his purposes, choosing the most egalitarian years on record for the 1980s and 1990s and then presenting data for the 2010s that appear unrelated to any verifiable source, as the Swedish economists Malin Sahlén and Salim Furth have shown.[519] As the two authors comment drily, Piketty's calculations are "obviously very useful for debaters who want to see a reinstated estate tax or a tax on wealth and property".[520]

What Sweden really needs is the exact opposite – further-reaching pro-market reforms. As Sanandaji argues, Sweden is among a number of European welfare states that are not very good at integrating new immigrants into the labour market. In the US, where welfare benefits are far more limited, the employment rate is higher by 4% for foreign-born than for native-born residents – in Sweden it is lower by 15%.[521] In Sweden, highly educated immigrants are 8% more likely to be unemployed than native-born residents with low education levels. In the US, unemployment among highly educated immigrants is only 1% higher than among highly educated native-born residents.[522]

Among other reasons, the Swedish welfare state offers even unemployed migrants a standard of living far higher than in their countries of origin. During the 2015 refugee crisis, countries with comprehensive welfare systems topped the list of the most popular destinations for refugees and other migrants. Sweden, which along with Germany initially took in large numbers of migrants, had to introduce changes to its overly generous immigration laws in 2016.

Compounding the problems is the disastrous housing shortage caused by Sweden's rent-control legislation. While this is disproportionately hitting low-income migrants, it is also hurting the economy. In 2016, the founders of Swedish tech giant Spotify threatened to move jobs elsewhere if the government failed to take urgent action to tackle the housing crisis. According to a *Neue Zürcher Zeitung* report, the lack of suitable housing for employees had already forced a German start-up to abandon plans for a new office in Stockholm in 2015.[523]

These issues notwithstanding, the overall economic outlook for Sweden is very positive. With strong economic growth, Sweden is one of the few countries that would currently meet the strict criteria for eurozone membership – which a majority of Swedes are opposed to, for good reason. Although contemporary Sweden remains a traditional welfare state in some respects (e.g. it has comparatively high tax rates), successive governments since the early 1990s have consistently chosen more freedom over more equality, more market over more state. Following the obvious failure of the socialist experiment, the balance between capitalism and socialism has shifted towards capitalism.

CHAPTER 8

Economic Freedom *Increases* Human Welfare

Taking what we've learned from the first seven chapters of this book, one thing becomes absolutely clear – people's lives are much better where there is more economic freedom. The population of South Korea are doing better than their neighbours across the border in North Korea; life was far better in the Federal Republic of Germany than it ever was in the German Democratic Republic; Chileans are better off than Venezuelans. The expansion of economic freedoms through free-market reforms – in China under Deng Xiaoping, in the UK under Margaret Thatcher and in the US under Ronald Reagan – increased economic prosperity for the majority of citizens in each of these countries.

There are two different ways to approach the question of whether it is more state intervention or greater market freedom that promotes people's prosperity: you can take a theoretical approach and discuss the advantages and disadvantages of different economic systems. Or you can take a more practical approach and determine which system works better in practice. At any given time, a host of social experiments are being conducted all over the world, some of which are described in this book. The result has consistently been the same: a planned economy and heavy-handed state intervention always lead to worse results than a market economy. This is true not only for the countries described in this book but in general, as demonstrated by the Index of Economic Freedom, which has been compiled by the Heritage Foundation every year since 1995.

The index, most recently published in February 2018, measures and ranks economic freedom in 180 countries. The Index of Economic Freedom could also be described as an index of capitalism, as the sociologist Erich Weede points out.[524] Even the briefest glance at the index reveals a clear correlation between capitalism and prosperity.

According to the 2018 index, the 25 most economically free countries are:

1.	Hong Kong	14.	Luxembourg
2.	Singapore	15.	Sweden
3.	New Zealand	16.	Georgia
4.	Switzerland	17.	Netherlands
5.	Australia	18.	United States
6.	Ireland	19.	Lithuania
7.	Estonia	20.	Chile
8.	United Kingdom	21.	Mauritius
9.	Canada	22.	Malaysia
10.	United Arab Emirates	23.	Norway
11.	Iceland	24.	Czech Republic
12.	Denmark	25.	Germany
13.	Taiwan		

The world's 20 least economically free countries are:

161. Sudan	171. Djibouti
162. Chad	172. Algeria
163. Central African Republic	173. Bolivia
164. Angola	174. Zimbabwe
165. Ecuador	175. Equatorial Guinea
166. Suriname	176. Eritrea
167. Timor-Leste	177. Republic of Congo
168. Togo	178. Cuba
169. Turkmenistan	179. Venezuela
170. Mozambique	180. North Korea

Of course, the degree of economic freedom as it is currently measured is not the only factor that contributes to a country's prosperity. For example, it stands to reason that countries such as Estonia, Latvia and Lithuania, which were only able to establish market economic systems once they emerged from communist rule in the early 1990s, should be less prosperous than Canada, Switzerland or the UK, all of which have very long traditions of economic freedom. In addition, this book has repeatedly shown that other criteria play an important role. These include cultural factors, such as a society's commitment to work and education.

It is impossible to measure economic freedom on the basis of just two or three indicators. For example, Sweden ranks 15th overall in the 2018 index, despite having one of the world's highest tax burdens. If this were the only criterion used to assess economic freedom, Sweden would rank fourth from bottom (177th) instead of 15th and would be considered one of the least economically free countries in the world. However, in other areas, the country scores highly and comes right near the top of the index. In terms of business freedom, Sweden ranks 11th; for property rights, it secures 3rd place.[525]

The index uses 12 equally weighted components to determine each country's level of economic freedom.

THE 12 COMPONENTS OF ECONOMIC FREEDOM MEASURED IN THE INDEX

PROPERTY RIGHTS

This component assesses the rights of citizens to own and accumulate private property. Can citizens be sure that their private property won't be unfairly expropriated? To what extent does the freedom to conclude and enforce contracts exist? Even where private property rights do formally exist, economic freedom suffers if, in fact, the state prevents its citizens from disposing of their assets as they see fit. Venezuela, for example, was awarded just 5.2 out of a potential 100 points in this category in 2018, while Switzerland scored 84.2 out of 100.[526]

JUDICIAL EFFECTIVENESS

Can citizens turn to the judicial system to effectively assert their legal rights? Is the country a fully developed state governed by constitutional law? Or do a country's citizens have to seriously worry about enforcing their legal rights because the judiciary is not always independent?

GOVERNMENT INTEGRITY

Corruption and crony capitalism are common in certain African, Latin American, Eastern European and Southern European countries and have a massive, negative impact on economic freedom. In this regard, the Scandinavian countries are exemplary – Sweden, for instance, scores 88.2 out of 100, whereas Zimbabwe only manages 18.9 points and ranks 175th.[527]

TAX BURDEN

Taxes are necessary to finance services and projects that benefit society as a whole. But the more income the state takes away from companies and individuals, the more it restricts their economic freedom. And this is not just a question of income or corporate taxes, but of all types of taxes, including indirect taxes, such as sales taxes. This is where the Scandinavian countries, which do extremely well in the other categories, lose a lot of points.

GOVERNMENT SPENDING

A great deal of government expenditure, including investments in domestic security, defence, infrastructure and education, is absolutely necessary and even promotes economic prosperity. Nevertheless, the state should not see itself as an entrepreneur. When states do so, they often fail, distorting markets to the detriment of private-sector companies.

FISCAL HEALTH

Large deficits and debts are a problem for many countries today and are clearly detrimental to economic freedom. Although additional debt may appear to have a positive impact in the short term (e.g. to finance stimulus programmes), it has a number of negative side effects that damage the economy in the long term.

BUSINESS FREEDOM

This category primarily measures how difficult it is to establish and run a business. In Hong Kong, all an entrepreneur has to do is fill out a form and in a few hours their company is fully licensed. In Africa, India and many countries in South America, the same process can take weeks, or even months, and involve time-consuming appointments at one public authority after another, some of which only work efficiently after they have been appropriately bribed. Even once a company is up and running, the extent of state regulation varies significantly from country to country.

LABOUR FREEDOM

Some governments take a very active role in regulating their labour markets. Regulations can include statutory minimum wages, restrictions on hiring and firing, and other top-down regulations. Such constraints frequently lead to higher unemployment. Let's take France as an example: France ranks 71st overall, but in terms of labour freedom it only reaches 148th in the rankings.[528] It is no surprise that President Emmanuel Macron made labour market reform one of his key priorities when he took office in 2017. Germany doesn't fare much better and only manages to score 53.3 points in this category, which equates to 116th out of 180 countries.[529]

MONETARY FREEDOM

Economic freedom cannot exist without monetary stability. There is clear evidence that having an independent central bank is the best way to achieve currency stability. In contrast, high inflation and government price controls pose serious threats to economic freedom.

TRADE FREEDOM

The free flow of goods is another key contributor to economic freedom and growth. Protectionist measures – such as excessive import duties or other restrictions on free trade – only harm a country in the long run, even when these measures are intended to protect the domestic economy from undesirable competition in the short term.

INVESTMENT FREEDOM

Every individual and company should be free to choose where and how they invest their capital. The more restrictions a country imposes on such freedoms, the fewer opportunities there will be for economic growth. Companies and individuals should have access to a free and open investment environment, both domestic and international.

FINANCIAL FREEDOM

It is the state's job to provide a regulatory framework for banks and other financial service providers to ensure a high level of transparency and honesty. Over-regulation of the banking sector, on the other hand, often achieves exactly the opposite of what the legislator intended.

In the 2018 index, only six countries in the world are classed as economically 'free' and 28 countries are rated as 'mostly free'. This group includes many of the countries discussed in this book, such as the UK (8th), Sweden (15th), the US (18th), Chile (20th) and Germany (25th). The 'moderately free' category comprises 61 countries, while 63 are described as 'mostly unfree'. North Korea and Venezuela are among the 21 countries rated as economically 'repressed'. Economies rated 'free' or 'mostly free' enjoy income levels and economic growth far higher than those in the 'mostly unfree' and 'repressed' countries.

Asia-Pacific is unique among the index's global regions in terms of its massive variations in economic freedom and prosperity. The four economically 'free' countries have an average GDP per capita of USD 58,093. This far exceeds the average of USD 10,836 in the region's economically 'repressed' countries.[530] The three freest countries in the Americas have an average GDP per capita of more than USD 42,000, almost four times the USD 11,519 reported for the region's five 'repressed' economies.[531] There are also striking variations across Europe and Africa.[532] In the countries rated as 'free' by the Heritage Foundation, GDP per capita averages USD 60,194, compared with an average of just USD 8,058 in the index's 'repressed' economies.[533]

There is also a documented correlation between increased economic freedom and stronger economic growth. We have already seen this from the examples of China, Sweden, the UK, the US and Chile in this book. The same holds true when we consider the impact of expanded economic freedom on economic growth across the globe.[534] Here are just a few examples.[535]

Hong Kong and Singapore have topped the economic freedom rankings for years. Both countries registered dramatic growth in economic freedom between 1975 and 2008. During this period, GDP per capita as a percentage of GDP in Western Europe rose from 56% to 130% in Singapore and from 61% to 146% in Hong Kong.

In Chile, GDP per capita in 1975 was just over a third (37%) of the GDP of Western Europeans. In 2008, this figure had risen to 61%. Conversely, in 1975 the GDP per capita in Venezuela stood at 91% of that of Western Europeans but had fallen to half (49%) by 2008. In Chile, the degree of economic freedom increased significantly during this period, while in Venezuela it decreased.

In India, the degree of economic freedom increased significantly in the period between 1975 and 2008, which fuelled a substantial rise in real GDP per capita. Taken as a percentage of GDP per capita in Western Europe, GDP per capita in India rose from 8% in 1975 to 14% in 2008.

In South Korea, economic freedom increased significantly in the period between 1975 and 2008, and GDP per capita rose from 28% to 97% of GDP per capita in Western Europe.

Economic freedom benefits almost everyone. Research has demonstrated time and again that the greater the economic freedom, the wealthier an economy. Freer economies are more likely to achieve higher rates of economic growth and higher incomes for the poorest 10% of their populations.[536] One of the most persuasive arguments in favour of capitalism is that economically free countries have lower poverty rates and have been able to reduce poverty faster.

The World Bank regularly publishes data on global poverty trends, although these are only reported for developing countries, not for industrialized, high-income countries. In 2005, the rate of extreme poverty in the world's most repressed economies stood at 41.5%, which contrasts to just 2.7% in the freest economies. The rate of 'moderate poverty' was 57.4% for the quartile of the least economically free countries, compared to 3.6% for the quartile of the world's most economically free countries.[537]

Correspondingly, life expectancy is also significantly higher in countries with greater economic freedom than in countries with lower levels of economic freedom. In the quartile of the least economically free countries, life expectancy at birth was 60.7 years in 2009, while in the quartile of the world's most economically free countries it was higher by almost 20 years at 79.4.[538]

One indicator of economic prosperity is the percentage of overall consumer spending on food. In the US today – a country not known for its restraint when it comes to eating – food accounts for approximately 6% of overall consumer spending. A hundred years ago, spending on food in the US was at 40% of overall consumer spending, as much as it is today in many developing countries. A 2017 study showed that, in percentage terms, the countries with the lowest spending on food are the US, Singapore, the UK, Switzerland, Canada, Ireland, Austria, Australia, Germany and Denmark – all countries that are classed as (mostly) economically free. The populations that spend the greatest proportion on food are all in countries with low levels of economic freedom. Here, spending on food averages 40%, rising to 59% in extreme cases.[539]

It has also been documented that freer economies rarely experience civil wars. They also enjoy greater political stability, lower murder rates, fewer human rights violations and lower levels of militarization, and they have populations that feel safer and more secure.[540] It would be an interesting task for researchers to analyse the correlation between global refugee movements and economic freedom. There are many reasons for people to flee a country: political oppression, economic hardship, wars and civil wars. If we look at the Heritage Foundation's Index of Economic Freedom and compare the top 20 countries with the bottom 20, one thing is instantly obvious: no one is fleeing countries such as New Zealand, the UK, the Netherlands or Sweden for any of the above reasons. On the contrary, a majority of the countries that are rated 'mostly free' are popular destinations for refugees, including Germany, Austria and Sweden.

At the other end of the scale, a range of problems have caused people to flee from many of the world's 20 most economically 'repressed' countries – except where they have been forcibly prevented from doing so, as they have in North Korea. This is true not only for countries such as Sudan, where civil war rages, but also for countries such as Venezuela, which has seen millions of people leave, fleeing the disastrous effects of socialist policies.

Despite the laudable progress made in sub-Saharan Africa, many of the region's 48 countries are still economically 'repressed'. Only one of the region's countries is classed as 'mostly free', eight are 'moderately free', 26 are 'mostly unfree' and 12 are among the most 'repressed' countries in the world.[541] It is therefore not difficult to understand why a majority of the world's refugees come from Africa. Sub-Saharan Africa suffers from the greatest lack of economic freedom. Correspondingly, the region's populations are the most desperate in the world. On the one hand, much has been done to reduce poverty in many African countries over the past few decades, as we have already seen in Chapter 2. Unfortunately, this hasn't reduced the number of refugees, as politicians would have us believe when they talk about "eliminating the causes of migration and flight". In any case, the poorest of the poor can't afford to pay people smugglers, whose services often cost several thousand dollars. On the contrary, people who can afford to be smuggled out are often those who are more prosperous, having previously benefited from the economic gains in their home countries.

THE HUMAN DEVELOPMENT INDEX

There are numerous other indices and rankings that assess the quality of life in countries around the world. The Human Development Index (HDI), which has been published by the UN since 1990, is among the most prominent. Developed by the Pakistani economist Mahbub ul Haq, the HDI is a composite index and is designed to be a more comprehensive 'prosperity indicator' than traditional economic indicators. The methodology underpinning the index has changed repeatedly over the years and it now includes criteria such as education and life expectancy alongside per-capita income indicators to rank countries' achievements in human development.

In principle, it certainly makes sense to include indicators beyond GDP per capita. After all, GDP per capita only provides a snapshot of the total value of goods and services produced by an economy in a single year, which means it is not suitable as the sole measure of economic and social prosperity. It is a good measure of income but doesn't reflect a country's level of well-being. Of course, in order to determine a country's prosperity, we also need to consider factors such as life expectancy. Nevertheless, the HDI's methods and findings would, at least in some respects, appear to be questionable. In 2016, Cuba and Venezuela ranked 68th and 71st out of 105 nations, well ahead of Mexico (77th) and Brazil (79th).[542]

Despite some questionable methods and findings in measuring prosperity, there is a strong correlation between the HDI ranking and the Index of Economic Freedom. Almost all of the top 20 countries in the UN's HDI[543] also appear among the top 30 of the Heritage Foundation's most economically 'free' nations (with the exception of Israel and Macau, which rank 31st and 34th in the Index of Economic Freedom). Conversely, not a single country in the bottom 20 of the HDI index (a group that includes the Maldives, Samoa and Uzbekistan) is rated as 'economically free' or 'mostly free' by the Heritage Foundation's index.

CHAPTER 9

The Financial Crisis: A Crisis *of* Capitalism?

In my view, the Index of Economic Freedom is a fairly reliable measure of relative economic freedom. No one can deny that Australia is economically freer than France or that France is freer than Venezuela. However, the index does not reflect negative developments that restrict economic freedom in capitalist countries worldwide, leading to serious crises such as the subprime mortgage crisis in the US in 2007–2008, which in turn triggered a global financial crisis. The massively increased power of the central banks in particular represents an increasing threat to economic freedom.

Opponents of capitalism like to cite the financial crisis as evidence of the damage done by 'neoliberal politics' with its excessive 'deregulation' of the markets. The logical corollary of their diagnosis is a demand for more government intervention in economic affairs and more regulation of the financial sector. In fact, the opposite is required, as I will show in this chapter. The financial crisis brought the international financial system to the brink of collapse. Understanding its causes is essential to understanding its implications for the future.

FEDERAL RESERVE INTERVENES
TO DISASTROUS EFFECT

The financial crisis was triggered by developments on the American residential property market, which had their roots in political interventions and the policies of the US Federal Reserve, the Fed for short. The US National Home Price Index measures the development of home prices in the US. It was first published in 1987 and the index was calculated back to 1890; it rose almost constantly from 5 points in 1941 to 184 points in 2006. It is striking that it more than doubled in the seven years from 1999 to 2006, from 92 to 184 points. Today we know that this was one of the largest asset bubble formations in history.[544]

So, how did this extreme development come about in just seven years? To understand the housing price bubble, we first need to understand the preceding stock market bubble. At the end of the 1990s, there was a stock market bubble that was, at least in part, fuelled by the policies of the central banks. In 2000, this stock market bubble burst. In September 2002, the British weekly news magazine *The Economist* stated: "Without easy credit the stock market bubble could not have been sustained for so long, nor would its bursting have had such serious consequences. And unless central bankers learn their lesson, it will happen again."[545]

From its peak in 2000, the Nasdaq index fell 74% and the S&P 500 Index, a composite index of the 500 most important American stocks, lost 43%.[546] In response, the Fed under its then chairman, Alan Greenspan, lowered short-term interest rates from 6.25% to 1.75% in 2001, and the money supply was expanded by more than 10% during this period. By mid-2003, Greenspan had further reduced interest rates to 1%.[547]

Artificially low interest rates always have undesirable side effects. Prices – including interest rates, which represent the price of money lent – usually provide valuable information for market participants and encourage capital to flow where it is needed. If interest rates are kept artificially low or even abolished (i.e. set to zero), this mechanism can no longer take effect. Investors are then driven to put their capital into increasingly risky stocks and bonds, because when the prices of bonds issued by sound companies and creditworthy countries fall, institutional investors, who have promised certain returns to their investors, are forced to invest in riskier bonds, shares and real estate, whose prices then rise.

In addition, the prospect of earning a lot of money very quickly in certain markets attracts increasing numbers of investors without specialist expertise. These investors, who no longer buy shares or real estate in order to hold them in the long term but instead to resell them quickly at a much higher price, strengthen the price bubble and force experienced and long-term-oriented investors out of the market because they are not willing to pay such absurd prices.

Years before the American house price bubble burst, a number of forward-looking economists warned of the link between low interest rates and rising house prices. William R. White, a proponent of the market-oriented Austrian school of economics, warned in August 2003 that "the unusually buoyant behavior of housing prices in the current slowdown may well be related to the substantial monetary easing undertaken by central banks… [This] has encouraged a further rise in indebtedness in the household sector in a number of countries, raising the risk of contributing to balance sheet overextension there, especially if housing prices were to soften."[548] In 2006, he again warned that "persistently easy monetary conditions can lead to the cumulative build-up over time of significant deviations from historical norms – whether in terms of debt levels, saving ratios, asset prices or other indicators of 'imbalances'".[549]

It is notable how a leading American economist who is more sympathetic to active market interventions than White saw the matter. In an opinion piece for the *New York Times* in 2002, Nobel Prize winner Paul Krugman even *recommended* to the Fed the very strategy White had *warned against*: "To fight the recession the Fed needs more than a snapback; it needs soaring household spending to offset moribund business investment. And to do that, as Paul McCulley of Pimco put it, Alan Greenspan needs to create a housing bubble to replace the Nasdaq bubble."[550] The Fed should therefore pursue a low-interest policy in order to create a house price bubble to *replace* the dot-com bubble.

It is at this point that a more fundamental problem becomes clear: celebrated by the media as the 'master of the universe', Greenspan believed that his task was to steer the economy and financial markets. He was proud to have doubled the number of data series monitored by the Fed to over 14,000 within ten years of taking office in 1987. His employees joked that these included data series that only their boss understood. "This enabled him to spot economic shifts long before anyone else and quickly change the direction of monetary policy. This adulation is an expression of the dream of the planned economy – the idea that some enlightened man in a bathtub will understand the market better than all the millions of market players and that he will be able to use this insight to steer them in the right direction."[551]

Greenspan's interventionism was seen by market participants as a guarantee against falling market prices. Many stock market investors relied on the 'master' to intervene in good time or, after a downturn, to do everything necessary to ensure that prices rose again. On the stock market, the term 'Greenspan put' became a common phrase. This referred to the fact that Greenspan had already used his power several times in the past to prevent stock market catastrophes: in 1987 after the stock market crash, in 1998 after the Russian debt crisis and the collapse of the Long-Term Capital Fund, and when he took steps to prevent the Y2K crisis in the run-up to the turn of the millennium. "It was thought that he had proven through his actions that he would never let the market fall sharply,"[552] said Robert J. Shiller, American economist and Nobel Prize winner in economics.

The Fed's interventionist policy of extremely low interest rates certainly cannot be classed as a 'market failure'. Quite the contrary. Rather than limiting themselves to creating the conditions for monetary stability and letting markets run their course, central banks around the world have increasingly taken it upon themselves to smooth out or cushion the normal ups and downs of the economy and the financial markets. When the stock market bubble burst, the Fed reacted with even lower interest rates, which triggered the next, far worse bubble, this time in the American real estate market.

There were many reasons for the influx of money into the housing sector. In addition to low interest rates, the real estate boom was fuelled by high tax benefits. Tax incentives for consumer loans (e.g. for cars) had already been abolished in the 1980s and 1990s, but the deduction of home mortgage interest was maintained. In 1997, the capital gains tax on real estate (up to USD 500,000 for a married couple) was abolished, while it remained in force for other investments (such as stocks). The then head of the Internal Revenue Service was surprised: "Why insist in effect that they put it in housing to get that benefit? Why not let them invest in other things that might be more productive, like stocks and bonds?"[553] A study by the Fed showed that the number of real estate transactions between 1997 and 2006 was 17% higher than it would have been without these tax incentives.[554] In particular, it fired up the rapid trading of houses by so-called 'flippers', who entered the market for entirely speculative reasons.

Extremely low interest rates combined with tax benefits for real estate investments were one reason for the bubble. However, this bubble did not develop all across the US, but only in about a dozen states. Studies show that this primarily affected states that used strong regulations to restrict the supply of real estate. Between 2000 and 2006, prices in heavily regulated states such as California and Florida rose by more than 130%, while in unregulated Georgia and Texas they rose by only 30%.[555]

POLITICALLY CORRECT LENDING

The house price bubble was also fuelled by the fact that a growing number of home mortgages were granted to unqualified borrowers. In fact, this was precisely what politicians wanted. It is worth mentioning in this context that the Community Reinvestment Act (CRA) initially had little impact when it was passed under Jimmy Carter in 1977. It was only during the Clinton administration (1993–2001) that this law was considerably expanded and used to force banks to finance homebuyers who would previously have been considered uncreditworthy.

This was done in the name of racial equality and to protect blacks, Hispanics and other economically deprived groups from discrimination.

Under the CRA, banks ran the risk of being sued for discriminating against minorities unless they met certain quotas for lending to minorities. They were only able to achieve these quotas by relaxing the risk assessments they used to approve home loans.[556] Banks ran the risk of having mergers or new branch openings blocked if they violated the provisions of the CRA.[557] And of course no bank wanted to be pilloried in the media for alleged discrimination against minorities.

Banks had to publish their CRA grades and publicly state whether they had issued enough mortgage loans to minorities and low-income homebuyers. Those who did not meet the targets were lambasted in aggressive campaigns by left-wing political associations such as Acorn, a national association of municipal activists. Acorn's aim was to use public pressure to force financial service providers to relax lending conditions. Two major banks, Chase Manhattan and J.P. Morgan, donated hundreds of thousands of dollars to this organization so as not to jeopardize their upcoming merger in November 2001.[558] In 2009, federal support for Acorn was discontinued after video footage from a hidden film camera purported to show Acorn employees giving tips on how to organize child prostitution, evade taxes and smuggle girls from El Salvador into the country.[559] Shortly afterwards, the organization went bankrupt.

The Department of Housing and Urban Development also forced financial services providers to conclude anti-discrimination agreements based on the principle of 'affirmative action', i.e. giving preference to minorities, in this case when granting loans. It was openly acknowledged that qualifying people for mortgages who did not normally meet lending standards would increase credit risk.[560]

At a conference, Edward M. Gramlich, a member of the Board of Governors of the Fed, cited studies showing that low-income households and members of minorities who traditionally had difficulties in obtaining mortgage loans would now receive loans in record numbers. Between 1993 and 1998, the volume of conventional mortgages increased by 75% for low-income borrowers, 78% for Hispanics and as much as 95% for African Americans. Overall, the volume of conventional mortgages only increased by 40% in the same period.[561]

The companies Fannie Mae and Freddie Mac played a major role in these developments. The Federal National Mortgage Association (FNMA) was founded in 1938 as a state bank and formally 'privatized' in 1968. At that time, the company was rebranded as Fannie Mae, from the abbreviation FNMA.

Thanks to regulatory privileges and tax benefits, the company remained close to the state even after it was formally privatized. Its counterpart, Freddie Mac (Federal Home Loan Mortgage Corporation), buys mortgage loans from banks and packages them for the financial market as mortgage-backed securities. Freddie Mac is also a government-sponsored enterprise and is supervised by the Office of Federal Housing Enterprise Oversight. Government-sponsored enterprises are particularly dangerous because they allow private investors to take every conceivable risk while knowing that the state – i.e. the taxpayer – will pay for their losses in a worst-case scenario.[562]

The two companies had an extremely high and inexpensive refinancing credit line with the US Treasury. Because they were guaranteed by the state, their refinancing bonds were treated as 'government securities' with low interest rates similar to government bonds.[563] The two quasi-state banks fell back on this state guarantee in 2008–2009.

Fannie Mae and Freddie Mac were the largest mortgage banks in the world and guaranteed the lion's share of US mortgage loans. Following their effective bankruptcy in 2008, they were formally nationalized. Without them, the rapid spread of subprime loans – i.e. risky mortgages to low-income homebuyers – would never have been possible. They had a close relationship with Countryside, a financial services provider notorious for its subprime activities, which, at its peak, had 60,000 employees and 90 branches and was the largest seller of mortgages to Fannie Mae. At the time, real estate insiders joked that Countryside was a subsidiary of Fannie Mae.[564]

The two quasi-state banks played an important role in implementing the requirements for politically correct lending. As early as September 1999, the *New York Times* reported that Fannie Mae had relaxed the requirements for the loans it bought, thus making it possible "to extend home mortgages to individuals whose credit is generally not good enough to qualify for conventional loans". Fannie Mae would stand "under increasing pressure from the Clinton administration to expand mortgage loans among low and moderate-income people". One of the aims was "to increase the number of minority and low-income owners who [tended] to have worse credit ratings than non-Hispanic whites". Even then, the *New York Times* pointed to the considerable risks this would entail, especially in economic downturns.[565]

In 1996, the Department of Housing and Urban Development demanded that 12% of all mortgages purchased by Fannie and Freddie should be 'special affordable' loans, typically granted to very low-income homebuyers. That number was increased to 20% in 2000 and to 22% in 2005. The goal for 2008 would have been 28%. The two state-affiliated companies implemented these requirements.[566] Fannie Mae bought USD 1.2 billion in subprime loans in 2000, USD 9.2 billion in 2001 and USD 15 billion in 2002. By 2004, Fannie Mae and Freddie Mac together had already spent USD 175 billion on subprime loans.[567] In 2008, Paul Krugman defended the two companies against their critics and stressed that they had never granted a single subprime loan.[568] Mortgage lending was not the job of the two state-affiliated banks anyway, but without them the real estate crisis would never have occurred, as they were by far the largest and most reckless buyers of subprime loans. More than 40% of the mortgage loans that the two companies bought between 2005 and 2007 were subprime loans or so-called Alt-A loans, which was usually just a nicer label for subprime loans.[569]

The politically motivated relaxation of the conditions for granting loans to lower-income groups or minorities, combined with government lending targets, was the trigger for the increase in loans made to borrowers whose creditworthiness and credit history indicated that they were unlikely to be able to repay their home loans in the long term. It was the combination of the Fed's low-interest policy and the politically driven expansion of subprime loans that ultimately fuelled the house price bubble and financial crisis. In his autobiography, Alan Greenspan defended the easing of lending standards by saying: "I was aware that the loosening of mortgage credit terms for subprime borrowers increased financial risk, and that subsidized homeownership initiatives distort market outcomes. But I believed then, as now, that the benefits of broadened homeownership are worth the risk."[570]

In retrospect, it becomes clear just how absurd this was as the American house price crisis triggered an international financial crash. Incidentally, the target was never achieved, because the post-crash homeownership rate in the US was lower than before, as a result of homebuyers with poor credit ratings losing their homes due to foreclosures. It is obvious that foreclosure is often a traumatic experience for any household. This is one of many examples of how political intervention in the market often leads to exactly the opposite of what politicians originally intended.

The volume of 'politically correct' subprime loans granted primarily to minorities continued to increase. In 1994, the volume of subprime mortgages stood at only USD 35 billion. By 2005, it had grown to USD 625 billion. For 2006, the *New York Times* estimated Wall Street's share of the overall mortgage financing market at 60%. Investment banks bought subprime mortgages from the mortgage lenders, packaged them by the thousands and sold them in the form of securities.[571] Because the banks and other financial service providers did not usually keep the loans on their own books but resold them either to Fannie Mae or elsewhere, there was no longer any limit to the number of loans that could be granted.

In all of this, investors thought they could rely on the rating agencies that provided ratings on securitized mortgage loans. As it turned out later, these ratings were far too generous. But the failure of the rating agencies is no proof that the market failed. The market has never been free because of the (ongoing) oligopoly of a few rating agencies (above all S&P, Moody's and Fitch), whose ratings determine which bonds institutional investors are allowed to buy. In fact, the state has entrusted them with certain tasks, thereby reducing the individual responsibility of investors for their decisions. Power, especially power legitimized by the state, often leads to the abuse of power, and this is exactly what happened during the irrational house price bubble, because the rating agencies awarded overly positive ratings and thus gave investors a false sense of security.

Extremely low interest rates and lax lending standards meant that more and more Americans entered the housing market and prices soared higher and higher. In the aforementioned practice known as 'flipping', buyers only acquired houses in order to sell them immediately at a profit. The housing market mirrored a stock market boom: prices rose steeply and everyone expected that prices would keep on rising and that they would be able to sell at an even higher price.

Between 1997 and 2002, house prices in the US rose by 42%. In New York City they rose by as much as 67%, in Boston by 69%, in Jersey City by 75% and in San Francisco by 88%.[572] House price increases even did the American economy good at first: many homeowners used the increased value in their homes to withdraw equity for personal consumption, thus providing the economy with a short-term boost.

Mortgage lenders and homebuyers were in a real state of euphoria. All rules of logic and serious business conduct were suspended. Studies have shown that in almost 60% of all stated income loans, i.e. loans for which no written proof of income was required from the borrower, the declared income was exaggerated by at least 50%. According to a Credit Suisse analysis, USD 276 billion of loans were granted in the US in 2006 for which no or little proof of income was provided. So-called 2/28 mortgages, which had two years of low interest rates followed by 28 years at very high interest rates, were particularly popular.[573]

As with all bubble formations, the boom increasingly attracted fraudsters who saw an opportunity to make a quick buck. The television station ABC reported on the example of an old man with ailing health who applied for a small amount of consumer credit. What he got instead was a USD 50,000 home mortgage.

After 17 days, even before the first instalment was due, his loan repayments were rescheduled and the period over which he was expected to repay his loan was extended. In the following four years, the lender rescheduled the loan 11 times and charged a financing fee of 10% each time. After the man was unable to pay the instalments, the lender foreclosed on his home.[574] Although this may have been an extreme case, fake income statements and expert opinions that overestimated the value of houses and other fraudulent practices were the order of the day.

The subprime loans were securitized as Collateralized Debt Obligations (CDOs) and sold to investors. Bankers driven by the prospect of high bonuses were rightly criticized for creating such products and reselling them to naive investors. Investors, including state-owned German banks, invested with great enthusiasm in such products and did not question their value but relied blindly on the ratings (Americans spoke of "stupid German money"). Since real estate prices had never fallen nationwide and certainly not in recent decades, the mathematical, historical likelihood of default for these securities seemed extremely low.

As soon as property prices started to fall, these statistical calculations were not worth the paper they were written on. And this is exactly what happened in the following years: the Case-Shiller Home Price Index for 20 regions in the US fell by 35% between July 2006 and February 2012. In San Francisco house prices fell 46%, in Tampa 48%, in Detroit 49% and in Miami 51%.[575] When adjusted for inflation, the drops were even more drastic.

Many homebuyers who had bought at the height of the house price bubble lost their homes and all of the equity they had invested in their properties. The market value of many properties often fell below the outstanding amount of the mortgages secured on them, which meant that homeowners who were unable to raise additional equity had to watch as their banks foreclosed on their homes.

This is what triggered the global financial crisis. The securitized real estate loans, which had been awarded such good ratings by the rating agencies, collapsed in value because house prices fell and many borrowers were no longer able to service their loans. This caused serious difficulties for banks, insurance companies and funds, and led to a chain reaction that culminated in the collapse of Lehman Brothers in September 2008.

How did government and central banks respond? Now, shocked by the after-effects of the Lehman bankruptcy, they artificially kept banks and insurance companies alive with hundreds of billions of taxpayers' money. This was understandable because they wanted to prevent a complete market collapse but had seriously detrimental side effects in the long term because it delayed the sorely needed market shakeout. Many homeowners were ultimately protected from foreclosure by legal regulations. At the same time, central banks radically lowered interest rates further, to zero, and the Fed launched by far the biggest bond-buying programme in history.

THE EUROZONE CRISIS: THE PRIMACY OF POLITICS

A similar development occurred in Europe about two years after the outbreak of the financial crisis, where Greece and other hopelessly over-indebted Southern European countries triggered the eurozone crisis in 2010. This crisis was also by no means an expression of market failure but of government and political failure.

The embodiment of very specific political motives, the euro was initially adopted as the single currency by 14 European countries between 1999 and 2002. At the time, economic concerns were ignored, as countries such as France and Italy hoped that the currency union would 'tame' Germany, while the German chancellor, Helmut Kohl, saw the euro as a vehicle for advancing European unity. "Kohl and the other European leaders were guided by their belief in the primacy of politics – something they understood and put their hopes on – over economic laws, which they were barely able to grasp and whose existence they only reluctantly acknowledged," as the German economist Hans-Werner Sinn puts it.[576]

Kohl gained approval for the euro in Germany thanks, in large part, to the 'no bail-out' clause contained in the Maastricht Treaty, which guaranteed that no country would be obliged to settle another country's debts. Economists such as the renowned monetary theorist Peter Bernholz warned even before the euro's introduction that the laws of economics would prove themselves stronger than contractual clauses. Milton Friedman added his voice to those speaking out against the treaty,[577] and 155 German economists signed a public declaration against the premature introduction of the euro.

But Europe's politicians believed that their visions and political goals were stronger than the laws of the market and swept aside all concerns as they subordinated market economics to the primacy of politics. Incidentally, the same arguments were used to justify Greece's membership of the eurozone, despite the fact that it was clear to everyone that Greece had falsified financial data and, if it had reported honestly, would have grossly failed to meet the conditions for admission.

The southern Europeans were delighted that, after the introduction of the euro, they benefited from interest rates that were only marginally lower than Germany's. Before the introduction of the euro, the interest Athens was paying was roughly 15 percentage points higher than the rate paid by Berlin. Instead of using savings from drastically reduced interest rates to pay down debt, however, the already lavish government sector expanded massively. For example, the number of civil servants in Greece surged by 16% between 2000 and 2008[578] and their wages skyrocketed. In the years 2007 to 2010 alone, Greece's national debt increased from 240 billion to 330 billion euros. Incidentally, Greece has a tradition of unsound economics, having been insolvent for more than half of its existence as an independent state since the First Hellenic Republic was founded in 1829 – longer than any other country in the world.[579]

After the introduction of the euro and before the financial crisis, large numbers of banks and investors poured money into bonds issued by Greece and other Southern European countries because of their attractive interest rate premiums. Although the premium was now much lower than in the past, it remained economically advantageous, especially as EU member states had stipulated (in addition to the Basel Accords, which specified banks' capital requirements) that investments in Greek bonds were to be given the same weighting as investments in German bonds. Even highly indebted countries were given hugely preferential treatment over investments in highly solvent companies and real estate by these regulations, which Sinn described as "regulatory capriciousness".[580] This is certainly a good example of regulation that does nothing to help create a reasonable regulatory framework for the market but serves the self-interest of states. The same applies, incidentally, to state regulations for insurance companies, which are designed to favour investments in government bonds in a way that can also best be explained by the self-interest of the state.

However, in the wake of the financial crisis, and given Greece's excessive debts, investors lost all confidence in the country and interest rates on Greek government bonds rose sharply. After all, Greece was on the brink of bankruptcy. Of course, politicians and the media did not blame the state, which had become increasingly bloated, but 'speculators', who had done nothing more than exposing existing problems. This is as logical as blaming your doctor's thermometer when you are told that you have a fever. So, what did the Greeks do? They elected a radical socialist government that blamed international finance for their disastrous economic situation.

Greece was rescued from bankruptcy by its European neighbours – again for political reasons. Numerous provisions of the Maastricht Treaty were violated, in particular the no-bail-out provision mentioned above. The economic situation also became critical in Italy, Portugal and Spain, among others. They were all 'saved' by a package of loans and guarantees put together by the euro states and the European Central Bank (ECB), which continued to lower interest rates – to zero. When none of this helped, the ECB began to buy government bonds (and even corporate bonds), which was a serious market intervention.

As with so many other politically motivated projects, in many respects the introduction of the euro achieved the opposite of its stated objective, i.e. to accelerate European unity. At the time the euro was introduced, European countries had been growing ever closer, both politically and economically, for decades. The eurozone crisis actually drove them further apart again. Southern European countries, such as Greece, felt unbearably patronized by the Germans, and the German population was offended by the perceived ingratitude shown by the 'Club Med' and was extremely anxious about being asked to foot the bill for other countries' unsound budgetary policies.

A MARKET FAILURE?

Neither the house price bubble in the US and the resulting financial crisis, nor the eurozone crisis in Europe, have anything to do with a 'market failure' or a crisis of capitalism. On the contrary, both were caused by politicians and central banks. Politicians tried to implement certain political projects (increasing the homeownership rate among minorities in the US, and unifying Europe via the introduction of the euro) and intervened in the market for this purpose. The crises were also the result of irresponsible debt expansion at the expense of future generations and of drastic market intervention by the respective central banks, the Fed and the ECB, whose zero-interest-rate policies have largely nullified market mechanisms.

Of course, politicians and central banks did not want to accept responsibility for the financial and eurozone crises. Like a perpetrator crying 'Stop, thief!' to divert attention from himself, they blamed 'market failure' and 'unbridled capitalism' for what had happened. Bankers, whose greed was to blame for the financial crisis, were pilloried by the media and populists. Of course, there were some overly greedy bankers and fraudulent practices, as there have been in the run-up to every market bubble in history – just think of the euphoria that fuelled the dot-com bubble in the late 1990s, which attracted plenty of fraudsters. Despite the fact that pinning the blame for the financial crisis on greedy bankers may be a satisfying explanation for those who do not understand the complex causes, which are indeed difficult for laypeople to understand, it is actually no more convincing than pinning the blame for a plane crash on gravity.

Performance-related bonuses clearly incentivized bankers to pursue mistaken and risky strategies that only rewarded short-term profits, a practice that has been rightly and extensively criticized. However, this has little to do with a 'market failure', as bonuses based exclusively on short-term profits are ultimately not in the interest of any company or bank. In fact, such bonuses actually violate capitalist principles as financial theory defines profit maximization as maximizing the present value of the sum of all future cash flows, including those in the distant future.[581] This is even more relevant when interest rates are low. After all, the lower current interest rates are, the greater the impact of cash flows in the very distant future within the discounting formula for calculating present values. Remuneration systems that are based on distorted incentives are not in the best interests of any company or bank. However, these distortions have often been recognized as such, and subsequently corrected by banks and companies themselves – with no need for top-down directives or political interventions.

Such incentivized remuneration systems clearly distort the market, but they are also easy to fix. The implicit state guarantees given to an ever greater number of 'systemically relevant' banks are a far greater problem. These banks are deemed 'too big to fail' by politicians, which means they can be fairly sure that they will be bailed out by the state, with taxpayers' money, if they get into trouble as a result of speculative activities. This, too, is not the result of a 'market failure'. In fact, it is the exact opposite and actually encourages overly risky business models. After all, the market would normally punish banks for their misconduct, but it is prevented from functioning by these implicit state guarantees. Rather than collapsing, the banks in question are kept afloat. One of the most important principles of capitalism is that the market, by a process of survival of the fittest, decides which market participants are inefficient and economically unfeasible. The less this principle applies, the more we move away from capitalism. Talk of 'casino capitalism' in this context is absurd: there is not a single casino in the world that would guarantee to compensate gamblers for their losses.

Politicians, the media and anti-capitalists have claimed that the financial crisis was triggered by irresponsible, laissez-faire capitalism and the 'neoliberal deregulation' that began in the 1980s under Ronald Reagan. They claim that the financial crisis was the nail in the coffin of laissez-faire capitalism. In fact, there was never any such thing as laissez-faire capitalism in the financial system. Even before the financial crisis, 12,190 people in Washington, D.C., alone were employed to supervise and regulate the financial markets, five times as many as in 1960. Since the 1980s, when the laissez-faire phase allegedly began, US spending on the federal authorities that regulate the financial market has increased from USD 725 million to an inflation-adjusted USD 2.3 billion a year.[582] International banking regulations – such as Basel I, II and III – triggered many of the problems that led to the financial crisis, as Johan Norberg demonstrates in his book on the subject.[583] Ever tighter regulations lead to ever greater complexity, which makes the financial system ever more susceptible to crises.

Misdiagnosing the causes of the financial crisis means that the proposed therapies are also wrong. The financial crisis was caused by excessively low interest rates, heavy-handed market interventions and over-indebtedness. Are we seriously to believe that the right therapy involves even lower interest rates, stronger market interventions and more debt? These measures may well have a short-term impact, but markets are becoming increasingly dependent on low interest rates. Such low interest rates do nothing to solve the underlying problems – they only suppress the symptoms and push them into the future. The current combination of overly excessive regulation and interest rates of zero will cause considerable medium-term problems for many banks and is the breeding ground for new, even more severe crises.

If the ECB were to raise interest rates, countries such as Italy would be in big trouble. Stock markets have become so accustomed to low interest rates that they are almost like drug addicts. When drug addicts get a fix, they feel better in the short term because their withdrawal symptoms disappear. But no one with a modicum of common sense would claim that they are healed as a result.

Which is why I disagree with the Heritage Foundation: in recent years, economic freedom has not increased around the world – it has actually decreased significantly. In Europe, it has become increasingly clear that the ECB has long since lost its independence, even though it remains independent on paper. The ECB's role can no longer be compared to the position once held by the Deutsche Bundesbank. In fact, the ECB has become an instrument of public financing, despite being forbidden from doing so.

As a result, I worry that at some point we will face a new financial crisis. And even this will probably not serve as a wake-up call for change towards a true market economy. If anything, the opposite will happen: politicians and the media will cite such a crisis as proof of the inherent failures of the capitalist system and conclude once again, as they have done so many times before, that the state needs to intervene even more intensively in the economy. In my opinion, these interventions are the greatest threats capitalism faces.

The financial sector is less based on market economics and more strongly regulated than any other industry, perhaps with the exception of healthcare. The fact that precisely the two areas of the economy that are most strictly regulated by the state are the most unstable should give anti-capitalists food for thought. Of course, some regulation is needed in these areas. But the idea that increased regulation achieves more is plainly wrong. On the contrary. Richard Bookstaber concludes that increased regulation has exacerbated the problems in the financial sector: "Attempts at that point to add safety features, to layer on regulations and safeguards, will only add to the complexity of the system and make the accidents more frequent."[584] As with other forms of state intervention, all too often regulation does exactly the opposite of what is intended. It is therefore essential neither to overestimate what regulatory intervention can achieve nor to underestimate the danger of undesirable side effects.

CHAPTER 10

Why Intellectuals *Don't* Like Capitalism

First a heads-up: even readers who broadly agree with the arguments presented in this book so far may well find the following chapter harder to stomach. This goes for intellectuals with strong anti-capitalist sentiments as well as those who wouldn't consider themselves anti-capitalists at all. Although critiquing the motivations of others is part of their job description, intellectuals tend to dislike being subjected to critical scrutiny themselves – let alone having the extra-academic motivations behind their attitudes analysed. Journalists, for example, take pleasure in criticizing everything and everyone around them without pulling their punches – but are far less happy when the media themselves are at the receiving end of such criticism. Judging by my own experience and observations, even most intellectuals who would never define themselves as anti-capitalists share some anti-capitalist sentiment. For them, an anti-capitalist attitude appears to be an integral part of their identity – independent of any other political views they may hold.

There is no consistent definition of what constitutes an 'intellectual', but nor do the arguments made in this chapter require one. For the purpose of the following discussion, it will be sufficient to define intellectuals as professional thinkers who are more skilled at expressing their thoughts than most other people. They are also well read and well educated in one or more academic disciplines (typically, in the arts and humanities rather than engineering or other 'hard sciences') and, inasmuch as we are talking about intellectuals in the narrow sense discussed below, participate in public debates.

Along similar lines, the American historian and literary scholar Paul Hollander defines intellectuals as "well-educated, idealistic people of a social-critical disposition and high expectations, preoccupied with moral, cultural, political, and social issues, mainly employed (at the present time) by academic institutions in departments of humanities and social sciences".[585] Another defining trait is their tendency to "see themselves as the moral conscience of society".[586]

This sense of their mission as morally superior social critics is widely shared among intellectuals and seen as a defining trait that differentiates them from the business elite.

A further distinction may be drawn between a narrow sense and a broader sense of the term. This latter sense is given a polemic twist in Friedrich August von Hayek's description of intellectuals as "secondhand dealers in ideas" in his 1949 essay on "The Intellectuals and Socialism". Their function, he argues, "is neither that of the original thinker nor that of the scholar or expert in a particular field of thought. The typical intellectual need be neither: he need not possess special knowledge of anything in particular, nor need he even be particularly intelligent, to perform his role as intermediary in the spreading of ideas. What qualifies him for his job is the wide range of subjects on which he can readily talk and write, and a position or habits through which he becomes acquainted with new ideas sooner than those to whom he addresses himself."[587] Hayek's broad use of the term includes "journalists, teachers, ministers, lecturers, publicists, radio commentators, writers of fiction, cartoonists and artists" as well as those he labels "technicians, such as scientists and doctors, who … because of their expert knowledge of their own subjects, are listened to with respect on most others".[588] The convictions and opinions of this group "operate as the sieve through which all new conceptions must pass before they can reach the masses", thereby determining "the views on which society will act in the not too distant future".[589]

In my view, Hayek's use of the term is both too limited, since it excludes intellectuals in the narrow sense, and too broad in its inclusion of any inter-mediary who is in any way involved in the transfer of knowledge or opinions. These varying definitions are a reflection of the lack of a precise demarcation between intellectuals and other communities of practice.

ANTI-CAPITALISM AS A SECULAR RELIGION

Unfortunately, there are no empirical studies or surveys on the political beliefs and worldviews of intellectuals. What we do have is data on individual professions such as university lecturers and journalists. These consistently demonstrate a predominance of left-wing beliefs.[590] Even in the absence of hard statistical evidence, there can be little doubt that most intellectuals' attitude towards capitalism is critical to some extent. "Indeed, anti-capitalism is the most widespread and widely practiced spiritual commitment among intellectuals," as the historian

Alan S. Kahan puts it.[591] In a 2012 essay on "Intellectuals and Resentment towards Capitalism", the sociologist Thomas Cushman agrees: "Anti-capitalism has become, in some ways, a central pillar of the secular religion of the intellectuals, the *habitus* of modern critical intellectuals as a status group."[592]

"Why ... is it easier to find a thousand Western intellectuals who admire Communist China than one who admires the dramatic economic achievements of Taiwan?" asked the political scientist and historian Edward Luttwak as early as the 1970s in polemical exaggeration born of exasperation.[593] "The ideal that all wealth is acquired through stealing is popular in prisons and at Harvard," as the American sociologist George Gilder suggests in his 1981 study *Wealth and Poverty.*[594] He blames the "public establishment of ideas" – formed of "government officials, academic social scientists, and media leaders" – for disseminating this "impoverishing creed".[595]

Even readers who take issue with the contention that the majority of intellectuals are outright anti-capitalists will hardly disagree with the observation that a critical stance vis-à-vis capitalism is widely shared among their ranks. This attitude is prevalent among leftists as well as conservative or right-wing thinkers.

Alain de Benoist is one of the most prominent and prolific proponents of the French 'Nouvelle Droite' movement, which takes its inspiration from the 'Conservative Revolution' in 1920s Germany. In *On the Brink of the Abyss: The Imminent Bankruptcy of the Financial System*, he claims "that it is impossible to reduce the capitalist system to a simple economic form and to envisage the capitalist system only in its financial aspect. There is an anthropology of capitalism, a type of capitalist man, a capitalist imagination, a capitalist 'civilization', a capitalist lifestyle and, as long as one has not broken with capitalism as a 'total social fact' ... it will be futile to claim to be fighting capital."[596] In 2017, Benoist reiterated that "my principal enemy has always been capitalism in economic terms, liberalism in philosophical terms and the bourgeoisie in sociological terms".[597]

Anybody who still needs convincing that intellectuals have an affinity to anti-capitalism could do worse than pick up a copy of *Mind vs. Money: The War Between Intellectuals and Capitalism* by Alan S. Kahan or *From Benito Mussolini to Hugo Chavez: Intellectuals and a Century of Political Hero Worship* by Paul Hollander. Both writers provide plenty of evidence and examples in support of this assumption.

Having said this, my use of the term 'intellectuals' throughout this chapter is merely a convenient shortcut and not intended to imply that *all* intellectuals are anti-capitalists – fortunately, there are exceptions. It is also worth noting that anti-capitalism comes in various guises. On both sides of the political spectrum, it manifests as a critique of globalization variously directed against free trade and its allegedly exploitative practices, cultural levelling or capitalism's supposed complicity in creating poverty in Africa. Alternatively, it may take the form of anti-American resentment that regards the US as the epitome of the heartless and mercenary worldview that is capitalism. Since the 1970s, it has also reared its head in the environmentalist movement, which blames capitalism for climate change and the destruction of the natural environment. At the end of the 1960s and into the 1970s, Marxism experienced a renaissance. From the end of the 1990s, Marxism was increasingly supplanted by an 'anti-globalization' ideology. In more recent years, there are signs that Marxist though is starting to enjoy a renewed renaissance. Fashions may have changed – from Marxism to ecologism and anti-globalization – the enemy has remained the same: capitalism.

Anti-capitalist attitudes among intellectuals are not a recent phenomenon, nor are they confined to one particular region. European intellectuals are no less critical of capitalism than their peers in the US – if anything, pro-capitalist attitudes are more prevalent in the US (among intellectuals as well as in the general population) than they are in France, for example. According to Kahan, the "war between intellectuals and capitalism" has been "a constant of modern history" for over 150 years.[598]

Intellectual suspicion of wealth and the wealthy, however, dates back much further than the emergence of capitalism. Among ancient Greek and Roman philosophers, attitudes "run the gamut from violent rejection through indifference to an acceptance mediated to varying degrees by critical reflection, but ... always seem to remain close to total indifference". The fact that most ancient philosophers were wealthy men themselves didn't stop them from expressing their contempt for material riches or arguing that wealth was unimportant or even dangerous.[599]

In *The Republic*, Plato has Socrates pose the (rhetorical) question: "Isn't virtue in tension with wealth, as though each were lying in the scale of a balance, always inclining in opposite directions?"[600] However, on closer inspection these critical views conceal an "unambiguous approval of wealth", as Robert Velten has shown.[601] The hostility expressed in this and similar remarks was directed against trade and commerce rather than against wealth as such. While sharing a "massive disdain" of wealth gained from labour, trade and commerce, thinkers such as Plato and Aristotle took a far more positive view of inherited and property-based wealth.[602]

A defining trait of the utopian societies envisioned by writers including Tommaso Campanella and Johann Valentin Andreae is their belief in the beneficial effects of egalitarianism. In most utopian novels, private ownership of the means of production has been abolished along with any other distinctions between the poor and the rich. The citizens of these utopias all dress the same and even the buildings they live in look the same.[603]

In the eponymous founding text of the utopian genre, Thomas More affirms: "I am entirely convinced that no just and even distribution of goods can be made, nor any perfect happiness be found among human beings, until private property is utterly abolished. While it lasts, for most of humanity, and not the worst, there will remain a heavy and intolerable burden of poverty and anxiety."[604] He references Plato's belief that "states will be happy only if philosophers are kings or kings turn to philosophy", to which his fictional interlocutor responds that "rulers must be ready to take good advice" from philosophers.[605]

Intellectuals have been complaining for centuries about the trials and tribulations of making a living from the fruits of their intellectual labour, compared to the happy-go-lucky existence of a successful businessperson. In his essay "De commodis litterarum atque incommodis" (The Use and Abuse of Books, ca. 1430), the Italian humanist Leon Battista Alberti lists all the hardships awaiting aspiring scholars – a spartan existence of burning the midnight oil poring over learned tomes that affords no time or money for more worldly pleasures – and asks why it is that so many scholars are reduced to such miserable conditions. Alberti even provides figures to prove that only three out of 300 men of letters will ever attain any success worth mentioning, while crooks have no trouble at all making it to the top.[606] The 1839 painting *The Poor Poet* by the German artist Carl Spitzweg vividly illustrates the self-pity that fuels complaints by artists and intellectuals airing their grievances about their own economic and financial misery.

In the early 1940s, the Austrian economist Joseph Schumpeter tried to answer the question of why so many intellectuals hold such hostile views of capitalism. Unsurprisingly for an economist, he turned to economics for an explanation: the increase in the percentage of those who enter higher education creates a large number of university graduates who are surplus to the demand for white-collar professionals but overqualified for manual jobs, and who then drift into vocations where standards are less clearly defined. "They swell the host of intellectuals in the strict sense of the term whose numbers hence increase disproportionately. They enter it in a thoroughly discontented frame of mind. Discontent breeds resentment. And it often rationalizes itself into that social criticism which ... is in any case the intellectual spectator's typical attitude toward men, classes toward men, classes and institutions especially in a rationalist and utilitarian civilization." This "group interest shaping a group attitude", he goes on to argue, "will more realistically account for hostility to the capitalist order than could the theory ... according to which the intellectual's righteous indignation about the wrongs of capitalism simply represents the logical inference from outrageous facts".[607]

I don't completely buy his explanation, which is not to say that there isn't a kernel of truth in it. If anything, it is even more true today than when Schumpeter's study was published in 1942. There are definitely academics who would find it hard to get a job in business and who therefore have no choice but to take employment on the public-sector payroll, at the taxpayers' expense. Yet, there are also plenty of others who appreciate the job security and social benefits of public-sector employment, or who prefer writing books to starting their own business.

However, it is also true that countries such as the US and Germany have experienced a sharp increase in the number of academics over the past 50 years, which in turn led to a decline in prestige for what used to be a highly respected educated elite. Understandably, this loss of respect and prestige accorded to academic professions may be a painful experience for some. In conjunction with the widening income and wealth gap between their own community and the business elite, this may help to explain why intellectuals are prone to anti-capitalist resentment.

On the other hand, the attempt to explain anti-capitalist attitudes among intellectuals purely in economic terms doesn't quite cut it, given that – as Kahan rightly points out – these attitudes are particularly prevalent among the most professionally successful and high-earning academics. "If you want to find intellectuals who don't like capitalism, the best places to look for them are the liberal arts faculty at Harvard or Oxford or the Collège de France."[608] For a true understanding of the enmity between intellectuals and capitalism, it is necessary to dig deeper.

THEORETICAL CONSTRUCTS VERSUS SPONTANEOUS EMERGENCE

The failure of many intellectuals to understand the nature of capitalism as an economic order that emerges and grows spontaneously is one key factor. Unlike socialism, capitalism isn't a school of thought imposed on reality. As the example of China (see Chapter 1) shows, free-market capitalism largely evolves spontaneously, growing from the bottom up rather than decreed from above.

Leaders such as Deng Xiaoping came to play a role in this process by not doing anything to stop growth from happening, as their predecessors had done. This also explains why capitalism works better in contemporary China than it does in Russia. In both countries, it supplanted a socialist planned economy – but while Chinese capitalism grew from the bottom up and, inasmuch as it was promoted by the government, developed by trial and error within Special Economic Zones and specific social segments, Russia abolished economic planning in a kind of 'shock therapy', replacing it with a different system that was labelled 'free-market economy'.

Likewise, Western leaders such as Margaret Thatcher didn't impose an artificial system devised and perfected over years of deliberation. In fact, by abolishing regulations, breaking up encrusted structures and thus allowing the spontaneous forces of the market to develop freely, they did the exact opposite.

Capitalism has grown historically, in much the same way as languages have developed over time as the result of spontaneous and uncontrolled processes. Esperanto, invented in 1887 as a planned language, has now been around for over 130 years without gaining anything like the global penetration its inventors were hoping for. Socialism shares some of the characteristics of a planned language, a system devised by intellectuals. Having devised the system, the proponents of socialism then attempt to gain the political power required to put their ideas into action.

In its purest form, this approach informs Lenin's reflections on the role of theory and the party in his landmark essay "What Is to Be Done?" Lenin sharply criticizes "*all* worship of the spontaneity of the working-class movement".[609] His vision of an elite cadre guided by revolutionary theory stands in stark contrast to the spontaneous approach advocated by his opponents within the movement. "The history of all countries shows that the working class, exclusively by its own effort, is able to develop only trade union consciousness, i.e., the conviction that it is necessary to combine in unions, fight the employers, and strive to compel the government to pass necessary labour legislation, etc. The theory of socialism, however, grew out of the philosophic, historical, and economic theories elaborated by educated representatives of the propertied classes, by intellectuals. By their social status the founders of modern scientific socialism, Marx and Engels, themselves belonged to the bourgeois intelligentsia."[610]

In support of his argument, Lenin goes on to quote the "profoundly true and important words of Karl Kautsky on the new draft program of the Austrian Social-Democratic Party". Kautsky said: "Modern socialist consciousness can arise only on the basis of profound scientific knowledge ... The vehicle of science is not the proletariat, but the *bourgeois intelligentsia*. Thus, socialist consciousness is something introduced into the proletarian class struggle from without and not something that arose within it spontaneously."[611]

Oddly, Lenin, Kautsky and Hayek all agree on this point. Here's what Hayek has to say: "Socialism has never and nowhere been at first a working-class movement. It is by no means an obvious remedy for the obvious evil which the interests of that class will necessarily demand. It is a construction of theorists, deriving from certain tendencies of abstract thought with which for a long time only the intellectuals were familiar; and it required long efforts by the intellectuals before the working classes could be persuaded to adopt it as their program."[612]

It's hardly surprising that Marxism was considered such an attractive proposition by many 20th-century intellectuals – after all, it was a theory that originated in the heads of intellectuals and that, packaged into complicated systems, then had to be communicated to the 'masses' (first and foremost to the workers) by way of constant revolutionary agitation and propaganda. Once the elite of those who were able to understand the theory had seized power, it would become their job to implement it in the real world by destroying existing, organically grown orders – including the market economy as well as traditions and social norms – and installing a 'scientific' and rational system in their place.

Once we've grasped this essential difference between capitalism as a spontaneously evolving order and socialism as a theoretical construct, the reasons why many intellectuals have a greater affinity to the latter – in whatever form – suddenly become obvious. After all, devising mental constructs and using their linguistic skills to shape and communicate them, both in writing and in rousing speeches, is what they do for a living. Since their own livelihood depends on their ability to think and communicate ideas that are rational and coherent, they feel a greater affinity to an artificially planned and constructed economic order than to one that allows for unplanned, spontaneous development. The notion that economies work better without active intervention and planning is alien to many intellectuals.

Some anti-capitalist intellectuals design ideal social systems that they then compare to current reality – unsurprisingly, to the detriment of the latter. They deliberately eschew the route I have taken in this book – namely, a comparison between existing social systems. Since capitalism emerges as the unequivocal winner in any such comparison, anti-capitalist intellectuals prefer to devise a utopian vision of an *ideal* society, which they then hold up as a standard against which *existing* societies are bound to fail. Their utopias tend to be extremely egalitarian societies that give a lot of power to the state and very little room to the free play of market forces.

These utopias are not necessarily planned economies in the traditional sense, which have after all been comprehensively discredited by the collapse of the Soviet Union and other Eastern Bloc systems. Many intellectuals dislike capitalism without being able to articulate an alternative. Nor do they deny the fact that socialist alternatives to capitalism have failed everywhere they've been tried. Confronted with arguments along these lines, they will typically argue that none of these failed experiments ever stayed true to the spirit of 'genuine' socialism and that they must therefore be repeated until the lofty ideal of a 'fairer' – read: (more) egalitarian – society has finally been achieved.

Intellectuals typically frame their objections to capitalism as critical interventions on behalf of 'deprived' communities, or of a 'common' or 'public interest' that must be defended against the 'heartless' laws of the market. They present their motivation as driven by an altruistic concern for this 'public interest' – which is, of course, defined in their own terms – and for the interests of the 'deprived', the workers, minorities, the environment, etc., while accusing capitalists of putting their own material interests first.

This contention conveniently overlooks the fact that entrepreneurs prosper under capitalism only by serving the interests of a majority of consumers, i.e. by offering products or services for which there is demand. Artists, writers and scholars, on the other hand, earn less in many cases because consumer demand for their products and services is much lower in comparison. From the lofty vantage point of intellectual anti-capitalism, the gap in earnings between the publisher of a tabloid newspaper and a writer who pens elegant essays is evidence that there's something wrong with the laws of the market, while a strong sense of moral superiority is derived from the crass juxtaposition between the altruistically motivated intellectual and the capitalist driven by self-interest.

Anti-capitalism is an attitude rather than a coherent school of thought, which makes it hard to define. In many cases, it presents as little more than a vague feeling of resentment, an aversion against the existing social order and its representatives, and an expression of profound distrust in the mechanics of the market, which is usually unencumbered by any kind of clear vision of a desirable alternative. This lack of a clear vision has the benefit of being open to interpretation – a vague idea that allows for the projection of a myriad of different desires for an ideal and 'fair' society. The same also applies to Marxism: Karl Marx restricted himself to analyzing and criticizing capitalism, but nowhere did he describe the economic order that should replace it.

On the other hand, thinkers in the utopian tradition – including the proponents of 'utopian socialism' maligned by Marx and Engels – frequently went into great detail when describing their egalitarian visions of a utopian society.

Anti-capitalist intellectuals are attracted to economic orders that accord a lot of power to the state. These include the social democratic welfare state, which generously redistributes resources in accordance with social policy objectives and uses fiscal policy, government regulation and Keynesian measures to control the economy.

There's a paradox between the demand for strong government intervention in economic affairs and the critical attitude vis-à-vis the state many intellectuals like to assume in all other respects. 'Left-wing liberals' want the state to be weak where it needs to be strong – i.e. in the protection and defence of national security interests – and strong where it needs to be weak – i.e. in the active pursuit of economic policy. In any case, they put more faith in the state – which is to say, in politicians and government officials – than in the market or, in other words, the consumers and their individual decisions, which no central planning can ever account for.

Not all anti-capitalist intellectuals reject the free-market economy outright – in fact, many profess to be pro-market without fully understanding how a free-market system works. However, paying lip service to free-market principles doesn't demonstrate an actual commitment to these principles any more than calling an autocratic regime 'democratic' is irrefutable evidence of its leaders' commitment to democracy. After all, even communists and other opponents of democracy have been known to invoke democratic pretensions.

Thomas Piketty, whose 2013 global bestseller *Capital in the Twenty-First Century* has been widely adopted as a kind of anti-capitalist bible in spite of its myriad serious mistakes,[613] claims to have been "vaccinated for life against the conventional but lazy rhetoric of anticapitalism".[614] However, his radical ideas about redistribution of wealth by way of exorbitant income and wealth taxes for high earners[615] suggest otherwise.

There are two ways of fighting a system – by discrediting the concepts of one's enemy or by co-opting them. 'Newspeak', the language developed by the totalitarian regime in George Orwell's *1984*, is an example of what happens when concepts are robbed of their original meanings. In much the same way as the proponents of capitalism in China have turned the concept of 'socialism' on its head while continuing to pay lip service to Marxism, its opponents in Western countries have co-opted and repurposed the concept of the 'market economy'.

Any proponent of a system that allows the state to interfere in economic affairs wherever and whenever it pleases – rather than confining the role of government to creating a legal framework for free competition, safeguarding private property and providing the required infrastructure – has not understood what market economics means. Any self-professed 'supporter of the free market' who gives precedence to politics over economics and harbours a profound distrust of the spontaneous forces of the market has failed to grasp the essence of this economic system.

A lack of economic expertise on the part of many intellectuals is sometimes held responsible for their rejection of the free-market economy. It is true that many intellectuals are economically illiterate. Mention the market price mechanism or other key structural elements of capitalism – or anything to do with figures or statistics, for that matter – and you might as well be speaking a foreign language. However, ignorance of economics alone doesn't explain the strength of anti-capitalist resentment among intellectuals. After all, most other participants in a market economy only have a basic grasp of economic theory – nor are they required or expected to know more – without sharing the intellectual distaste for capitalism.[616]

It is also a fact that there are critics of capitalism even among the world's most renowned economists – including Nobel laureate Joseph E. Stiglitz, whose recommendations for China suggest that he fails to be swayed by compelling factual evidence. After more than three decades of success in China, where the influence of the state has increasingly been pushed back in favour of market forces, Stiglitz now recommends that the Chinese do exactly the opposite in future, namely expand the influence of the state, push back the market and focus on more redistribution.

Even Stiglitz has to admit: "No country in recorded history has grown as fast – and moved as many people out of poverty – as China over the last 30 years."[617] However, he then strikes a cautionary note, adding that "embracing America's profligate materialist lifestyle would be a disaster for China – and the planet".[618] Against the advice of the Chinese economist Zhang Weiying, who identifies excessive government intervention as the root cause of many problems in contemporary China (see Chapter 1), Stiglitz warns that a "more market-based system is not the direction in which China should be going".[619] Instead, he advocates for more government and tax increases[620] – which would be tantamount to abandoning the path the People's Republic has been pursuing so successfully for three decades. As this example shows, a knowledge of economics is no foolproof protection against anti-capitalist views.

While it is certainly true that many intellectuals working in the arts and humanities have at best a very limited understanding of economics, this doesn't fully explain their grudge against capitalism.

In order to understand why so many intellectuals hold anti-capitalist views, it is important to realize that they are an elite, or at any rate a community of practice that defines itself as such. Their anti-capitalism is nurtured by their resentment of and opposition to the business elite. In this sense, the rivalry between the two groups is simply that – a competition between different elites vying for status in contemporary society. If a higher level of education doesn't automatically guarantee higher incomes and more privileged positions, then the markets that allow this imbalance to happen are seen as unfair from the intellectuals' perspective – or "in any case a source of the most profound discontent", as Roland Baader puts it. "A society in which it is possible for a worker's or tradesman's sweaty shirt, or even that of a businessman 'sweaty with profit', to earn more than a philosopher's deep wisdom seems to them topsy-turvy."[621] Living in a competitive system that consistently awards the top prizes to others – a system where even the owners of medium-sized businesses achieve more income and wealth than a tenured professor of philosophy, sociology, cultural studies or art history – leads to a general scepticism against an economic order based on competition.

This also explains the seeming contradiction between the comfortable lifestyle enjoyed by many intellectuals and their despair at the injustice of the capitalist system.[622] A group that considers itself part of the elite, but whose lifestyle is significantly less affluent than that of a competing – entrepreneurial – elite, will rail against the perceived injustice of the system, and this is only compounded by the intellectual elite's sense of superiority bestowed by their higher level of education. In other words, anti-capitalist attitudes are partly fuelled by envy of the business elite.

In his best-selling study of *The Rich and the Super-Rich*, the American sociologist Ferdinand Lundberg makes the following telling observations: "As to the general human type of American wealth-builder, new and old, it can be said that he is usually an extrovert, given to little reflection ... He is more often unschooled than schooled, and unread, and has for the most part a naïve view of the world and his role in it ... By his position alone he is alienated."[623] Sneeringly, he refers to the "fortune-builders of more recent date" – many of them, he claims, "high school dropouts [or] grade-school dropouts" who "like their nineteenth-century forerunners, had little interest in school even when it was available to them" – as "truants from high culture".[624]

The disdain expressed in this assertion compellingly demonstrates the extent to which intellectuals tend to set their own value standards as absolutes. Lundberg judges others by their level of education and cultural capital, and accordingly considers it deeply unfair that "wealth-builders" with little formal education and no interest in high culture should amass great fortunes, while well-educated and well-read academic scholars have to make do with comparatively little. It is hardly surprising that the world seems upside down to him. After all, intellectuals derive their own sense of superiority from being better educated, more knowledgeable and better able to express themselves verbally.

It is worth noting in this context that academic scholars conducting research into elite formation consider academic recruitment processes to be far more transparent, rational and 'democratic' than recruitment processes in the business world. Michael Hartmann, who is one of Germany's leading scholars in this field, highlights the degree to which academic selection processes (specifically, appointment to full professorships) are formalized and subject to "democratic influences". He goes on to argue that there is "greater social mobility" in academia, where selection is based on universally transparent formal qualifications (degrees, publications) than in the recruitment of business elites, where "relatively ill-defined personality traits" play a key role.[625] Hartmann's line of argument implies that he believes academic standards and selection processes to be superior to those of the business world.

Hartmann's refusal to accord the processes by which the business elite recruits new members as much democratic legitimacy as the procedures by which academic institutions appoint new members of faculty is completely groundless. After all, who decides whether an entrepreneur makes a profit? It's up to consumers to buy the company's products and services – or not, as the case may be. The misconception that this daily vote of confidence by consumers is somehow less democratic than the appointment of an academic by a committee of other academics is partly based on Hartmann's exclusive focus on salaried executives rather than entrepreneurs who run their own businesses – a focus he shares with other researchers who have studied elite formation.[626]

I believe envy to be only one reason for the popularity of anti-capitalism among intellectuals. As the German sociologist Helmut Schoeck has shown in his important book on the subject,[627] envy is a constant of human existence. However, I'm not convinced that the propensity to envy is stronger among intellectuals than among other communities of practice. Moreover – since it tends to be bred by proximity – envy would more likely be directed towards fellow intellectuals than members of the business community. So, while I agree that anti-capitalism is partly motivated by envy, I want to propose a more far-reaching explanation – namely that many intellectuals' hostility towards capitalism is driven by the unjustified supremacy they assign to their own definition of 'knowledge' and 'knowledge acquisition', which renders them blind to the existence of other types of knowledge and other methods of knowledge acquisition that are far more relevant to economic success.

OVER-RELIANCE ON EXPLICIT LEARNING

Understandably, intellectuals tend to equate knowledge acquisition with academic education and book learning. Psychology uses the term 'explicit knowledge' to refer to this type of knowledge, which is acquired by means of 'explicit learning'. However, there is a different kind of knowledge acquired by 'implicit learning', which is far more primordial and often more powerful, although many intellectuals are unaware of its existence. Since this is the route to knowledge acquisition taken by the majority of entrepreneurs, it's important to understand the differences between the two forms of learning and knowledge.

Hayek uses the example of small children who are able to apply the rules of grammar and idiomatic language without consciously knowing them.[628] "The child who speaks grammatically without knowing the rules of grammar not only understands all the shades of meaning expressed by others through following the rules of grammar, but may also be able to correct a grammatical mistake in the speech of others."[629] Similarly, the skills of a craftsperson or athlete – which involve *knowing-how* rather than *knowing-what* – are acquired implicitly rather than explicitly. "It is characteristic of these skills that we are usually not able to state explicitly (discursively) the manner of acting which is involved."[630]

More recently, the term 'tacit knowledge' was reintroduced by the Hungarian-born British philosopher Michael Polanyi, who coined the much-quoted phrase "we can know more than we can tell" in his book *The Tacit Dimension* (1966).[631] For Polanyi, this represents a central problem of communication. "Our message had left something behind that we could not tell, and its reception must rely on it that the person addressed will discover that which we have not been able to communicate."[632] Polanyi clarifies the difference between implicit and explicit knowledge – between skill on the one hand and theoretical knowledge on the other. "The skill of a driver cannot be replaced by a thorough schooling in the theory of the motorcar; the knowledge I have of my own body differs altogether from the knowledge of its physiology;

and the rules of rhyming and prosody do not tell me what a poem told me, without any knowledge of its rules."[633]

In other words, learning is not necessarily the result of the conscious and systematic acquisition of knowledge, but often the result of unconscious processes. In an experiment, test subjects assumed the role of a factory manager in a computer simulation. They were tasked with maintaining a specific volume of sugar production by making adjustments to factory staffing levels. The system's underlying functional equation was not revealed to the test subjects. During the learning phase, they didn't know that they would subsequently be required to take a knowledge test. The test showed that the test subjects were able to regulate production in the sugar factory without being able to explain exactly how they did so.[634]

My study "The Wealth Elite", based on the findings of entrepreneurship research carried out in the US in conjunction with my own original research, demonstrates that formal education only plays a secondary role in the development of entrepreneurial skills. Entrepreneurial success is determined by factors other than academic qualifications. Key among these are sales skills, which, although rarely taught at academic institutions, respondents considered an essential prerequisite for their successful careers as entrepreneurs or investors. Many respondents started their first business when they were still at school or university, which allowed them to test the waters and acquire comprehensive implicit knowledge, which would be key to their subsequent economic success.[635]

Implicit learning is not documented in the same way as explicit learning, which can be demonstrated in the form of directly comparable certificates and academic qualifications. By an intellectual's standards, an entrepreneur who may not have read a lot of books or shown much promise at college or university has nothing to show for himself that would compare to a doctorate or a list of publications. That's why – on a platform developed and run by intellectuals – a professor with an average list of publications has a better chance of being considered worthy of a Wikipedia entry than an investor who transacts billions of dollars on the property market.

At best, the outcomes of entrepreneurial learning can be seen indirectly by looking at the performance of a company or the standard of living enjoyed by its owner. Intellectuals are unable to understand why a college dropout with an 'inferior intellect', who has only read a fraction of what they've read, ends up making a lot more money, living in a much bigger house and driving a far better car. They feel offended in their sense of what is 'fair' and thus vindicated in their belief in a malfunction of capitalism or the market, which needs to be 'corrected' by means of redistribution on a massive scale. By divesting the rich of some of their 'undeserved wealth', intellectuals console themselves with the fact that, even if they can't abolish the brutal capitalist system altogether, they can at least 'correct' it to some extent.

Casting about for explanations that would account for the entrepreneur's far greater economic success in spite of their lack of formal education and qualifications, anti-capitalist intellectuals typically come up with two assertions. The first one rests on their fundamental conviction that the market produces 'unfair' results. The second concerns the insinuation that most riches are ill-gotten gains acquired by means that are ethically and morally questionable. There's a kind of solace in this since it affords non-wealthy intellectuals the luxury of taking the moral high ground. They can now explain away their own lack of economic success as a sign of greater moral integrity marked by the refusal to resort to unethical methods in their pursuit of happiness. For a community that regards itself as the moral conscience of society, this is a doubly compelling and deeply satisfying notion.

There is another type of explanation, which ascribes the wealthy entrepreneur's success to 'pure luck'. As demonstrated by the high turnover of books – written, of course, by intellectuals – that put the greater success of some individuals over others down to 'luck' or 'accident',[636] this idea is particularly popular whenever people are confronted with the effects of causes they don't fully comprehend. When these various attempts at explaining the uneducated entrepreneur's economic success prove inconclusive, intellectuals eventually decide that any 'system' capable of producing such questionable outcomes must be fundamentally flawed. Much of their anti-capitalist sentiment derives from this conviction.

In a 1998 essay, the libertarian philosopher Robert Nozick tackles the question: "Why Do Intellectuals Oppose Capitalism?"[637] His explanation is based on the assumption that intellectuals feel superior to other members of society. Ever since the days of Plato and Aristotle, intellectuals have been telling us that their contribution to society is more valuable than that of any other group. Where, Nozick asks, does this sense of entitlement come from?

His answer is: it starts at school, where intellectual brilliance is rewarded with praise and good grades. By the time 'verbally bright children' graduate from formal education, they have been inculcated with a sense of their greater value in comparison to their less intellectually gifted peers, which then leads them to expect society at large to operate according to the same norms. The subsequent realization that the market economy doesn't hold their particular skills in the same regard leads to feelings of frustration and resentment that fuel hostility to the capitalist system as such.

I would argue that the seeds of these beliefs are planted even earlier. Intellectuals are more likely to grow up in a middle-class milieu where a lot of emphasis is placed on education, with parents or other relatives who are academics, than in working-class or entrepreneurial families. From early childhood onwards, the message drummed into them is that education, book learning, and social and/or political engagement are far worthier goals than striving for material riches. The education system, which Nozick holds responsible for instilling these values, emphatically reinforces them, confirming what the child has already learned at home: book learning, verbal skills and intellectual brilliance will earn the highest accolades.

Another question worth exploring is to what extent these contentions are true for both American and European intellectuals. Although the two groups share a strong affinity to anti-capitalist views, sociologists including Seymour Martin Lipset in the US and Ralf Dahrendorf in Europe have pointed to differences in regard to the esteem in which intellectuals are held. In his 1967 work on *Society and Democracy in Germany*, Dahrendorf quotes Lipset's observation that Europeans accord equal respect to professors, engineers and factory owners, while Americans are too committed to an ideal of equality to pay deference to anybody on the grounds of social status: "Ironically some of the reasons why American intellectuals do not get the signs of respect for which they crave spring from the strength of the egalitarian standards which they espouse."[638] Dahrendorf agrees with this analysis, adding that the "tension between the anti-intellectualism of the actors and the longing of intellectuals for action" – which he considers universal – may well be most pronounced in a culture like the US, "whose dominant traits are painted in economic colours".[639]

In 1956, the influential Austrian-born American economist Ludwig von Mises had already described differences between the US and Europe in a similar vein: "Access to European society is open to everybody who has distinguished himself in any field ... The stars of the Parisian salons are not the millionaires, but the members of the Académie Française. The intellectuals prevail and the others feign at least a lively interest in intellectual concerns. Society in this sense is foreign to the American scene. What is called 'society' in the United States almost exclusively consists of the richest families."[640] These families, von Mises goes on to argue, take little interest in cultural matters, preferring to talk about sports. As a consequence, American intellectuals "are prone to consider the wealthy businessman as a barbarian, as a man exclusively intent upon making money". Professors of philosophy feel affronted by the higher salary commanded by the coach of the football team.[641]

It's worth noting that Mises holds the rich partly responsible for these hostile attitudes: "If a group of people secludes itself from the rest of the nation, especially also from its intellectual leaders, in the way American 'socialites' do, they unavoidably become the target of rather hostile criticisms on the part of those whom they keep out of their own circles. The exclusivism practiced by the American rich has made them in a certain sense outcasts," kindling "animosities which make the intellectuals inclined to favor anti-capitalistic policies".[642]

These comments by Lipset, Dahrendorf and Mises date back to the 1950s and 1960s. Although there's certainly some truth to their observations, they fail to account for the affinity of European intellectuals – then and now – to anti-capitalist views, and thus only provide a partial explanation for a phenomenon that, regional differences notwithstanding, persists on both sides of the Atlantic and has been puzzling observers for over half a century.

It would be interesting to explore the following hypothesis: over the past 60 years, European society has become increasingly Americanized in many respects and the criticism of 'Anglo-Saxon capitalism' that has spread since the financial crisis has done little to change this. In Europe too, the traditional intellectual elites, and the professions in which they tend to be heavily represented, have lost some of their exclusivity and prestige. Many gripes by European intellectuals about the Americanization of European culture may well be in part motivated by the fear of losing status – which might also help to explain the frequent entanglement between anti-American and anti-capitalist sentiments. The feeling of having lost some of their privileged status is accompanied by the fear of sliding down the socio-economic scale, and 'neoliberal policies' are held responsible for both.

Those who hold anti-capitalist views may of course wonder why the affinity of intellectuals to such views would even require explanation: whether it isn't merely an appropriate response to the flaws and deficiencies inherent in the capitalist system itself. As Cushman argues, most intellectuals fail to reflect on the need to subject their hostility towards capitalism to critical analysis.[643] Rather, they mistake their own views for objective truth that requires no more explanation than the observation that most people prefer warm sunshine to bitterly cold weather.

In this book, I have demonstrated that capitalist systems are superior to other systems and that greater economic growth and greater wealth are more likely to result from *more capitalism* than from *more government intervention*.

It's worth noting, however, that most critics of capitalism fall into two traps: Firstly, they attribute imperfections that have arisen in every age and under every social system to capitalism, despite the fact that these have nothing to do with any inherent flaws in capitalism itself. Secondly, they rail against undesirable outcomes that, based on a more objective analysis, are actually the result of government interference in the market and have nothing to do with the capitalist system.

In response to the first point: Is there inequality, corruption and poverty in capitalist countries? Of course there is. But the real question we need to ask is whether these can be specifically linked to a market-based economic order, or whether they are in fact anthropological constants that have always existed across all historical periods and different models of society.

In recent years, the diesel emissions scandal triggered a public outcry about the shortcomings of the capitalist system in the wake of the detection of fraudulent software deployed by several major carmakers. But are fraud and deception really a capitalist invention, or rather a human impulse that is present in any socio-economic system?

In fact, fraud detection works better in a market economy than in other systems. In a capitalist economy, abusing customers' trust is likely to result in a loss of business, while, in a state-controlled economy, consumers don't have the choice of buying from a more trustworthy competitor. For example, consumers in the US are free to buy whatever make of car they prefer. In socialist East Germany, Trabant and Wartburg had a near monopoly. If those two companies had equipped their cars with fraudulent software, prospective buyers wouldn't have had the option of taking their custom elsewhere – assuming that their fraudulent behaviour would even have been a public issue, which is unlikely in the absence of a free press. In a market economy, on the other hand, it is in every company's interest not to disappoint consumer confidence and thereby damage the value of their brand. But of course, there are companies – as well as individuals – that act against their own long-term interests.

Is there inequality in capitalism? Of course there is. Inequality has always existed across the centuries and around the world. It might even be worth asking whether a society without inequality, as conceived in utopian novels, would be desirable. However, inequality is frequently less pronounced in capitalist than in state-controlled economies.

Another question is whether the level of inequality in a given economy is the most reliable indicator of human welfare. Would you rather be poor in a country where both living standards and levels of inequality are higher across the population, or poor in a country with less inequality and lower standards of living for everybody?

To reiterate a point I made in the introduction: neither socialism nor capitalism have ever existed in a pure form. However, as my discussion of the recent financial crisis in Chapter 9 shows, it is perfectly possible to demonstrate that many alleged contemporary 'problems of capitalism' are in fact the result of violations of the very principles of capitalism. Any critique of capitalism that takes these issues as its point of departure is flawed from the outset.

The weak premises of its key arguments notwithstanding, intellectual anti-capitalism is influential in contemporary debates primarily because, far from being confined to discussions between members of an aloof elite or academic seminars, it has a formative impact on the attitudes and views of a key group of public opinion shapers. In the era of mass communication, where the power of the media goes far beyond their traditional 'fourth estate' role, intellectual anti-capitalism influences political behaviour because politicians are dependent on the goodwill of the media. It will be interesting to observe the extent to which the erosion of traditional, agenda-setting monopolies in recent years will reshape the relationship between politics and media as public debate increasingly moves online.

Anti-capitalism in its various shapes and guises, of which environmentalism is currently the most influential, has succeeded in putting the business elite under enormous pressure. Less gifted with eloquence than their opponents, and more used to acting on gut feeling than on theoretical abstractions, the members of this elite have surrendered to the anti-capitalist resentment espoused by career intellectuals. Since entrepreneurial success is contingent on the ability to adapt to changing market conditions, they frequently fail to realize that adapting to objectionable political realities isn't always a sustainable survival strategy.

This isn't a recent dilemma. In 1961, the Russian-born American writer and 'objectivist' thinker Ayn Rand – best known for her novel *Atlas Shrugged* (1957), which depicts a libertarian utopia – published her first nonfiction book, *For the New Intellectual*, which includes the following admonition: "No man or group of men can live indefinitely under the pressure of moral injustice: they have to rebel or give in. Most of the businessmen gave in; it would have taken a philosopher to provide them with the intellectual weapons of rebellion, but they had given up any interest in philosophy. They accepted the burden of an unearned guilt; they accepted the brand of 'vulgar materialists' ... Starting as the most courageous class of men in history, the businessmen have slipped slowly into the position of men motivated by chronic fear – in all the social, political, moral, *intellectual* aspects of their existence. Their public policy consists of appeasing their worst enemies, placating their most contemptible attackers, trying to make terms with their own destroyers, pouring money into the support of leftist publications and 'liberal' politicians, placing avowed collectivists in charge of their public relations and then voicing – in banquet speeches and full-page ads – socialistic protestations that selfless service to society is their only goal, and altruistic apologies for the fact that they still keep two or three percent of profit out of their multi-million-dollar enterprises."[644]

Intellectual anti-capitalism was able to become as powerful as it did only because the business elite has so far been unable to muster an intellectually adequate response. Pro-capitalist intellectuals – economists such as Mises, Hayek and Friedman as well as writers such as Rand – have tried to take up the battle that the business elite itself is unwilling or unable to fight, whether out of lack of courage or intellectual wherewithal and verbal agility. However, supporters of capitalism have always been outsiders among their fellow intellectuals.

Hayek argued that this is because a proponent of liberalism[645] and the market economy is regarded "merely as a timid apologist of things as they are" by the majority of intellectuals.[646] It is important to note that Hayek doesn't use the terms 'liberalism' and 'liberal' in the same way an American would (i.e. as a commitment to leftist ideology), but in a traditional European sense (i.e. as a commitment to limited government and free-market economic policies). Nevertheless, traditional liberalism, he suggested, lacked the utopian visions that made socialism so seductive for many. Accordingly, Hayek called for a liberal utopia that went beyond a defence of the status quo.[647] He may have been right to think that a radical vision to counter the dominant anti-capitalist ideology is the only way to break the hold of that ideology. The problem is, however, that anti-capitalist utopias will always be able to capture the imagination in a way that liberal utopias can't, simply because at the core of leftist thinking is the ability to envisage an ideal society without any basis in the realities of human nature. Liberals, on the other hand, tend to be sceptical of any promises of paradise on earth predicated on a 'new man' because humanity, as it is, is not up to the job.

While no love was lost between leading 20th-century thinkers and the proponents of capitalism, admiration for dictators of Stalin's and Mao Zedong's ilk ran high in certain circles. These were not outsiders or misfits, but members of the intellectual elite, whose hatred of capitalism was so strong that it drove them to revere some of the worst mass murderers of the 20th century. The French writers Henri Barbusse and Jean-Paul Sartre are just two examples of many.

Barbusse, whose World War I novel *Under Fire* (1916) had been translated into more than 60 languages and won him a Prix Goncourt, went on to write a sycophantic biography of Stalin, of whom he says: "His history is a series of victories over a series of tremendous difficulties. Since 1917, not a single year of his career has passed without his having done something which would have made any other man famous. He is a man of iron. The name by which he is known describes it: the word Stalin means 'steel' in Russian."[648]

Writing in the July 1950 issue of *Les Temps modernes*, Sartre, the playwright and founder of existentialist philosophy and one of the leading French intellectuals of the 20th century, defended his silence on the subject of the gulags by saying: "As we were neither members of the [Communist] party nor its avowed sympathizers, it was not our duty to write about Soviet labor camps; we were free to remain aloof from the quarrel over the nature of this system, provided that no events of sociological significance had occurred."[649] On his return from a trip to the Soviet Union in 1954, he made the absurd assertion that Soviet citizens enjoyed the full freedom to criticize the measures implemented by the regime.[650] Sartre and his partner Simone de Beauvoir, whose feminist manifesto *The Second Sex* had made her France's best-known female intellectual, were fervent admirers of Mao Zedong, whose revolutionary violence they praised as "regenerative" and "profoundly moral".[651] Sartre would worship anybody who opposed or attacked capitalism in any form, from Che Guevara to the members of the German terrorist organization the Red Army Faction (also known as the Baader-Meinhof Gang) to the Palestinian terrorists who murdered 11 Israeli athletes during the 1972 Olympics in Munich[652] to the Cambodian dictator Pol Pot, who had 20% of the population of his country killed, a total of 2 million people.

This did nothing to diminish the adulation accorded to Sartre himself by fellow intellectuals. The same goes for Noam Chomsky, one of the leading critics of capitalism in the US, who stated that Pol Pot's mass killings had claimed no more than "a few thousand" victims and had been grossly exaggerated as part of the mainstream media's anti-communist propaganda campaign.[653] In a 1971 televised debate with Chomsky, the French philosopher Michel Foucault, one of the most important proponents of post-structuralism and the founder of discourse analysis, vented his own rage against the capitalist elite: "The proletariat doesn't wage war against the ruling class because it considers such a war to be just. The proletariat makes war against the ruling class because, for the first time in history, it wants to take power. When the proletariat takes power, it may be quite possible that the proletariat will exert toward the classes over which it has triumphed a violent, dictatorial and even bloody power. I can't see what objection could possibly be made to this."[654]

It is a tragic paradox that intellectuals – who have tended to start out as the designers, creators or at least chief defenders of anti-capitalist systems (in all too many cases, cruel dictatorships) – have always ended up among their victims. In his book on the history and origins of communism, Gerd Koenen reflects on "the fate of the many poets, makers of theatre and film, painters and scholars – exhausted or silenced, deported or shot – whose truncated or mutilated biographies make up a disproportionate share of Soviet cultural history".[655] Wherever it came to power, anti-capitalism destroyed – along with economic wealth – the political and mental freedom on which intellectuals thrive.

It is nothing but blind knee-jerk hatred of capitalism that could have made a leading intellectual such as Lion Feuchtwanger – one of the most successful German-language writers of the 20th century – pen these lines in his travelogue about a visit to Moscow, published in 1937: "One breathes again when one comes from this oppressive atmosphere of a counterfeit democracy and hypocritical humanism into the invigorating atmosphere of the Soviet Union. Here there is no hiding behind mystical, meaningless slogans, but a sober ethics prevails, really 'more geometrico constructa,' and this ethics alone determines the plan according to which the Union is being built up."[656] Elsewhere in the same text, he says: "The establishment of socialism would never have been possible with an unrestricted right to abuse."[657] It is worth noting that this was written as a response to the Stalinist show trials taking place in Moscow at the time of Feuchtwanger's visit.

Leading intellectuals including Feuchtwanger, Brecht, Barbusse, Sartre and Chomsky, among countless others, engage in a consistent denial of, firstly, the atrocities perpetrated in the name of communism, which in the course of the 20th century claimed an estimated 100 million casualties, as well as, secondly, of the civilizing achievements of capitalism, a system that has done more to eliminate poverty than any other economic order in human history. It is true that in most countries the admirers of Stalin, Mao and Chávez have never represented a majority even among intellectuals. However, they have constituted a powerful and influential group within the intellectual community. Their positions are extreme expressions of a general attitude that does reflect a majority opinion among intellectuals – resentment of capitalism.

The collapse of communism happened less than 30 years ago. The former communist countries have never engaged in critical reflection and public debate on the level of post-war Germany's struggle to come to terms with the legacy of the Third Reich. In contemporary China, a portrait of Mao still looms large over Tiananmen Square, while in Russia the cult of Stalin is more alive and thriving today than it was a few decades ago.[658] In light of all the damage communism has caused – the human tragedies, material devastation and wasted opportunities for development – this is bewildering, to say the least. Never in human history has there been another political movement that "has extended its reach across all continents and countries in the world and exerted such a decisive influence on global politics for such a long period of time".[659] Even more problematic than the disturbingly small number of convictions brought against those responsible for the atrocities committed in the name of communism[660] is the lack of sufficient critical reflection and debate on the spiritual roots of communism. First and foremost, these roots are to be found in a furious anti-capitalism, which – far from becoming less virulent in the 21st century – has merely been channelled into new forms of expression. For many intellectuals, this anti-capitalist worldview constitutes a political religion from which they derive a sense of identity, orientation and moral superiority.

Intellectuals like to think of themselves as unconventional free thinkers swimming against the tide, individualists who detest any form of 'uncritical' conformity. In truth, like most people, they typically exhibit a high degree of conformity within their own community of reference. Very few of them have the courage to position themselves on the outside of their own community.

Intellectuals usually find it easier to turn their backs on left-wing beliefs and adopt a conservative world view than to mentally overcome their deeply ingrained anti-capitalist resentments. Thus, converts who have swapped the far-left politics of their youth for a conservative outlook (not many take the opposite route) will often hold on to their anti-capitalist convictions even after changing their minds on almost everything else. Even for ex-communist renegades, this tends to be the one red line they will not cross. The German journalist Marco Carini has retraced the history of these renegades over more than half a century, starting with the 1949 essay collection *The God that Failed*, in which six prominent writers and journalists – including, most notably, Arthur Koestler – discuss the reasons for their radical break with communism. For all their harsh disillusionment with communist ideology and practice, the majority of these renegades still remain true to their anti-capitalist beliefs.[661]

One of my key motivations for writing this book – and this chapter in particular – was the hope that it may persuade some intellectuals to radically question the beliefs and attitudes that have guided their lives so far. The real contribution intellectuals make does not lie in constructing convoluted theories designed to keep their fellow citizens guessing what they might possibly be getting at. Wouldn't it be far more useful to society as a whole if instead they came up with verifiable, evidence-based criteria for identifying and defining the conditions required for the growth of freedom and prosperity for as many people as possible? This task, however, would be impossible without critical reflection on the extent to which their own judgement might be clouded by socio-psychological factors, as well as by the experiences and norms shared, however subconsciously, among intellectuals as a group.

CHAPTER 11

An Urgent Appeal *for* Pro-capitalist Reforms

This book makes an urgent plea for pro-capitalist reforms. The objective of such reforms would be to increase the influence of capitalism in contemporary economic systems where elements of free-market capitalism are combined with elements of socialist economic planning. It is worth pointing out that the state does have a very important role to play in creating the framework for economic activity. Even Friedrich August von Hayek warned against mistaking free-market thinking for "a dogmatic *laissez faire* attitude".[662] Contrary to common misconception, he didn't oppose redistribution as a matter of principle, either – a point on which Anthony de Jasay and other libertarian thinkers took him to task for being inconsistent.[663]

However, there isn't anywhere in the world today where an excess of economic freedom is creating problems. There are many places where the opposite is true. From China, officially still a socialist country, to the US, allegedly a capitalist paradise,[664] from African nations to the European welfare states, plenty of problems and crises are caused by a lack of capitalism. In Chapters 1 to 8, I have provided ample evidence to show that chancing more capitalism is worth the risk.

There are plenty of books that explain why capitalism works. Interesting as these theoretical explanations may be, they play at best a very minor role in this book. My own answer to the question 'Why capitalism?' is far simpler: because it works better than other economic systems. Of course, there are reasons for this – but, in my view, knowing *that* something works is more important than knowing *why* it works. After all, you're probably quite happy to drive your car, or to use your smartphone, without understanding the technology involved. In the same way, people can benefit from capitalism without having heard of Adam Smith, Friedrich August von Hayek, Ludwig von Mises or Milton Friedman – let alone having read their writings. At least, this is true as long as the economy is thriving. As I will argue below, the majority's ignorance of how capitalism works can become a problem in times of crisis.

You don't need to read a lot of economic theory to decide which system is better. All you need to do is look at economic history, as this book does. Every time socialist economic planning and free-market capitalism have been in direct competition with each other – e.g. in the rivalry between North and South Korea, or West and East Germany – the result has been unequivocal.

History is full of experiments. Socialist systems have been tested in all imaginable shapes and guises. Soviet-style socialism was different from that in China, Yugoslavia's economic system from North Korea's. Most recently, Venezuela conducted an experiment with a home-grown variant of '21st-century socialism', while the democratic, comparatively moderate forms of socialism tried in the post-war UK and 1970s Sweden were different again. In Africa, various models of 'African socialism' have worked no better than the Latin American, European and Asian versions.

Although many people around the world will probably agree with this assessment, there is a widespread delusion which holds that socialism is a good idea in principle that has been implemented badly in practice. In truth, what's wrong with socialism is not only the practice but the principle, and the sooner this truth is generally acknowledged, the better. There is far too little awareness in Western countries today that capitalist reforms lead to more prosperity than redistribution ever has and ever will.

REDISTRIBUTION OR ECONOMIC GROWTH?

In principle, there are only two ways in which social issues can be ameliorated in actual fact or public perception: by redistribution or by economic growth. Although the two frequently go hand in hand, political opinion is divided as to which should be prioritized. Those who put a stronger emphasis on redistribution often tend to regard national or global economies as a zero-sum game – an attitude most concisely expressed in a poem titled "Alfabet" by the German writer Bertolt Brecht, in which two men – one rich, one poor – come face to face:

> Said the poor man with a twitch:
> Were I not poor, you wouldn't be rich.[665]

This image of economic life is popular among intellectuals. According to this logic, rich countries must share their wealth with poorer nations, and the rich must be forced to give some of their money to the poor. The fact that poverty continues to exist is blamed on egotism and lack of empathy on the part of the rich. It's true that, in the past, a lot of wealth was based on theft in societies where small minorities grew rich at the expense of the majority. However, this is not how free markets work. The logic of the market rewards those who are able to meet the needs of a large number of consumers.

A look at the wealthiest people in the world shows that none of them became rich by taking something away from others. Rather, their entrepreneurial activities created value for the whole of society. Amazon founder Jeff Bezos made his fortune in e-commerce, Bill Gates pioneered the software we all use today and Warren Buffett's fortune is based on investments in highly profitable brands, including McDonald's and Coca Cola as well as several large insurance companies. These three men built their fortunes on good ideas and great brands that meet the needs of billions of consumers. It was us – the consumers – who made them rich.

It is also worth noting that, far from safely stashing away their billion-dollar fortunes in savings accounts or spending them on personal pleasures, by far the largest part of these people's wealth is invested in shares of productive businesses. The full list of the top 15 richest people in the world (May 2018) is as follows:

1. Jeff Bezos, Amazon, USD 134 billion, self-made entrepreneur
2. Bill Gates, Microsoft, USD 92.7 billion, self-made entrepreneur
3. Warren Buffett, Berkshire Hathaway, USD 81.9 billion, self-made entrepreneur
4. Mark Zuckerberg, Facebook, USD 76.0 billion, self-made entrepreneur
5. Bernard Arnault, LVMH, USD 74.5 billion
6. Amancio Ortega, Zara, USD 70.9 billion, self-made entrepreneur
7. Carlos Slim, telecom, USD 56.3 billion, self-made entrepreneur
8. Larry Page, Google, USD 52.6 billion, self-made entrepreneur
9. Larry Ellison, Oracle, USD 52.5 billion, self-made entrepreneur
10. Sergey Brin, Google, USD 51.3 billion, self-made entrepreneur
11. Jack Ma, Alibaba, USD 49.3, self-made entrepreneur
12. Françoise Bettencourt-Meyers, USD 47.9 billion
13. David Koch, Koch Industries, USD 46.8 billion
14. Charles Koch, Koch Industries, USD 46.8 billion
15. Jim Walton, Walmart, USD 40.7 billion, inherited.[666]

Because the economy isn't a zero-sum game, the idea that redistribution will resolve social issues is a naive one. Historically, redistribution has done far less to eliminate poverty than economic growth. Frequently, its only impact on social issues has been to exacerbate them.

One of the most impressive books I've read in the past few years is *Please Stop Helping Us* by the African American *Wall Street Journal* journalist Jason L. Riley. Riley demonstrates that social welfare policies such as the introduction of the minimum wage have made African Americans worse off than they were before.[667] Conversely, they saw their wages rise more sharply than whites under the Reagan administration's pro-market reforms.

These effects translate from the national to the international scale. As I've shown in Chapter 1, economic growth led to improved standards of living for hundreds of millions of China's poor as well as to an increase in inequality and the creation of a new class of very wealthy multi-millionaires and billionaires. Chapter 2 goes on to demonstrate that half a century of foreign aid has done very little for Africa – in fact, in many cases its impact has been the exact opposite of what the donors intended.

And even systems explicitly predicated on the ideal of equality have never succeeded in creating a society of equals, which can only exist in the fictions of utopians such as Thomas More and Tommasso Campanella. George Orwell's *Animal Farm*, published in 1945, memorably explores what happens when good intentions lead to more inequality.

EXPANSION OF GOVERNMENT INTERFERENCE

Over time, economies that are initially committed to free-market principles often tend to restrict the free play of market forces while expanding the influence of the state. This happens not just because of the lobbying activities of particular interest groups and the social welfare programmes promised by politicians hoping to maximize their voter base, but also due to government reactions to the boom-and-bust cycles that are an inevitable feature of capitalism. Governments frequently respond to these by launching stimulus packages, new regulations and a general expansion of state intervention in the economic sphere.

Crises are as integral to economic life as periods of physical weakness and illnesses are to the lives of human beings, animals and plants. The human immune system and powers of self-healing are able to cope with most illnesses we suffer over the course of our lives. Given time, our bodies are able to recover from illnesses such as the common cold without any outside interventions.

Over the medium and long term, capitalist economies are strengthened by crises, which lead to the disappearance of unproductive companies. Unpleasant as their immediate effects may be for businesses and employees, they serve a positive, cleansing function.

However, a doctor who sends patients home without a prescription, simply advising them to stay in bed for a few days and allow the cold to take its course, would be regarded as incompetent by many. In the same way, no politician would ever win an election by advising voters to wait out the crisis and take the long view – "The final outcome will be positive even though some large companies are bound to go bankrupt along the way." The opposition would take every opportunity to denounce the politician as being either heartless or incompetent, or both, and most voters would probably agree.

To push the analogy further, some people think prescribing antibiotics, antipyretics and cough suppressants to cure minor illnesses is the hallmark of a good doctor. They are unaware that the short-term benefits of making them well again come at the risk of adverse side effects, delaying the healing process or even causing serious long-term complications. Fever and coughing are natural responses by which the human body fights infection. Although specific circumstances may sometimes mandate medical treatment, usually it's best to let them take their course. Suppressing these responses in order to feel better interferes with the body's powers of self-healing. Fighting minor illnesses with antibiotics may lead not only to adverse side effects but also to the build-up of antibiotic resistance.

A majority of people appear to have internalized the belief that taking action is always better than doing nothing. In truth, there are many scenarios where taking a conscious decision to do nothing is preferable to acting for the sake of acting. Getting patients to see this is as near impossible as asking voters to understand that waiting out crises that occur naturally as part of the economic cycle and having faith in the economy's powers of self-healing would be a far better course of action than stimulus programmes, government intervention and 'quantitative easing'. While these measures may provide short-term relief, they do more harm than good in at least three respects – by triggering adverse side effects, delaying economic recovery and weakening long-term economic growth.

Japan provides a sad reminder of the damage governments can do by interfering rather than allowing a crisis to take its course. In the wake of the bursting of the bubble on the Japanese property and stock markets in 1990, the Japanese attempted to avert economic pain by increasing public debt, rather than reforming their economic system in order to allow the self-healing powers of the market to take effect. By 2017, public debt stood at a staggering 237% of GDP – even more than in Greece (182%), Italy (131%) and the US (108%).[668] Tellingly, at 4.37% Japan's annual growth rate in social welfare spending between 1980 and 2003 was also higher than in any other comparable country (US 2.84%, Germany 1.94%).[669]

While doing nothing would in many cases be the most sensible response to cyclical crises or bursting bubbles, severe crises with deeply rooted, structural causes demand a more proactive political response. Again, the medical analogy is useful – unlike common colds, serious illnesses do need to be treated. As discussed in Chapter 5, Margaret Thatcher and Ronald Reagan were able to lead their respective countries out of deep economic crises during the 1980s by introducing measures designed to give freer rein to the powers of the market: privatization, tax cuts and deregulation.

On a smaller scale, similar reforms took place in Sweden during the 1990s to rectify the earlier excesses of taxation and regulation and to restore economic growth (see Chapter 7). Many other countries have experienced similar outcomes of pro-market reforms resulting in more growth and prosperity – including Germany, where the reforms instigated by Gerhard Schröder in the early 2000s led to economic recovery and helped to bring unemployment down.

Unfortunately, reforms of this kind happen far too rarely. It's easier to win an election with promises to increase welfare benefits and launch new redistribution schemes than by announcing pro-market reforms that frequently go hand in hand with welfare spending cuts. In their attempts to win and keep voters by promising them generous rewards, political parties are constantly on the lookout for new 'social injustices' to address in their election manifestos.

As William Voegeli has demonstrated, the long-term trend towards increasing redistribution and social spending is universal across Western countries. Between 1980 and 2003, per-capita social expenditure in proportion to GDP rose from 10.9% to 17.9% in Australia, from 20.8% to 28.7% in France, from 23.0% to 27.3% in Germany, from 18.0% to 24.2% in Italy, from 15.5 to 20.3% in Spain, from 16.6% to 20.6% in the UK and from 13.3% to 16.2% in the US.[670] During this period, the annual growth rate of welfare expenditure was significantly higher in the US and the UK than in classic welfare states such as Denmark and Sweden.[671] This growth in welfare spending was financed at the expense of future generations, by increasing public debt. 'Sustainability' is a buzzword today's politicians like to bandy about the better to hide the truth, which is that their policies are anything but sustainable.

As far as most politicians are concerned, there is no limit to the expansion of the welfare state – it never takes long for each new level to be perceived as inadequate. Politicians are forever sniffing out new 'injustices' (read: inequalities), which they then propose to correct by way of redistribution or increasing national debt in the hope that these proposals will win them votes in the next elections. However, the benefits of these measures – to anybody but the victorious candidates themselves – are highly dubious. In Chapter 2, we've already seen that foreign aid has done more harm than good for poor countries.

The German journalist René Zeyer demonstrates that the fight against poverty only creates more poverty and helps the 'aid industry' more than those who actually need help. In Germany, the aid industry, which includes nonprofits such as the Workers' Welfare Association (Arbeiterwohlfahrt) and the Catholic charity Caritas, employs a workforce of 1.5 million – three times the size of the entire German car industry – and incurs staff and administrative expenses of between EUR 80 billion and EUR 140 billion per year, which are largely funded by the taxpayer.[672] Less than half of the EUR 49 billion the German government spent on helping low-income households in 2010 actually reached the intended beneficiaries.[673] Efficiency, impact, cost–benefit analysis – all key terms in economic life – suddenly lose their meaning when it comes to poverty management. "Asking these questions of the private nonprofits is regarded as the equivalent of bursting into laughter at a memorial service."[674] Similar observations about the inefficiency of redistribution in the fight against poverty apply to the US[675] and the UK,[676] as James D. Gwartney and colleagues and Kristian Niemietz have shown. In these countries, too, redistribution has frequently widened rather than narrowed existing income gaps, while more market-oriented policies might have done far more to fight poverty.

Despite the overwhelming evidence of its ill effects, the trend towards greater government influence appears almost irreversible. At best, it is interrupted by short intervals of less rapid growth in government interference and welfare spending. The 'political economy of reforms' theory has shown why governments generally refrain from taking comprehensive reform measures. Most significantly, reforms initially tend to cause pain, which increases the risk of reformers being voted out of office. In the pro-market reforms discussed in this book in Germany (under Erhard), the US (under Reagan), the UK (under Thatcher) and Chile (under Pinochet), the short-term deterioration of economic conditions following the introduction of the reforms was reflected in rising unemployment and/or inflation. In China, too, price reform initially resulted in inflation. In many cases, reforms reveal pre-existing issues –

take Sweden, for example, where the introduction of reforms made hidden unemployment visible.

Measures liable to create more growth and employment in the medium or long term frequently cause short-term unemployment or even a recession. This, in turn, causes the popularity of their instigators to plummet in opinion polls. Nor are they able to rely on reaping the benefits of their reforms in time for the next elections – as was the case with Germany's chancellor Gerhard Schröder, who was voted out of office, leaving his successor Angela Merkel to benefit from the effects of his reforms.

Accordingly, would-be reformers need to be prepared to introduce radical measures in the immediate aftermath of their election victory and hope for the best – namely, that it won't take more than one or two difficult years for their reforms to take effect and noticeably improve conditions for the majority of voters. Longer election cycles of at least five to six years would make this easier to do, though at the risk of exacerbating existing economic problems under incompetent governments.

For all the variations between the pro-market reforms in different parts of the world discussed in this book, there is a common factor: in all cases – from Deng's China to the US under Reagan, from Chile to Sweden – reforms were instigated at a time of extreme, sometimes catastrophic economic difficulties. The economists Allan Drazen and Vittorio Grilli have used arithmetic functions to argue that a crisis is a prerequisite for economic reforms: "The welfare losses associated with economic distortions and crises enable societies to enact measures that would be impossible to enact in less distortionary circumstances. In other words, distortions and crises may raise welfare if they are the only way to induce necessary policy changes."[677]

There is of course no guarantee that voters will draw the right conclusions in times of extreme crisis. If anything, they are likely to respond by putting their faith in simplistic slogans and following those who offer them scapegoats. During the Great Depression in the early 1930s, a majority of Germans gave their votes to the National Socialist and Communist parties,[678] both of whom blamed the crisis on capitalism and successfully used anti-capitalist slogans to win votes.

In *Hitler: The Policies of Seduction*, I demonstrate the importance of socialist and anti-capitalist elements in Hitler's worldview for the National Socialists' success. Hitler was alarmingly modern in that he intended to subordinate private property and the free-market economy to the 'primacy of politics' – unlike the communists, who wanted to completely abolish them.[679] As early as 1941, the German economist and sociologist Friedrich Pollock argued that, although the National Socialists had formally maintained private property rights, they had destroyed all key features of private property except one – the legal title to property as such, which was powerless against state control over all-important aspects of industrial production "even when it is based on ownership of the majority stake".[680]

This is why thinkers such as the German-born Austrian School economist Hans F. Sennholz insist on equating private ownership and sole right of disposition in an economic order based on private property and free trade: "The owner himself [rather than the state] decides on the use of any economic resources he owns."[681] Many people are no longer aware of how essential this is. Democratic systems are not immune to the dangers of the erosion of key features of private property due to increasing regulatory intervention in the economy – a process accelerated by occasional crises.

The majority of voters are unable to grasp the full complexity of a crisis like the subprime mortgage and financial crisis that started in 2007–2008. Since the same goes for the majority of politicians, it is far easier to denounce 'greedy bankers' as scapegoats than to analyse the underlying causes of the crisis and draw the appropriate conclusions. Coming back to the observations I started this chapter with, in times of crisis the ignorance of the majority of voters, politicians and media as to the inner workings of capitalism does become a problem.

Governments tend to respond to these crises by expanding their own activities – which may ease the problems and even stimulate economic growth in the short run but will almost certainly exacerbate the situation in the long run. An additional problem is that with each new crisis, the level of public debt becomes more unsustainable as politicians attempt to solve the problems by borrowing more money. According to the October 2017 *Global Financial Stability Report*, published by the International Monetary Fund (IMF), total nonfinancial sector debt in the G20 economies has reached a record level of over USD 135 trillion, or about 235% of aggregate GDP.[682]

While interest rates of zero have slowed down the accumulation of public debt in Germany, the same is not true for the rest of the world, where debt levels are rising even faster, precisely because the money is (almost) free. States, companies and private households are even more heavily in debt than before the beginning of the financial crisis. According to the IMF, public debt in the US alone increased by USD 11.1 trillion between 2006 and 2016, while the debt owed by Chinese companies increased by USD 14.4 trillion during the same period. Debts are also rising faster than GDP. In the US, public debt doubled from around USD 10 trillion in 2009 to over USD 21 trillion in 2018.

In fact, public debt is even higher than reflected in the official figures, which do not take into account implicit debt, e.g. future pension rights of public servants vis-à-vis the public authorities.

With ordinary levels of economic growth no longer enough to get out of the debt trap, governments have little choice but to resort to time-honoured responses to exorbitant public debt: inflation, currency reform or sovereign default. The economists Kenneth S. Rogoff and Carmen M. Reinhart have documented a total of at least 250 sovereign defaults on external debt since 1800, as well as 68 domestic debts defaults, where debt is denominated in the local currency and held mainly by residents.[683] Some countries are more frequently affected than others. Spain and Venezuela top the list with 13 and 10 defaults respectively, while Australia, Canada, Norway and the US are among the countries that have never experienced sovereign default.[684]

The central banks' low-interest-rate policy exacerbates the debt problem by allowing governments to borrow money practically free of charge. For a number of years, Germany and other European countries have been issuing government bonds with negative interest rates. Under such conditions, taking on new debts appears to be no big deal and the parties can continue to distribute social benefits on a large scale to keep their voters happy. However, the zero-interest-rate policy has dramatic consequences. With prices for real estate, bonds, shares and other assets continuing to rise sharply, new bubbles are likely to form.

Private and institutional investors alike start to take greater risks in order to achieve any return at all. In this market, anything goes – including 100-year bonds issued by Argentina, Iraqi debt securities and 40-year Amazon bonds for any investor who isn't happy with interest rates in the US or Germany. Faced with dwindling returns and core investments selling out quickly, real estate investors, too, find themselves taking ever greater risks.

The zero-interest-rate policy puts banks at risk as well. The October 2017 IMF *Global Financial Stability Report* warns that nearly one third of systemically important global banks, representing USD 17 trillion in assets, will struggle to achieve sustainable profitability to ensure ongoing resilience, with half of them not even reaching their own targets.[685] This is a direct result of the decision to bail out the banks, almost all of which are now considered 'too big to fail'. The selection mechanism – crucial to the functioning of a market economy – has been suspended in the financial system, which is more regulated than any other sector of the economy. If the economy and stock markets collapsed, many banks would be on the brink of collapse and would 'need' to be saved again by taxpayers' money, which would further increase public debt.

At the same time, pension funds are on the brink of collapse. Public pension funds organized on a pay-as-you-go basis can no longer cope with the rate of demographic change in many Western countries, especially as politicians are reluctant to raise the pension age to the extent that would be necessary to even start addressing the problem. With a severe crisis of the statutory pension insurance system already a certainty, privately funded old-age provision becomes even more important. However, private life insurance companies and company pension funds are also struggling as a result of the zero-interest-rate policy, as they can't even come close to achieving the returns previously calculated on the basis of higher interest rates. The growing realization among the population that the risk of old-age poverty is rising rapidly increases social discontent.

Massive public borrowing and economic intervention by governments and central banks are exacerbating current problems by pushing them into the future. This will continue until the system either recovers through radical capitalist reforms – or collapses, giving rise to demagogues whose promises of salvation mobilize the masses and lead them into bondage. My motivation for writing this book is twofold: to provide politicians, journalists and other citizens who are willing to speak up with arguments to oppose the wrong-headed and short-sighted policies described above – and to show that neither the current problems nor the impending dramatic crises can be solved unless we have the courage to undertake radical reforms and to chance more capitalism.

Acknowledgments

I am grateful to friends and experts who read and discussed earlier versions or parts of this manuscript with me. My discussions with Dr. Gerd Kommer, the late Dr. Thomas Löffelholz and Dr. Helmut Knepel were particularly intense. Dr. Gerd Kommer is the author of the best books about the financial markets I know. The managing director of Gerd Kommer Invest GmbH, he supported me throughout the writing of this book and his feedback and advice have been invaluable. My discussions with Dr. Helmut Knepel, who is a former member of the board of directors and the advisory board of Feri EuroRating AG, and Dr. Thomas Löffelholz, who was the publisher and editor-in-chief of *Die Welt* during my stint of working as an editor, were particularly useful in forcing me to sharpen my thinking.

I have Christian Hiller von Gaertringen to thank for valuable comments on the Africa chapter (and beyond). After working as an editor at *Frankfurter Allgemeine Zeitung* for 16 years, he now works as a consultant for companies that invest in Africa. Professor Dr. Karl-Werner Schulte, who is the founder of the first academic programmes in Germany to offer executive education courses for real estate practitioners and of the IREBS Foundation for African Real Estate Research, also gave me invaluable feedback and support.

Prof. Dr. André Steiner, from the Potsdam Centre for Contemporary History and the author of the standard reference work on the East German planned economy, was kind enough to read the chapter on the East German economy. I am also grateful to Dr. Stefan Wolle, who has been the academic director of the GDR Museum in Berlin since 2005 and has written a number of books on East German history, for his support.

Werner Pascha, who is Professor for East Asian Economic Studies / Japan and Korea at the University of Duisburg-Essen, gave me invaluable advice on the South Korean economy. Rüdiger Frank, who is Professor for East Asian Economy and Society at the University of Vienna, generously shared his knowledge on North Korea. Prof. Dr. Stefan Rinke, the director of the Institute of Latin America Studies at the Free University of Berlin, and Matthias Rüb, who is the Latin America correspondent at *Frankfurter Allgemeine Zeitung*, were kind enough to cast a critical eye over the chapter on Chile and Venezuela.

Notes

INTRODUCTION

1   Zhang Weiying, *The Logic of the Market: An Insider's View of Chinese Economic Reform* (Washington, DC: Cato Institute, 2015), 12.

2   Friedrich August von Hayek, *The Constitution of Liberty: The Definitive Edition* (Chicago: University of Chicago Press, 2011), 111.

3   Ibid., 117.

4   See Chapter 8.

5   Georg Wilhelm Friedrich Hegel, *Lectures on the Philosophy of History* (London: George Bell and Sons, 1902), 19.

6   See *Hollander, Paul. From Benito Mussolini to Hugo Chavez: Intellectuals and a Century of Political Hero Worship.* Cambridge: Cambridge University Press, 2016, 253–259, for examples of adulation of Chávez among leading intellectuals.

7   Thomas Mayer, *Die neue Ordnung des Geldes. Warum wir eine Geldreform brauchen*, 3rd ed. (Munich: FinanzBuch Verlag, 2015), 228.

8   These findings are quoted in Samuel Gregg, *Becoming Europe: Economic Decline, Culture, and How America Can Avoid a European Future* (New York: Encounter Books, 2013), 266 et seq.

9   Cal Thomas, "Millennials Are Clueless about Socialism (Call It the 'Bernie Sanders effect')," *Fox News Opinion* (20 October 2016), accessed 20 June 2018, www.foxnews.com/opinion/2016/10/20/millennials-are-clueless-about-socialism-call-it-bernie-sanders-effect.html.

10 Bernie Sanders, *Our Revolution: A Future to Believe In* (New York: Thomas Dunne Books, 2016), 265, emphasis in original.

11 Klaus Schroeder and Monika Deutz-Schroeder, *Gegen Staat und Kapital – für die Revolution! Linksextremismus in Deutschland: Eine empirische Studie* (Frankfurt: Peter Lang / Internationaler Verlag der Wissenschaften, 2015), 568.

12 Ibid., 574–575.

13 Ibid., 580–581.

14 Thomas Piketty, *Capital in the Twenty-First Century* (Boston: Harvard University Press, 2014), 41.

15 Ibid., 42.

16 Ibid., 20.

17 For more detail, see Jean-Philippe Delsol, Nicholas Lecaussin and Emmanuel Martin, eds., *Anti-Piketty: Capital for the 21st Century* (Washington, DC: Cato Institute, 2017).

18   See Tom G. Palmer, "Foreword," in *Anti-Piketty: Capital for the 21st Century*, edited by Jean-Philippe Delsol, Nicholas Lecaussin and Emmanuel Martin (Washington, DC: Cato Institute, 2017), xv.

19   Kristian Niemietz, "Der Mythos vom Globalisierungsverlierer: Armut im Westen," in *Das Ende der Armut: Chancen einer globalen Marktwirtschaft*, edited by Christian Hoffmann and Pierre Bessard (Zürich: Liberales Institut Zürich, 2012), 152.

20   See Jean-Philippe Delsol, "The Great Process of Equalization of Conditions," in *Anti-Piketty: Capital for the 21st Century*, edited by Jean-Philippe Delsol, Nicholas Lecaussin and Emmanuel Martin (Washington, DC: Cato Institute, 2017), 8–9.

21   Karl Marx, *A Contribution to the Critique of Political Economy*, translated by S. W. Ryazanskaya (Moscow: Progress Publishers, 1859), 15.

22   As calculated by the University of California economist J. Bradford DeLong, quoted in Zhang, *The Logic of the Market*, 24–25.

CHAPTER 1

23   Quoted in Jung Chang and Jon Halliday, *Mao: The Unknown Story* (London: Jonathan Cape, 2005), 519.

24   Frank Dikötter, *Mao's Great Famine: The History of China's Most Devastating Catastrophe*, 1958–62 (London: Bloomsbury, 2010), 27.

25   Ibid., 32.

26   Quoted in Chang and Halliday, *Mao*, 529.

27   Ibid., 529–530.

28   Felix Wemheuer, *Der große Hunger: Hungersnöte unter Stalin und Mao* (Berlin: Rotbuch Verlag, 2012), 194–195.

29   Dikötter, *Mao's Great Famine*, xii.

30   Ibid., xiii.

31   Wemheuer, *Der große Hunger*, 203.

32   Quoted in Felix Lee, *Macht und Moderne: Chinas großer Reformer Deng Xiaoping – Die Biographie* (Berlin: Rotbuch Verlag, 2014), 80.

33   Dikötter, *Mao's Great Famine*, 320–321.

34   Chang and Halliday, *Mao*, 533.

35   Wemheuer, *Der große Hunger*, 169.

36   Chang and Halliday, *Mao*, 531.

37   Dikötter, *Mao's Great Famine*, 57.

38   Ibid., 61.

39   Chang and Halliday, *Mao*, 526.

40   Dikötter, *Mao's Great Famine*, 60.

41   Chang and Halliday, *Mao*, 526.

42   Ibid., 527.

43   Ronald Coase and Ning Wang, *How China Became Capitalist* (New York: Palgrave MacMillan, 2012), 15.

44   Chang and Halliday, *Mao*, 520.

45   Ibid., 15.

46   Dikötter, *Mao's Great Famine*, 128.

47   Ibid., 137.

48 Chang and Halliday, *Mao*, 525.

49 Wemheuer, *Der große Hunger*, 189.

50 Dikötter, *Mao's Great Famine*, 133.

51 Wemheuer, *Der große Hunger*, 193.

52 Quoted in ibid., 181.

53 Dikötter, *Mao's Great Famine*, 117.

54 Ibid., 92.

55 Quoted in Chang and Halliday, *Mao*, 535.

56 Quoted in ibid., 535.

57 Quoted in Dikötter, *Mao's Great Famine*, 100.

58 Coase and Wang, *How China Became Capitalist*, 32.

59 Ibid., 33.

60 Lee, *Macht und Moderne*, 165.

61 Coase and Wang, *How China Became Capitalist*, 33.

62 Tobias ten Brink, *Chinas Kapitalismus: Entstehung, Verlauf, Paradoxien* (Frankfurt: Campus Verlag, 2013), 106.

63 Coase and Wang, *How China Became Capitalist*, 34.

64 Lee, *Macht und Moderne*, 159.

65 Coase and Wang, *How China Became Capitalist*, 47.

66 Ibid., 49.

67 Ibid., 54.

68 Ten Brink, *Chinas Kapitalismus*, 118.

69 Ibid., 84.

70 Ibid., 170.

71 Coase and Wang, *How China Became Capitalist*, 58.

72 Ibid., 68.

73 Ibid., 75–78.

74 Ibid., 60.

75 Lee, *Macht und Moderne*, 188–189.

76 Ibid., 191.

77 Ten Brink, *Chinas Kapitalismus*, 177.

78 Ibid., 178.

79 Coase and Wang, *How China Became Capitalist*, 92.

80 Amnesty International, *China: The Massacre of June 1989 and Its Aftermath*, accessed 20 June 2018, https://www.amnesty.org/download/Documents/200000/asa170091990en.pdf, 5.

81 Lee, *Macht und Moderne*, 256.

82 Ibid., 258.

83 Quoted in Coase and Wang, *How China Became Capitalist*, 117.

84 Quoted in ibid., 120–121.

85 Ibid., 123.

86 Ibid., 124.

87 Ten Brink, *Chinas Kapitalismus*, 123.

88   Coase and Wang, *How China Became Capitalist*, 143.
89   Ten Brink, *Chinas Kapitalismus*, 126–127.
90   Zhang, *The Logic of the Market*, 79.
91   Ibid., 61 et seq.
92   Ibid., 75–76.
93   Ibid., 79.
94   Ten Brink, *Chinas Kapitalismus*, 114.
95   Ibid., 269.
96   Zhang, *The Logic of the Market*, 286.
97   Ibid., 287.
98   Ibid., 288.
99   Ibid., 290.
100   Heritage Foundation, *2018 Index of Economic Freedom* (Washington, DC: Institute for Economic Freedom, 2018), 39–40.
101   See ibid., 5.
102   Zhang, *The Logic of the Market*, xii–xiii.
103   Ibid., 158.
104   Ibid., 162.
105   Ibid., 177.
106   Ibid., 185 et seq.
107   Ibid., 161.
108   Ibid., xiii–xiv.
109   Ibid., 18.

CHAPTER 2

110   Andreas Freytag, "Ist Afrikas wirtschaftliche Entwicklung nachhaltig?" in *Praxishandbuch Wirtschaft in Afrika*, edited by Thomas Schmidt, Kay Pfaffenberger and Stefan Liebing (Wiesbaden: Springer Gabler, 2017), 43.
111   World Food Programme, "Zero Hunger," accessed 20 June 2018, http://de.wfp.org/hunger/hunger-statistik.
112   Jonathan Berman, *Success in Africa: CEO Insights from a Continent on the Rise* (Brookline, MA: Bibliomotion, 2013), 18.
113   Quoted in ibid., 19
114   Ibid., 9.
115   Quoted in Dambisa Moyo, *Dead Aid: Why Aid Is Not Working and How There Is a Better Way for Africa* (New York: Farrar, Straus & Giroux, 2009), 108.
116   Ibid., 5.
117   Ibid., 28.
118   Ibid., 36.
119   Ibid., 39.
120   Ibid., 5.
121   Ibid., 43.
122   Ibid., 55.

123 Quoted in David Signer, "Entwicklungshilfe statt Entwicklung? Die fragwürdige Bilanz eines überholten Konzeptes," in *Das Ende der Armut: Chancen einer globalen Marktwirtschaft*, edited by Christian Hoffmann and Pierre Bessard (Zürich: Liberales Institut Zürich, 2012), 94–95.

124 Quoted in ibid., 97–98.

125 William Easterly, *The White Man's Burden: Why the West's Efforts to Aid the Rest Have Done So Much Ill and So Little Good* (Oxford: Oxford University Press, 2006), 123.

126 Moyo, *Dead Aid*, 49.

127 Freytag, "Ist Afrikas wirtschaftliche Entwicklung nachhaltig?," 50.

128 Easterly, *The White Man's Burden*, 53.

129 Ibid., 78.

130 See Chapter 8.

131 Heritage Foundation, *2018 Index of Economic Freedom*, 63.

132 Ibid., 5 and 7.

133 Ibid., 3.

134 Transparency International, *Corruption Perceptions Index* 2017 (2018), accessed 29 May 2018, https://www.transparency.org/news/feature/corruption_perceptions_index_2017.

135 Quoted in Signer, "Entwicklungshilfe statt Entwicklung?", 88.

136 Berman, *Success in Africa*, 121.

137 Ibid., 117.

138 Signer, "Entwicklungshilfe statt Entwicklung?," 94.

139 Easterly, *The White Man's Burden*, 164.

140 To read these arguments, see Hernando de Soto, "Eigentumsrechte und Märkte," *LI-Paper* (May 2016), accessed 29 June 2018, www.libinst.ch/publikationen/LI-Paper-De-Soto-Eigentum.pdf.

141 These estimates are based on reports published between 2002 and 2006; see Vijay Mahajan, *Africa Rising: How 900 Million African Consumers Offer More than You Think* (New Jersey: Prentice Hall, 2009), 42 et seq.

142 Ibid., 42 et seq.

143 Kay Pfaffenberger, "Die Bedeutung regionaler Besonderheiten für das Geschäftsleben," in *Praxishandbuch Wirtschaft in Afrika*, edited by Thomas Schmidt, Kay Pfaffenberger and Stefan Liebing (Wiesbaden: Springer Gabler, 2017), 56.

144 Heritage Foundation, *2018 Index of Economic Freedom*, 7.

145 Ibid., 364, 292, 140, 112 and 384. Per capita GDP figures compiled in September 2017 from 2016 data.

146 Hans Stoisser, *Der Schwarze Tiger: Was wir von Afrika lernen können* (Munich: Kösel-Verlag, 2015), 12–13.

147 Ruchir Sharma, *The Rise and Fall of Nations: Forces of Change in the Post-crisis World* (New York: Allen Lane, 2016), 396–397.

148 Ibid., 353.

149 Andreas Sieren and Frank Sieren, *Der Afrika-Boom: Die große Überraschung des 21. Jahrhunderts* (Munich: Carl Hanser Verlag, 2015), 190.

150 Ibid., 66–70.

151 Ibid., 93.

152 Paul Collier, *The Bottom Billion: Why the Poorest Countries Are Failing and What Can Be Done about It* (Oxford: Oxford University Press, 2007), 38 et seq.

153 See Fabian Urech, "Das Öl hat der Regierung den Kopf verdreht," *Neue Zürcher Zeitung* (11 August 2015), accessed 20 June 2018, https://www.nzz.ch/international/afrika/das-oel-hat-der-regierung-den-kopf-verdreht-1.18593317.

154 Thomas Scheen, "Ein Reformwunder mit Schönheitsfehlern," *Frankfurter Allgemeine* (7 January 2017), accessed 20 June 2018, www.faz.net/aktuell/wirtschaft/afrika-im-umbruch/ruanda-reformwunder-mit-schoenheitsfehlern-14592400.html.

155 Heritage Foundation, *2018 Index of Economic Freedom*, 4.

156 Ibid., 70.

157 I have Christian Hiller von Gaertringen to thank for the information on Kenya.

158 "M-Pesa Has Completely Transformed Kenya's Economy, This Is How...," *CNBC Africa* (4 January 2017), accessed 20 June 2018, https://www.cnbcafrica.com/news/east-africa/2017/01/04/mpesa-economic-impact-on-kenya.

159 Nambuwani Wasike, "M-PESA and Kenya's GDP Figures: The Truth, the Lies and the Facts," *LinkedIn Pulse* (2 March 2015), accessed 20 June 2018, https://www.linkedin.com/pulse/m-pesa-kenyas-gdp-figures-truths-lies-facts-wasike-phd-student-.

160 See www.88mph.ac/nairobi.

161 Christian Hiller von Gaertringen, *Afrika ist das neue Asien: Ein Kontinent im Aufschwung* (Hamburg: Hoffmann und Campe Verlag, 2014), 103.

162 The following is based on Hiller von Gaertringen, *Afrika ist das neue Asien*, 110 et seq.

163 Berman, *Success in Africa*, 35.

164 Source: ITU, based on national data, accessed on 20 June 2018, https://www.itu.int/en/ITUD/Statistics/Documents/statistics/2018/Mobile_cellular_2000-2016.xls

165 Berman, *Success in Africa*, 35.

166 Ibid., 35–36.

167 TNS poll for the European Commission, "SPECIAL EUROBAROMETER 353: The EU and Africa: Working towards closer partnership", November 2010, accessed 20 June 2016, http://ec.europa.eu/commfrontoffice/publicopinion/archives/ebs/ebs_353_en.pdf, 44-45.

168 Christian Hiller von Gaertringen, "Afrikas junge Unternehmer," in *Praxishandbuch Wirtschaft in Afrika*, edited by Thomas Schmidt, Kay Pfaffenberger and Stefan Liebing (Wiesbaden: Springer Gabler, 2017), 5.

169 Philipp von Carlowitz, "Unternehmertum in Afrika: Eine Bestandsaufnahme," in *Praxishandbuch Wirtschaft in Afrika*, edited by Thomas Schmidt, Kay Pfaffenberger and Stefan Liebing (Wiesbaden: Springer Gabler, 2017), 23. The figures on how long it takes to set up a business are taken from the World Bank, *Time Required to start a Business (days)*, accessed on 20 June 2018, https://data.worldbank.org/indicator/IC.REG.DURS?view=chart.

170 Johannes Dietrich, "Afrika liebt Champagner," *Der Westen* (29 April 2017), accessed 20 June 2016, https://www.derwesten.de/panorama/afrika-liebt-champagner-id7896047.html.

171 Knight Frank, *The Wealth Report 2016* (2016), accessed 20 June 2016, https://content.knightfrank.com/research/83/documents/en/wealth-report-2016-3579.pdf, 14.

172 Sieren and Sieren, *Der Afrika-Boom*, 50.

173 Helmut Asche, "Demografische und soziale Entwicklung: Chance oder Risiko?" In *Praxishandbuch Wirtschaft in Afrika,* edited by Thomas Schmidt, Kay Pfaffenberger and Stefan Liebing (Wiesbaden: Springer Gabler, 2017), 42.

174 Sieren and Sieren, *Der Afrika-Boom,* 50–51. Asche estimates that around 30 million households in Africa are middle class (at least USD 5,500 annual household income): Asche, "Demografische und soziale Entwicklung," 43.

175 Sieren and Sieren, *Der Afrika-Boom,* 50.

176 Ibid., 16.

177 Ibid., 41.

178 Dambisa Moyo, *Winner Take All: China's Race for Resources and What It Means for the World* (New York: Basic Books, 2012), 85.

179 Stefan Enders, "Investment in Afrika: Chinas und Indiens planvolle Präsenz," *IHK* (19 June 2017), accessed 20 June 2018, www.subsahara-afrika-ihk.de/blog/2017/06/19/investment-in-afrika-chinas-und-indiens-planvolle-praesenz.

180 Sieren and Sieren, *Der Afrika-Boom,* 21.

181 Ibid., 115.

182 Freytag, "Ist Afrikas wirtschaftliche Entwicklung nachhaltig?," 37.

183 Sieren and Sieren, *Der Afrika-Boom,* 15.

184 Moyo, *Winner Take All,* 166 et seq.

185 Sieren and Sieren, *Der Afrika-Boom,* 42–43.

186 Berman, *Success in Africa,* 117.

187 Ibid., 120.

188 Ibid., 118–119.

189 Ibid., 130–131.

190 See Zhang, *The Logic of the Market,* 161 et seq.

191 Moky Makura, *Africa's Greatest Entrepreneurs* (Century City, CA: Penguin, 2008).

192 Freytag, "Ist Afrikas wirtschaftliche Entwicklung nachhaltig?," 47.

193 Ibid., 46.

194 Georgetown University, "U2's Bono: Budget Cuts Can Impact Social Enterprise, Global Change" (13 November 2012), accessed 20 June 2018, https://www.georgetown.edu/news/bono-speaks-at-gu.html.

195 Louise Armitstead and Ben Harrington, "Bob Geldof to Front African Private Equity Fund," *The Telegraph* (3 September 2010), accessed 20 June 2018, www.telegraph.co.uk/finance/newsbysector/banksandfinance/privateequity/7978634/Bob-Geldof-to-front-African-private-equity-fund.html.

196 Mahajan, *Africa Rising,* 18.

197 Quoted in ibid., 21.

CHAPTER 3

198 André Steiner, *Von Plan zu Plan: Eine Wirtschaftsgeschichte der DDR* (Berlin: Aufbau Taschenbuch, 2007), 24.

199 Institut für Marxismus-Leninismus beim ZK der SED, *Revolutionäre deutsche Parteiprogramme: Vom Kommunistischen Manifest zum Programm des Sozialismus* (Berlin: Dietz Verlag, 1967), 196–197.

200 Steiner, *Von Plan zu Plan,* 46.

201 Ibid., 47.

202 Ibid., 80.

203 Ibid., 48.

204 Stefan Wolle, *Der große Plan: Alltag und Herrschaft in der DDR 1949–1951* (Berlin: Ch. Links Verlag, 2013), 118.

205 Quoted in Steiner, *Von Plan zu Plan*, 65.

206 Quoted in Wolle, *Der große Plan*, 116–117.

207 Steiner, *Von Plan zu Plan*, 79.

208 Ibid., 81.

209 Quoted in ibid., 83.

210 Wolle, *Der große Plan*, 376.

211 Steiner, *Von Plan zu Plan*, 86.

212 Ibid., 89.

213 Quoted in Wolle, *Der große Plan*, 271.

214 Ibid., 273–274.

215 Steiner, *Von Plan zu Plan*, 103.

216 Wolle, *Der große Plan*, 389.

217 Steiner, *Von Plan zu Plan*, 111.

218 Ibid., 114.

219 Ibid., 122–123.

220 Ibid., 123.

221 Rüdiger Frank, *Nordkorea: Innenansichten eines totalen Staates*, 2nd ed. (Munich: Deutsche Verlags-Anstalt, 2017), 148.

222 Steiner, *Von Plan zu Plan*, 124.

223 Wolle, *Der große Plan*, 390.

224 Steiner, *Von Plan zu Plan*, 131.

225 Wolle, *Der große Plan*, 390.

226 Steiner, *Von Plan zu Plan*, 131.

227 Wolle, *Der große Plan*, 391.

228 Steiner, *Von Plan zu Plan*, 132–133.

229 Ibid., 134–135.

230 Ibid., 135–136.

231 Wolle, *Der große Plan*, 391.

232 Steiner, *Von Plan zu Plan*, 128.

233 Ibid., 128.

234 Ibid., 118.

235 Ibid., 149.

236 Ibid., 165.

237 Ibid., 178.

238 Ibid., 180.

239 Ibid., 182.

240 Ibid., 184.

241 Ibid., 194–195.

242 Quoted in ibid., 194.

243 Ibid., 198.

244 Ibid., 200–201.

245 Henrik Eberle, *Mit sozialistischem Gruß: Eingaben, Briefe und Mitteilungen an die DDR-Regierung* (Berlin: Edition Berolina, 2016), 13–14.

246 Quoted in ibid., 14.

247 Quoted in ibid., 18.

248 Steiner, *Von Plan zu Plan*, 235.

249 Ibid., 221.

250 Ibid., 222.

251 Ibid., 225.

252 Ibid., 238.

253 Ibid., 239.

254 Ibid., 248.

255 Mark Spoerer and Jochen Streb, *Neue deutsche Wirtschaftsgeschichte des 20. Jahrhunderts* (Munich: De Gruyter Oldenbourg, 2013), 212–213.

256 Walter Wittmann, *Soziale Marktwirtschaft statt Wohlfahrtsstaat: Wege aus der Krise* (Zürich: Orell Füssli, 2013), 72.

257 Gerd Habermann, *Der Wohlfahrtsstaat: Die Geschichte eines Irrwegs* (Frankfurt: Propyläen Verlag, 1994), 331.

258 Karen Ilse Horn, Die Soziale Marktwirtschaft. Alles, was Sie über den Neoliberalismus wissen sollten (Frankfurt: Frankfurter Allgemeine Buch, 2010), 122.

259 Spoerer and Streb, *Neue deutsche Wirtschaftsgeschichte*, 265.

260 Ludwig Erhard, *Wohlstand für alle* (Düsseldorf: Econ, 1990), 10.

261 Habermann, *Der Wohlfahrtsstaat*, 332.

262 Quoted in Peter Gillies, "Ludwig Erhard: Ökonom der Freiheit," in Peter Gillies, Daniel Koerfer and Udo Wengst, *Ludwig Erhard* (Berlin: Be.bra Wissenschaft Verlag, 2010), 125–126.

263 Ibid., 126.

264 Spoerer and Streb, *Neue deutsche Wirtschaftsgeschichte*, 210.

265 Daniel Koerfer, "Ludwig Erhard: Der vergessene Gründervater," in Peter Gillies, Daniel Koerfer and Udo Wengst, *Ludwig Erhard* (Berlin: Be.bra Wissenschaft Verlag, 2010), 32.

266 Karen Ilse Horn, *Die Soziale Marktwirtschaft*, 123.

267 Koerfer, "Ludwig Erhard," 32.

268 Hans-Peter Schwarz, *Die Ära Adenauer: Gründejahre der Republik 1949–1957* (Stuttgart: Deutsche Verlagsanstalt, 1981), 86.

269 "Aufbauhilfe für das zerstörte Europa," *Frankfurter Allgemeine Zeitung* (3 April 2008).

270 Spoerer and Streb, *Neue deutsche Wirtschaftsgeschichte*, 219.

271 For the following data, see Statistisches Jahrbuch 1990 für die Bundesrepublik Deutschland, Statistisches Jahrbuch 1991 für das vereinigte Deutschland, Sozialreport 1990 (Daten und Fakten zur sozialen Lage in der DDR), Datenreport 2008.

272 Sources: "Bauen und Wohnen" building permits/completed constructions, Lange Reihen, Federal Statistical Office, 26 July 2017, Article no. 5311101167004; Chapters 4.2 (1990) and 4.3 (1991–1999)/EUR 84 billion: these are the aggregate costs quoted by the developers for buildings completed in the former GDR for the period between 1991 and 1999; "Bauen und Wohnen" building permits/completed constructions, construction costs, Lange Reihen dating back to 1962, Federal Statistical Office, 27 July 2017, Article no. 5311103167004; Neue Länder und Berlin, Chapter 3.

273 Erhard, *Wohlstand für alle*, 251–252.

274 Spoerer and Streb, *Neue deutsche Wirtschaftsgeschichte*, 262.

275 Gerhard Schröder, byline article for *Handelsblatt* (16 December 2002).

276 Quoted in Gregor Schöllgen, *Gerhard Schröder: Die Biografie* (Munich: Deutsche Verlags-Anstalt, 2015), 676.

277 Ibid., 684–685.

CHAPTER 4

278 Estimates for South Korea published by the International Monetary Fund in June 2017.

279 Since North Korea has good reasons not to publish any official figures, these are unofficial estimates and the real numbers may well be higher or lower. Productivity in North Korea is very difficult to gauge "because nobody knows exactly who produces what in North Korea. This is true of the public sector and the second industrial sector (the military) as much as of the growing quasi-private sector. We are finding it difficult even to analyze the data we do have because North Korean calculations are not based on dollar prices. The South Korean Bank of Korea issues calculations on the basis of South Korean factor prices, which is not always an optimal solution. I myself use North Korean data, but these only exist for growth rates and not for absolute GDP (information provided to the author by Prof. Rüdiger Frank, 21 August 2017).

280 Quoted in Frank, *Nordkorea*, 111.

281 Ibid., 68.

282 Ibid., 68–69.

283 Ibid., 62.

284 Ibid., 63.

285 Quoted in ibid., 63.

286 Ibid., 66.

287 Ibid., 183–184.

288 Ibid., 101.

289 Ibid., 115 et seq.

290 Ibid., 204.

291 Ibid., 397.

292 Ibid., 144.

293 Ibid., 145.

294 Ibid., 58.

295 Ibid., 207.

296 Ibid., 226.

297 Ibid., 228–229.

298 Ibid., 229 et seq.

299 Ibid., 405 et seq.

300 Ibid., 119.

301 Ibid., 163–164.

302 Heritage Foundation, *2018 Index of Economic Freedom*, 3.

303 Ibid., 7.

304 Dieter Schneidewind, *Wirtschaftswunderland Südkorea* (Wiesbaden: Springer Gabler, 2013), 109.

305 Patrick Köllner, "Südkoreas politisches System," in *Südkorea und Nordkorea: Einführung in Geschichte, Politik, Wirtschaft und Gesellschaft*, edited by Thomas Kern and Patrick Köllner (Frankfurt: Campus Verlag, 2005), 51.

306 Schneidewind, *Wirtschaftswunderland Südkorea*, 45.

307 Ibid., 138.

308 Ibid., 138.

309 Markus C. Pohlmann, "Südkoreas Unternehmen," in *Südkorea und Nordkorea: Einführung in Geschichte, Politik, Wirtschaft und Gesellschaft*, edited by Thomas Kern and Patrick Köllner (Frankfurt: Campus Verlag, 2005), 123.

310 Ibid., 136–137.

311 Ibid., 125.

312 Ibid., 134.

313 Werner Pascha, "Südkoreas Wirtschaft," in *Südkorea und Nordkorea: Einführung in Geschichte, Politik, Wirtschaft und Gesellschaft,* edited by Thomas Kern and Patrick Köllner (Frankfurt: Campus Verlag, 2005), 100.

314 Schneidewind, *Wirtschaftswunderland Südkorea*, 147.

315 Pohlmann, "Südkoreas Unternehmen," 142.

316 Ibid., 144.

317 Data for January 2018: Banks around the World, "The World's Top 50 Companies" (2018), accessed 4 June 2018, https://www.relbanks.com/rankings/worlds-largest-companies.

318 Pascha, "Südkoreas Wirtschaft," 96–97.

319 Schneidewind, *Wirtschaftswunderland Südkorea*, 124.

320 Comment made by Prof. Dr. Werner Pascha to the author on 10 August 2017.

321 Thomas Kern, "Südkoreas Bildungs- und Forschungssystem," in *Südkorea und Nordkorea: Einführung in Geschichte, Politik, Wirtschaft und Gesellschaft,* edited by Thomas Kern and Patrick Köllner (Frankfurt: Campus Verlag, 2005), 161.

322 Kooperation International, "Bildungslandschaft: Republik Korea (Südkorea)" (nd), accessed 20 June 2018, www.kooperation-international.de/laender/asien/republik-korea-suedkorea/bildungs-forschungs-und-innovationslandschaft/bildungslandschaft.

323 Kern, "Südkoreas Bildungs- und Forschungssystem," 166.

324 Kooperation International, "Bildungslandschaft."

325 Kern, "Südkoreas Bildungs- und Forschungssystem," 161. However, there is a flipside to this trend, which sees students pushing into top universities and white-collar jobs without considering alternative career paths. In many cases, the money invested in tuition fees could be better spent elsewhere. Many Koreans are now critical of these developments and very interested in alternative models such as the dual education

system practiced in German-speaking countries, which combines apprenticeships in a company and vocational education at a vocational school (comment made by Prof. Dr. Werner Pascha to the author on 10 August 2017).

326 Organisation for Economic Co-operation and Development, *PISA 2015: PISA Results in Focus* (2018), accessed 20 June 2018, https://www.oecd.org/pisa/pisa-2015-results-in-focus.pdf. According to the OECD's definition, top performers are students who achieve Level 5 or 6 in at least one subject (mathematics, science or reading). Low achievers are students whose performance is rated below Level 2 in all three subjects.

327 Frank, *Nordkorea*, 20.

328 Schneidewind, *Wirtschaftswunderland Südkorea*, 78–79.

329 Ibid., 79.

CHAPTER 5

330 Margaret Thatcher, *The Downing Street Years* (London: Harper Collins, 1993), 6.

331 This and the following passages are quoted from *Der Spiegel*, 14 January 1974.

332 Horst Poller, *Mehr Freiheit statt mehr Sozialismus: Wie konservative Politik die Krisen bewältigt, die sozialistisches Wunschdenken schafft* (Munich: Olzog, 2010), 46.

333 Thatcher, *The Downing Street Years*, 33.

334 Ibid., 33.

335 Ibid., 33.

336 Holger Schmieding, "Vor Thatcher war Großbritannien ein Trümmerhaufen," *Die Welt* (9 April 2013), accessed 20 June 2018, https://www.welt.de/wirtschaft/article115147486/Vor-Thatcher-war-Grossbritannien-ein-Truemmerhaufen.html.

337 Detlev Mares, *Margaret Thatcher: Die Dramatisierung des Politischen* (Gleichen: Hans Hansen-Schmidt, 2014), 34.

338 Ibid., 26.

339 Thatcher, *The Downing Street Years*, 104.

340 Ibid., 39–40.

341 Ibid., 93.

342 Ibid., 43–44.

343 Ibid., 40.

344 Ibid., 339.

345 Ibid., 343.

346 Ibid, 676.

347 Chris Edwards, "Margaret Thatcher's Privatization," *Cato Journal* 37, no. 1 (2017), 95.

348 Poller, *Mehr Freiheit statt mehr Sozialismus*, 52.

349 Edwards, "Margaret Thatcher's Privatization," 95.

350 Ibid., 89.

351 Thatcher, *The Downing Street Years*, 687.

352 Ibid., 668.

353 Poller, *Mehr Freiheit statt mehr Sozialismus*, 45.

354 Ibid., 50.

355 Walter Eltis, "The Key to Higher Living Standards," in *CPS Policy Study* no. 148 (London: Centre for Policy Studies, 1996), 26.

356 Ibid., 18. Real take-home pay; OECD data.

357 Figures (in constant, fiscal year 2000 dollars) are quoted from William Voegeli, *Never Enough: America's Limitless Welfare State* (New York: Encounter Books, 2010), 23–25.

358 Ibid., 39.

359 The following figures are all quoted from William A. Niskanen and Stephen Moore, "Supply-Side Tax Cuts and the Truth about the Reagan Economic Record," *Cato Policy Analysis* no. 261 (22 October 1996).

360 Interest rate on a 30-year mortgage.

361 Michael Schaller, *Ronald Reagan* (Oxford: Oxford University Press, 2011), 30.

362 Ibid., 34.

363 Quoted in Mark D. Brewer and Jeffrey M. Stonecash, *Dynamics of American Political Parties* (Cambridge: Cambridge University Press, 2009), 125; see also Ronald Reagan, "The President's News Conference," *The American Presidency Project* (12 August 1986), accessed 20 June 2018, www.presidency.ucsb.edu/ws/?pid=37733. Another two years later, Reagan offered a slightly different version of this quote in a speech to representatives of the Future Farmers of America when he said: "The nine most dangerous words in the English language are: I'm from the government, and I'm here to help" (https://www.reaganlibrary.gov/sites/default/files/archives/speeches/1988/072888c.htm).

364 Robert L. Bartley, *The Seven Fat Years: And How to Do It Again* (New York: Free Press, 1992), 100–101.

365 Ibid., 89–90.

366 The following statistics are quoted from Niskanen and Moore, "Supply-Side Tax Cuts," and based on the eight years in which Reagan's policies were in effect following his first budget proposal for fiscal year 1982. His 1981 tax cuts came into force on 1 January 1983.

367 Bartley, *The Seven Fat Years*, 4.

368 Ibid., 167.

369 In fiscal year 1987 dollars.

370 William A. Niskanen, *Reaganomics: An Insider's Account of the Policies and the People* (New York: Oxford University Press, 1988), 35.

371 Ibid., 25.

372 Niskanen and Moore, "Supply-Side Tax Cuts," np.

373 Ibid.

374 Voegeli, *Never Enough*, 23.

375 Ibid., 39.

376 Niskanen and Moore, "Supply-Side Tax Cuts," np.

377 Ibid.

378 Bartley, *The Seven Fat Years*, 45.

379 Ibid., 49.

380 Ibid., 99–100.

381 Figures in this and the following paragraphs are quoted from ibid., 135 et seq.

382 Ibid., 146–147.

383 Milton Friedman and Rose D. Friedman, *Two Lucky People: Memoirs* (Chicago: University of Chicago Press, 1998), 396.

384 Ibid., 394.

385 Ibid., 395–396.

386 See Gregg, *Becoming Europe.*

CHAPTER 6

387 Heritage Foundation, *2018 Index of Economic Freedom*, 3 and 7.

388 Ricardo Hausmann and Francisco Rodríguez, eds., *Venezuela before Chávez: Anatomy of an Economic Collapse* (University Park: Pennsylvania State University Press, 2014), 1.

389 See the articles in ibid.

390 Omar Bello and Adriana Bermúdez, "The Incidence of Labor Market Reforms on Employment in the Venezuelan Manufacturing Sector, 1995–2001," in *Venezuela before Chávez: Anatomy of an Economic Collapse,* edited by Ricardo Hausmann and Francisco Rodríguez (University Park: Pennsylvania State University Press, 2014), 117.

391 A. C. Clark, *The Revolutionary Has No Clothes: Hugo Chávez's Bolivarian Farce* (New York: Encounter Books, 2009), 55–56.

392 Stefan Wirner, "Die deutsche Linke nimmt sich Chávez als Vorbild," *Die Welt* (29 November 2007), accessed 20 June 2018, https://www.welt.de/politik/article1412494/ Die-deutsche-Linke-nimmt-sich-Chavez-als-Vorbild.html; see also "Reaktionen: Wagenknecht preist Chávez' Arbeit," Handelsblatt (3 March 2013), accessed 20 June 2018, www.handelsblatt.com/politik/deutschland/reaktionen-wagenknecht-pre-ist-wirtschaftsmodell-von-chvez/7887454.html.

393 Quoted in Hollander, *From Benito Mussolini*, 256.

394 Quoted in ibid., 256.

395 Quoted in ibid., 257.

396 Quoted in Clark, *The Revolutionary Has No Clothes*, 60.

397 Quoted in Raúl Gallegos, *Crude Nation: How Oil Riches Ruined Venezuela* (Lincoln: Potomac Books, 2016), 80.

398 Ibid., 81.

399 "Storm over Venezuela Oil Speech," *BBC News* (4 November 2006), accessed 7 November 2006, http://news.bbc.co.uk/1/hi/world/americas/6114682.stm.

400 Gallegos, *Crude Nation*, 84.

401 Harald Neuber, "Billiges Heizöl für 16 US-Bundesstaaten," *Amerika21* (12 December 2007), accessed 20 June 2018, https://amerika21.de/nachrichten/ inhalt/2007/dez/heizoel-fuer-usa; see also "Citgo–Venezuela Heating Oil Program" (nd), accessed 20 June 2018, www.citgoheatingoil.com/whoweserve.html.

402 Gallegos, *Crude Nation*, 84.

403 "Boykott: Venezuela kappt Exxon die Ölzufuhr," *Spiegel* (13 February 2008), accessed 20 June 2018, www.spiegel.de/wirtschaft/boykott-venezuela-kappt-exx-on-die-oelzufuhr-a-534931.html.

404 Gallegos, *Crude Nation*, 84.

405 Hans-Jürgen Burchardt, "Zurück in die Zukunft? Venezuelas Sozialismus auf der Suche nach dem 21. Jahrhundert," in *Venezuela heute: Politik, Wirtschaft, Kultur,* edited by Andreas Boeckh, Friedrich Welsch and Nikolaus Werz (Frankfurt: Vervuert Verlagsgesellschaft, 2011), 439–440.

406 Sven Schaller, "Wandel durch Persistenz (Teil 1): Eine Analyse der Wirtschaftspolitik von Hugo Chávez," *Quetzal* (March 2013), accessed 20 June 2018, www.quetzal-leipzig.de/lateinamerika/venezuela/venezuela-wirtschaftspolitik-hugo-chavez-erdoel-wirtschaftsstruktur-19093.html.

407 Gallegos, *Crude Nation*, 85.

408 Ibid., 83–84; Schaller, "Wandel durch Persistenz."

409 Carl Moses, "Der Öl-Caudillo," *Frankfurter Allgemeine* Zeitung (27 February 2007), accessed 20 June 2018, www.faz.net/aktuell/wirtschaft/wirtschaftspolitik/hugo-chavez-der-oel-caudillo-1118662.html.

410 Gallegos, *Crude Nation*, 24.

411 Clark, *The Revolutionary Has No Clothes*, 46–47.

412 Ibid., 48–49.

413 Alexander Rommel, "Sozialstruktur, Armut, Ungleichheit und soziale Klassen," in *Venezuela heute: Politik, Wirtschaft, Kultur,* edited by Andreas Boeckh, Friedrich Welsch and Nikolaus Werz (Frankfurt: Vervuert Verlagsgesellschaft, 2011), 72.

414 Ibid., 71.

415 Klaus Ehringfeld, "Venezuela droht der Kollaps," *Spiegel* (30 May 2017), accessed 20 June 2018, www.spiegel.de/wirtschaft/venezuela-droht-der-kollaps-a-1149662.html.

416 Matthias Rüb, "Telenovela über Hugo Chávez: Er konnte Menschen verführen," *Frankfurter Allgemeine* (1 February 2017), accessed 20 June 2018, www.faz.net/aktuell/feuilleton/medien/el-comandante-eine-serie-ueber-hugo-chavez-14799710.html.

417 Gallegos, *Crude Nation*, 23.

418 *Venezuela's Tragic Meltdown*, 34.

419 Gallegos, *Crude Nation*, 97.

420 Ibid., 37–38.

421 Ibid., 36–37.

422 Ibid., 44.

423 Venezuela: "Wenn Hunger Grenzen überschreitet", *Die Zeit* (6 July 2016), https://www.zeit.de/politik/ausland/2016-07/venezuela-krise-nahrung-grenze-kolumbien, accessed 6 July 2018.

424 "Venezuela: Von Hunger und Sterben" [broadcast], *NDR* (17 July 2017).

425 *Venezuela's Tragic Meltdown*, 29.

426 Ehringfeld, "Venezuela droht der Kollaps."

427 Gallegos, *Crude Nation*, 85.

428 *Venezuela's Tragic Meltdown*, 35.

429 Thomas Schweizer, "So regiert Maduro sein Land in den Abgrund," *Wirtschaftswoche* (25 May 2017), accessed 20 June 2018, https://www.wiwo.de/politik/ausland/venezuela-so-regiert-maduro-sein-land-in-den-abgrund/19850212.html.

430 *Venezuela's Tragic Meltdown*, 34–35.

431 Ibid., 29.

432 Patricio Meller, *The Unidad Popular and the Pinochet Dictatorship: A Political Economy Analysis* (London: Palgrave Macmillan, 2000), 28.

433 Ibid., 33.

434 Stefan Rinke, *Kleine Geschichte Chiles* (Munich: C. H. Beck, 2007), 146.

435 Ibid., 147.

436 Meller, *The Unidad Popular*, 39.

437 Ibid., 35.

438 Ibid., 55.

439 Rinke, *Kleine Geschichte Chiles*, 147.

440 Ibid., 149.

441 Meller, *The Unidad Popular*, 70.

442 Rinke, *Kleine Geschichte Chiles*, 149–150.

443 Ibid., 150.

444 Meller, *The Unidad Popular*, 33.

445 Rinke, *Kleine Geschichte Chiles*, 153–154.

446 Friedman, *Two Lucky People*, 398.

447 See ibid., 398–407.

448 Richard W. Kahn, "A Tale of Two Economies," *Washington Times* (2 July 2013), accessed 20 June 2018, https://www.washingtontimes.com/news/2013/jul/2/a-tale-of-two-economieschile-has-employed-free-mar.

449 Meller, *The Unidad Popular*, 76.

450 Ibid., 79.

451 Ibid., 80–81.

452 Ibid., 86.

453 Rinke, *Kleine Geschichte Chiles,* 163–164.

454 Meller, *The Unidad Popular*, 121.

455 Arnold Harberger, "The Miracle of Chile," in *Up for Debate: Reform without Liberty: Chile's Ambiguous Legacy* (nd), accessed 20 June 2018, www.pbs.org/wgbh/commandingheights/shared/minitextlo/ufd_reformliberty_full.html.

456 Meller, *The Unidad Popular*, 142.

457 Milton Friedman, "The Chicago Boys," in *Up for Debate: Reform without Liberty: Chile's Ambiguous Legacy* (nd), accessed 20 June 2018, www.pbs.org/wgbh/commandingheights/shared/minitextlo/ufd_reformliberty_full.html.

458 Sergio de Castro, "There's No Doubt They're Doing Better," in *Up for Debate: Reform without Liberty: Chile's Ambiguous Legacy* (nd), accessed 20 June 2018, www.pbs.org/wgbh/commandingheights/shared/minitextlo/ufd_reformliberty_full.html.

459 On a scale from 0 (most equal) to 100 (most unequal), Chile scored 50.5 and was ranked in 15th place among the most unequal countries in the world for the period between 2010 and 2015.

460 Martin Hutchinson, "Rückkehr zum Vollblutkapitalismus," *Handelsblatt* (19 January 2010), accessed 20 June 2018, https://www.handelsblatt.com/meinung/kolumnen/chile-rueckkehr-zum-vollblutkapitalismus/3348842.html.

461 Lisa Caspari, "Endstation Reichtum," *Die Zeit* (27 June 2017), accessed 20 June 2018, https://www.zeit.de/wirtschaft/2017-06/chile-neoliberalismus-armutsgrenze-wirtschaft-reichtum.

462 Ibid.

463 Alexander Busch, "Länderanalyse Chile: Gefangen in der Mittelschicht," *Neue Zürcher Zeitung* (22 February 2017), accessed 20 June 2018, https://www.nzz.ch/wirtschaft/laenderanalyse-chile-gefangen-in-der-mittelschicht-ld.146938.

464 Rinke, *Kleine Geschichte Chiles*, 176.

CHAPTER 7

465 Heritage Foundation, *2018 Index of Economic Freedom*, 3–7.

466 The following figures are quoted from Heritage Foundation, *2017 Index of Economic Freedom*, 287.

467 Nima Sanandaji, *Debunking Utopia: Exposing the Myth of Nordic Socialism* (Washington, DC: WND Books, 2016), 104.

468 Ibid., 88.

469 Ibid., 89.

470 Ibid., 94.

471 Assar Lindbeck, "The Swedish Experiment," *Journal of Economic Literature* 35, no. 3 (1997), 1285.

472 Sanandaji, *Debunking Utopia*, 95.

473 Philip Mehrtens, *Staatsschulden und Staatstätigkeit: Zur Transformation der politischen Ökonomie Schwedens* (Frankfurt: Campus Verlag, 2014), 80.

474 Sanandaji, *Debunking Utopia*, 38.

475 Ibid., 63.

476 Ibid., 64–66.

477 Mehrtens, *Staatsschulden und Staatstätigkeit*, 82.

478 Lindbeck, "The Swedish Experiment," 1274–1275.

479 Mehrtens, *Staatsschulden und Staatstätigkeit*, 91.

480 Lindbeck, "The Swedish Experiment," 1279.

481 Mehrtens, *Staatsschulden und Staatstätigkeit*, 92.

482 Ibid., 93–94.

483 Ibid., 96.

484 See Rüdiger Jungbluth, *Die elf Geheimnisse des IKEA-Erfolges* (Bergisch Gladbach: Bastei Lübbe (Bastei Verlag), 2008), 63 et seq.

485 Ibid., 85.

486 Quoted in ibid., 85.

487 Ibid.

488 Quoted in Daniel Hammarberg, *The Madhouse: A Critical Study of Swedish Society* (Daniel Hammarberg, 2011), 430–431.

489 Quoted in Henrik Berggren, *Underbara dagar framför oss: En biografi över Olof Palme* (Stockholm: Norstedt, 2010), 540.

490 The following passage is quoted from ibid., 540–541.

491 Ibid., 540.

492 Ibid., 541.

493 Jacob Sundberg, "Die schwedische Hochsteuergesellschaft: Eine Herausforderung an den Rechtsstaat," in *Lothar Bossle and Gerhard Radnitzky, Selbstgefährdung der offenen Gesellschaft* (Würzburg: Naumann, 1982), 180.

494 Ibid., 181.

495 Ibid., 181 et seq.

496 Lindbeck, "The Swedish Experiment," 1275.

497 Mehrtens, *Staatsschulden und Staatstätigkeit*, 99.

498 Ibid., 100.

499 Ibid., 180.

500 Sanandaji, *Debunking Utopia*, 134.

501 Mehrtens, *Staatsschulden und Staatstätigkeit*, 117.

502 Ibid.

503 Ibid., 128.

504 Ibid., 149.

505 Ibid., 128.

506 Frank Bandau, "Soziale Ungleichheit im sozialdemokratischen Musterland Schweden," *Verteilungsfrage* (30 March 2016), accessed 20 June 2018, http://verteilungsfrage. org/2016/03/soziale-ungleichheit-im-sozialdemokratischen-musterland-schweden; Mehrtens, *Staatsschulden und Staatstätigkeit*, 174 and 193.

507 Mehrtens, *Staatsschulden und Staatstätigkeit*, 194.

508 "Für deutsche Ohren mag es nach Überwachungsstaat klingen," *Süddeutsche Zeitung* (10 September 2014), accessed 20 June 2018, www.sueddeutsche.de/wirtschaft/ schweden-steuererklaerung-per-sms-1.1728167-2.

509 Assar Lindbeck, Per Molander, Torsten Persson, Olof Petersson, Agnar Sandmo, Birgitta Swedenborg and Niels Thygesen, *Turning Sweden Around* (Cambridge, MA: MIT Press, 1994), 2–4.

510 Ibid., 5.

511 Ibid., 207.

512 Ibid., 206.

513 Mehrtens, *Staatsschulden und Staatstätigkeit,* 150.

514 Ibid., 183.

515 Ibid., 195.

516 "Staatsquote im internationalen Vergleich" (2012), accessed 20 June 2018, https://www.tu-chemnitz.de/wirtschaft/vwl2/downloads/material/Staatsquote_2012.pdf.

517 Bandau, "Soziale Ungleichheit."

518 See Piketty, *Capital in the Twenty-First Century*, 344.

519 Malin Sahlén and Salim Furth, "Piketty Is Misleading about the Swedish Case," in *Anti-Piketty: Capital for the 21st Century,* edited by Jean-Philippe Delsol, Nicholas Lecaussin and Emmanuel Martin (Washington, DC: Cato Institute, 2017), 97–100.

520 Ibid., 97.

521 Sanandaji, *Debunking Utopia*, 151.

522 Ibid., 157.

523 Rudolf Hermann, "Finanzministerin Blind im 'Budget-Maserati,'" *Neue Zürcher Zeitung* (14 April 2016), accessed 20 June 2018, https://www.nzz.ch/wirtschaft/ wirtschaftspolitik/kraeftiges-wirtschaftswachstum-schweden-auf-der-ueberhol-spur-ld.13596.

CHAPTER 8

524 Erich Weede, "Wirtschaftliche Freiheit: Hintergrundbedingungen, Auswirkungen und Gefährdungen," *Wirtschaftspolitische Blätter* 3–4 (2014), 448.

525 Heritage Foundation, "Explore the Data," in *2018 Index of Economic Freedom* (2018), accessed 20 June 2018, https://www.heritage.org/index/explore.

526 Ibid.

527   Ibid.

528   Ibid.

529   Ibid.

530   Heritage Foundation, *2018 Index of Economic Freedom*, 40.

531   Heritage Foundation, *2018 Index of Economic Freedom*, 32.

532   Heritage Foundation, *2018 Index of Economic Freedom*, 48, 56 and 64.

533   Ibid., 19.

534   Ibid., 1.

535   The following figures are all from Kristian Niemietz, *Redefining the Poverty Debate: Why a War on Markets Is No Substitute for a War on Poverty* (London: Institute of Economic Affairs, 2012), 28.

536   Weede, "Wirtschaftliche Freiheit," 447.

537   James Gwartney, "Freiheit und Wohlfahrt: Ein globaler Zusammenhang," in *Das Ende der Armut: Chancen einer globalen Marktwirtschaft*, edited by Christian Hoffmann and Pierre Bessard (Zürich: Liberales Institut Zürich, 2012), 36–37 (poverty in 2005).

538   Ibid., 39 (life expectancy at birth, 2009).

539   Martin Lanz, "Je mehr Wohlstand, desto weniger anteilige Ausgaben für Essen: Ein positiver Zusammenhang?" *Neue Zürcher Zeitung* (2 November 2017), accessed 20 June 2018, https://www.nzz.ch/wirtschaft/je-hoeher-der-wohlstand-desto-klein-er-der-anteil-der-essensausgaben-ein-uneingeschraenkt-positiver-zusammen-hang-ld.1321011?mktcid=nled&mktcval=107_2017–11–2.

540   Weede, "Wirtschaftliche Freiheit," 448.

541   Heritage Foundation, *2018 Index of Economic Freedom*, 64.

542   United Nations Development Programme, *Human Development Report 2016* (New York: United Nations, 2016), 198.

543   This comparison is based on the two most recently published indexes: United Nations Development Programme, *Human Development Report 2016*, and Heritage Foundation, *2018 Index of Economic Freedom*.

CHAPTER 9

544   Home Price Index data accessed 4 June 2018, https://fred.stlouisfed.org/series/CSUSHPINSA.

545   Quoted in Jerry H. Tempelman, "Austrian Business Cycle Theory and the Global Financial Crisis: Confessions of a Mainstream Economist," *Quarterly Journal of Austrian Economics* 13, no. 1 (2010), 6.

546   William A. Fleckenstein and Frederick Sheehan, *Greenspan's Bubbles: The Age of Ignorance at the Federal Reserve* (New York: McGraw-Hill Professional, 2008), 125.

547   Adrian Ravier and Peter Lewin, "The Subprime Crisis," *Quarterly Journal of Austrian Economics* 15, no. 1 (2012), 49.

548   Quoted in Tempelman, "Austrian Business Cycle Theory," 5.

549   Quoted in Ibid., 5.

550   Quoted in Ravier and Lewin, "The Subprime Crisis," 57.

551   Johan Norberg, *Financial Fiasco: How America's Infatuation with Homeownership and Easy Money Created the Economic Crisis* (Washington, DC: Cato Institute, 2009), 12.

552 Robert J. Shiller, *Irrational Exuberance*, 3rd ed.
(Princeton: Princeton University Press, 2015), 62.

553 Norberg, *Financial Fiasco*, 6.

554 Ibid., 6.

555 Ibid., 8.

556 Thomas E. Woods Jr., *Meltdown: A Free-Market Look at Why the Stock Market Collapsed, the Economy Tanked, and Government Bailouts Will Make Things Worse* (Washington, DC: Regnery, 2009), 17.

557 Ravier and Lewin, "The Subprime Crisis," 55.

558 Norberg, *Financial Fiasco*, 28.

559 Scott Shane, "A Political Gadfly Lampoons the Left via YouTube,"
New York Times (18 September 2009), accessed 20 June 2018,
www.nytimes.com/2009/09/19/us/19sting.html.

560 Woods, *Meltdown*, 21.

561 Wolfgang Köhler, *Wall Street in Panik* (Murnau: Mankau Verlag, 2008), 45–46.

562 Norberg, *Financial Fiasco*, 26.

563 Ravier and Lewin, "The Subprime Crisis," 55–56.

564 Norberg, *Financial Fiasco*, 30.

565 Woods, *Meltdown*, 15.

566 Ravier and Lewin, "The Subprime Crisis," 55.

567 Norberg, *Financial Fiasco*, 33.

568 Ibid., 41.

569 Ibid., 42.

570 Alan Greenspan, *The Age of Turbulence: Adventures in a New World* (New York: Penguin, 2007), 233.

571 Köhler, *Wall Street in Panik*, 78.

572 Fleckenstein and Sheehan, *Greenspan's Bubbles*, 138.

573 With regard to the following statements, see Rainer Sommer, *Die Subprime-Krise: Wie einige faule US-Kredite das internationale Finanzsystem erschüttern* (Hanover: Heisoft, 2008), Chapters 1 and 2.

574 Köhler, *Wall Street in Panik*, 40–41.

575 For these and other statistics, see "Case–Shiller Index," *Wikipedia* (nd), accessed 20 June 2018, https://en.wikipedia.org/wiki/Case%E2%80%93Shiller_index.

576 Hans-Werner Sinn, *Die Target-Falle: Gefahren für unser Geld und unsere Kinder* (Munich: Carl Hanser Verlag, 2012), 27.

577 Ibid., 31.

578 Ibid., 88.

579 Bert Flossbach and Philipp Vorndran, *Die Schuldenlawine: Eine Gefahr für unsere Demokratie, unseren Wohlstand und ihr Vermögen* (Munich: FinanzBuch Verlag, 2012), 19–20, based on calculations by Carmen M. Reinhart and Kenneth S. Rogoff.

580 Sinn, *Die Target-Falle*, 127.

581 Konrad Hummler, "Von der Gier zum Anstand," in *Der Liberalismus: Eine zeitlose Idee – Nationale, europäische und globale Perspektiven*, edited by Gerd Habermann and Marcel Studer (Munich: Olzog, 2011), 209 et seq.

582 Norberg, *Financial Fiasco*, 132.

583 Ibid., 51 et seq.

584 Richard Bookstaber, *A Demon of Our Own Design: Markets, Hedge Funds, and the Perils of Financial Innovation* (New York: John Wiley & Sons, 2007), 257.

CHAPTER 10

585 Hollander, Paul. *From Benito Mussolini to Hugo Chavez: Intellectuals and a Century of Political Hero Worship.* Cambridge: Cambridge University Press, 2016, 9.

586 Alan S. Kahan, *Mind vs. Money: The War between Intellectuals and Capitalism* (New Brunswick: Transaction, 2010), 12.

587 Friedrich August von Hayek, *The Intellectuals and Socialism* [1949] (Reprinted from The University of Chicago Law Review (Spring 1949), pp. 417-420, 421-423, 425-433, The University of Chicago Press; George B. de Huszar ed., *The Intellectuals: A Controversial Portrait* (Glencoe, Illinois: the Free Press, 1960) pp. 371-84. The pagination of this edition corresponds to the Huszar edited volume.]), 371.

588 Ibid., 372.

589 Ibid., 374.

590 Hollander, *From Benito Mussolini,* 4.

591 Kahan, *Mind vs. Money,* 17.

592 Thomas Cushman, "Intellectuals and Resentment toward Capitalism," *Society* 49, no 3 (2012), 248.

593 Edward N. Luttwak, *Strategy and Politics: Collected Essays* (Piscataway: Transaction, 1980), 319.

594 George Gilder, *Wealth and Poverty* (New York: Basic Books, 1981), 97.

595 Ibid., 99.

596 Alain de Benoist, *On the Brink of the Abyss: The Imminent Bankruptcy of the Financial System* (Budapest: Arktos Media, 2015), 158.

597 Quoted in Thomas Wagner, *Die Angstmacher: 1968 und die Neuen Rechten* (Berlin: Aufbau Verlag, 2017), 65.

598 Kahan, *Mind vs. Money,* 22.

599 Robert Velten, "Die Soziologie der antiken Reichtumsphilosophie," in *Reichtum und Vermögen: Zur gesellschaftlichen Bedeutung der Reichtums- und Vermögens-forschung,* edited by Thomas Druyen, Wolfgang Lauterbach and Matthias Grund-mann (Wiesbaden: Verlag für Sozialwissenschaften, 2009), 245.

600 Quoted in ibid., 245.

601 Ibid., 245.

602 Ibid., 249.

603 See Rainer Zitelmann, "Träume vom neuen Menschen," in *Hat die politische Utopie eine Zukunft?,* edited by Richard Saage (Darmstadt: Wissenschaftliche Buchgesellschaft, 1992).

604 Thomas More, *Utopia,* edited by William P. Weaver (London: Broadview Press, 2011), 55.

605 Ibid., 46.

606 See Helmut Schoeck, *Envy: A Theory of Social Behaviour* (Indianapolis: Liberty Fund, 1966), 191–192.

607 Joseph Schumpeter, *Capitalism, Socialism and Democracy* (London: George Allen & Unwin, 1976), 153–154.

608   Kahan, *Mind vs. Money*, 20–21.

609   Vladimir I. Lenin, "What Is To Be Done? Burning Questions of Our Movement," in *Lenin's Collected Works* (Moscow: Foreign Languages Publishing House, 1961), Vol. 5, 382, emphasis in original.

610   Ibid., 375.

611   Kautsky quoted in ibid., 383–384, emphasis by Kautsky.

612   Hayek, *The Intellectuals and Socialism*, 371.

613   See the critique by Delsol et al.

614   Piketty, *Capital in the Twenty-First Century*, 31.

615   See ibid., Chapters 14 and 15.

616   See Kahan, *Mind vs. Money*, 21.

617   Joseph Stiglitz, *The Great Divide: Unequal Societies and What We Can Do about Them* (New York: W. W. Norton & Company, 2015), 346.

618   Ibid., 347.

619   Ibid, emphasis in original.

620   Ibid., 349.

621   Roland Baader, *Totgedacht: Warum Intellektuelle unsere Welt zerstören* (Gräfelfing: Resch-Verlag, 2002), 126.

622   See Hollander, *From Benito Mussolini*, 7.

623   Ferdinand Lundberg, *The Rich and the Super-Rich: A Study in the Power of Money Today* (New York: Lyle Stuart, 1968), 85.

624   Ibid., 83.

625   Michael Hartmann, "Der Mythos von den Leistungseliten: Spitzenkarrieren und soziale Herkunft," in *Wirtschaft, Politik, Justiz und Wissenschaft* (Frankfurt: Campus Verlag, 2002), 132–134.

626   For a more in-depth discussion, see the relevant passages in my doctoral thesis: Rainer Zitelmann, *The Wealth Elite: A Groundbreaking Study of the Psychology of the Super-Rich* (London: LID Publishing, 2018), 24–36.

627   See Schoeck, *Envy*.

628   Friedrich August von Hayek, "Rules, Perception and Intelligibility," in *Studies in Philosophy, Politics and Economics* (London: Routledge & Kegan Paul, 1967), 43.

629   Ibid., 4.

630   Ibid., 43.

631   Michael Polanyi, *The Tacit Dimension* (London: Routledge, 1966), 4.

632   Ibid., 6.

633   Ibid., 20.

634   Georg Hans Neuweg, *Könnerschaft und implizites Wissen: Zur lehr- und lerntheoretischen Bedeutung der Erkenntnis- und Wissenstheorie Michael Polanyis* (Münster: Waxmann, 2001), 25–26.

635   See Rainer Zitelmann, *The Wealth Elite: A Groundbreaking Study of the Psychology of the Super Rich* (London: LID Publishing, 2018), Chapter 13.

636   As evidenced by the popularity of Malcolm Gladwell's and Michael Mauboussin's books on the subject.

637   Robert Nozick, "Why Do Intellectuals Oppose Capitalism?", in *Socratic Puzzles* (Cambridge, MA: Harvard University Press, 1997).

638 Quoted in Ralf Dahrendorf, *Society and Democracy in Germany*
     (New York: Doubleday, 1967), 291.

639 Ibid., 282.

640 Ludwig von Mises, *The Anti-capitalist Mentality*, edited by Bettina Bien Greaves
     (Indianapolis: Liberty Fund, 2006), 11–12.

641 Ibid., 12.

642 Ibid., 12–13.

643 Cushman, "Intellectuals and Resentment toward Capitalism," 249.

644 Ayn Rand, *For the New Intellectual: The Philosophy of Ayn Rand* (New York:
     Random House, 1961), 40, emphasis in original.

645 Unlike modern American readers, who will associate liberalism with left-wing,
     social liberalism, Hayek used the term in the traditional European sense, i.e. as a
     commitment to limited government and laissez-faire economic policies.

646 Hayek, *The Intellectuals and Socialism*, 382.

647 Ibid., 384.

648 Henri Barbusse, *Stalin: A New World Seen through One Man*
     (London: Workers' Bookshop, 1935), 289.

649 Quoted in Hollander, *Political Pilgrims*, 423.

650 Mark Lilla, *The Reckless Mind: Intellectuals and Politics*
     (New York: New York Review Books, 2001), 164–165.

651 Hollander, *From Benito Mussolini*, 194.

652 Roger Scruton, *Fools, Frauds and Firebrands: Thinkers of the New Left*
     (London: Bloomsbury, 2016), 94.

653 Daniel Bultmann, *Kambodscha unter den Roten Khmer: Die Erschaffung des
     perfekten Sozialisten* (Paderborn: Verlag Ferdinand Schöningh, 2017), 15;
     Hollander, From Benito Mussolini, 201–202.

654 Quoted in Lilla, *The Reckless Mind*, 150.

655 Gerd Koenen, *Die Farbe Rot: Ursprünge und Geschichte des Kommunismus*
     (Munich: C. H. Beck, 2017), 991.

656 Lion Feuchtwanger, *Moscow 1937: My Visit Described for My Friends* (New York:
     Viking Press, 1937), 111.

657 Ibid., 55.

658 Andreas Rüesch, "Wieso es in Russland wieder salonfähig ist, Stalin zu verehren,"
     Neue Zürcher Zeitung (24 October 2017), accessed 20 June 2018, https://www.nzz.
     ch/international/stalin-und-die-sehnsucht-nach-der-starken-hand-ld.1323741?mkt-
     cid=nled&mktcval=107_2017-10-24.

659 Koenen, *Die Farbe Rot*, 1031.

660 Ibid., 1001.

661 Marco Carini, *Die Achse der Abtrünnigen: Über den Bruch mit der Linken* (Berlin:
     Rotbuch Verlag, 2012). See, for example, 21, 43, 52, 56, 61, 145–146. These passages
     demonstrate that many purported renegades haven't entirely abjured their faith in
     socialist doctrine, or at any rate remain extremely hostile towards 'neoliberalism'.

CHAPTER 11

662 Friedrich August von Hayek, *The Road to Serfdom* (London: Routledge 2001), 45.

663 Anthony de Jasay, "Über Umverteilung," in *Wider die Wohlstandsdiktatur: Zehn liberale Stimmen*, edited by Roland Baader (Munich: Resch-Verlag, 1995), 21–32.

664 See Voegeli, *Never Enough* – an excellent book on the subject.

665 Bertolt Brecht, "Alfabet" [1934], in *The Collected Poems of Bertolt Brecht*, translated by David Constantine and Tom Kuhn (New York: Liveright, 2018).

666 "Bloomberg Billionaires Index," accessed 29 May 2018, www.bloomberg.com/billionaires, plus additional information provided by the author.

667 Jason L. Riley, *Please Stop Helping Us: How Liberals Make It Harder for Blacks to Succeed* (New York: Encounter Books, 2014), 85–110.

668 Figures on debt as a percentage of GDP reported by the International Monetary Fund, accessed 29 May 2018, www.imf.org.

669 Voegeli, *Never Enough,* 47, Annual Growth Rate of Real Per Capita Public Social Expenditures, 1980–2003.

670 Ibid., 43.

671 Ibid., 47.

672 René Zeyer, *Armut ist Diebstahl: Warum die Armen uns ruinieren* (Frankfurt: Campus Verlag, 2013), 161.

673 Ibid., 53.

674 Ibid., 56.

675 James D. Gwartney, Richard L. Stroup, Dwight R. Lee, Tawni H. Ferrarini and Joseph P. Calhoun, *Common Sense Economics: What Everyone Should Know about Wealth and Prosperity*, 3rd ed. (New York: St. Martin's Press, 2016), 141–149.

676 Niemietz, *Redefining the Poverty Debate.*

677 Allan Drazen and Vittorio Grilli, "The Benefit of Crisis for Economic Reforms," *American Economic Review* 83, no. 3 (1993), 598.

678 At the parliamentary elections in November 1932, the National Socialist (NSDAP) and Communist (KPD) parties between them won 319 of 608 seats in the Reichstag.

679 See Rainer Zitelmann, *Hitler: The Policies of Seduction* (London: London House, 1999), 221–269.

680 Friedrich Pollock, "Ist der Nationalsozialismus eine neue Ordnung?," in Max Horkheimer et al., *Wirtschaft, Recht und Staat im Nationalsozialismus: Analysen des Instituts für Sozialforschung 1939–1942*, edited by Helmut Dubiel and Alfons Söllner (Frankfurt: Europäische Verlags-Anstalt, 1981), 113.

681 Hans F. Sennholz, "Über den Abbau von Armut und Ungleichheit," in *Wider die Wohlstandsdiktatur: Zehn liberale Stimmen*, edited by Roland Baader (Munich: Resch-Verlag, 1995), 123.

682 International Monetary Fund, *Global Financial Stability Report October 2017: Is Growth at Risk?* (2017), accessed 20 June 2018, https://www.imf.org/en/Publications/GFSR/Issues/2017/09/27/global-financial-stability-report-october-2017.

683 Kenneth S. Rogoff and Carmen M. Reinhart, *This Time Is Different: Eight Centuries of Financial Folly* (Princeton: Princeton University Press, 2009).

684 Flossbach and Vorndran, *Die Schuldenlawine*, 19–20, based on calculations by Kenneth Rogoff and Carmen M. Reinhart.

685 International Monetary Fund, *Global Financial Stability Report October 2017.*

Bibliography

Armitstead, Louise and Ben Harrington. "Bob Geldof to Front African Private Equity Fund." *The Telegraph* (3 September 2010). Accessed 20 June 2018. www.telegraph.co.uk/finance/newsbysector/banksandfinance/privateequity/7978634/Bob-Geldof-to-front-African-private-equity-fund.html.

Asche, Helmut. "Demografische und soziale Entwicklung: Chance oder Risiko?" In *Praxishandbuch Wirtschaft in Afrika*, edited by Thomas Schmidt, Kay Pfaffenberger and Stefan Liebing, 41–52. Wiesbaden: Springer Gabler, 2017.

Baader, Roland. *Totgedacht: Warum Intellektuelle unsere Welt zerstören.* Gräfelfing: Resch-Verlag, 2002.

Bandau, Frank. "Soziale Ungleichheit im sozialdemokratischen Musterland Schweden." *Verteilungsfrage* (30 March 2016). Accessed 20 June 2018. http://verteilungsfrage.org/2016/03/soziale-ungleichheit-im-sozialdemokratischen-musterland-schweden.

Banks around the World. "The World's Top 50 Companies" (2018). Accessed 4 June 2018. https://www.relbanks.com/rankings/worlds-largest-companies.

Barbusse, Henri. *Stalin: A New World Seen through One Man.* London: Workers' Bookshop, 1935.

Bartley, Robert L. *The Seven Fat Years: And How to Do It Again.* New York: Free Press, 1992.

Bello, Omar and Adriana Bermúdez. "The Incidence of Labor Market Reforms on Employment in the Venezuelan Manufacturing Sector, 1995–2001." In *Venezuela before Chávez: Anatomy of an Economic Collapse*, edited by Ricardo Hausmann and Francisco Rodríguez, 115–155. University Park: Pennsylvania State University Press, 2014.

Benoist, Alain de. *On the Brink of the Abyss: The Imminent Bankruptcy of the Financial System.* Budapest: Arktos Media, 2015.

Berggren, Henrik. *Underbara dagar framför oss: En biografi över Olof Palme.* Stockholm: Norstedt, 2010.

Berman, Jonathan. *Success in Africa: CEO Insights from a Continent on the Rise.* Brookline, MA: Bibliomotion, 2013.

Boeckh, Andreas, Friedrich Welsch and Nikolaus Werz, eds. *Venezuela heute: Politik, Wirtschaft, Kultur.* Frankfurt: Vervuert Verlagsgesellschaft, 2011.

Bookstaber, Richard. *A Demon of Our Own Design: Markets, Hedge Funds, and the Perils of Financial Innovation.* New York: John Wiley & Sons, 2007.

"Boykott: Venezuela kappt Exxon die Ölzufuhr." *Spiegel* (13 February 2008). Accessed 20 June 2018. www.spiegel.de/wirtschaft/boykott-venezue-la-kappt-exxon-die-oelzufuhr-a-534931.html.

Brecht, Bertolt. "Alfabet" [1934]. In *The Collected Poems of Bertolt Brecht,* translated by David Constantine and Tom Kuhn, New York: Liveright, 2018.

Brewer, Mark D. and Jeffrey M. Stonecash. *Dynamics of American Political Parties.* Cambridge: Cambridge University Press, 2009.

Bultmann, Daniel. *Kambodscha unter den Roten Khmer: Die Erschaffung des perfekten Sozialisten.* Paderborn: Verlag Ferdinand Schöningh, 2017.

Burchardt, Hans-Jürgen. "Zurück in die Zukunft? Venezuelas Sozialismus auf der Suche nach dem 21. Jahrhundert." In *Venezuela heute: Politik, Wirtschaft, Kultur,* edited by Andreas Boeckh, Friedrich Welsch and Nikolaus Werz, 427–450. Frankfurt: Vervuert Verlagsgesellschaft, 2011.

Busch, Alexander. "Länderanalyse Chile: Gefangen in der Mittelschicht." *Neue Zürcher Zeitung* (22 February 2017). Accessed 20 June 2018. https://www.nzz.ch/wirtschaft/laenderanalyse-chile-gefangen-in-der-mittelschicht-ld.146938.

Bylund, Per. "How the Welfare State Corrupted Sweden." *Mises Institute.* Accessed 31 May 2006. https://mises.org/library/how-welfare-state-corrupted-sweden.

Carini, Marco. *Die Achse der Abtrünnigen: Über den Bruch mit der Linken.* Berlin: Rotbuch Verlag, 2012.

Carlowitz, Philipp von. "Unternehmertum in Afrika: Eine Bestandsauf-nahme." In *Praxishandbuch Wirtschaft in Afrika,* edited by Thomas Schmidt, Kay Pfaffenberger and Stefan Liebing, 15–30. Wiesbaden: Springer Gabler, 2017.

"Case–Shiller Index." *Wikipedia* (nd). Accessed 20 June 2018. https://en.wikipedia.org/wiki/Case%E2%80%93Shiller_index.

Caspari, Lisa. "Endstation Reichtum." *Die Zeit* (27 June 2017).
Accessed 20 June 2018. https://www.zeit.de/wirtschaft/2017-06/
chile-neoliberalismus-armutsgrenze-wirtschaft-reichtum.

Castro, Sergio de. "There's No Doubt They're Doing Better."
In *Up for Debate: Reform without Liberty: Chile's Ambiguous Legacy*
(nd). Accessed 20 June 2018. www.pbs.org/wgbh/commandingheights/
shared/minitextlo/ufd_reformliberty_full.html.

Chang, Jung and Jon Halliday. *Mao: The Unknown Story.*
London: Jonathan Cape, 2005.

"Citgo–Venezuela Heating Oil Program" (nd). Accessed 20 June 2018.
www.citgoheatingoil.com/whoweserve.html.

Clark, A. C. *The Revolutionary Has No Clothes: Hugo Chávez's
Bolivarian Farce.* New York: Encounter Books, 2009.

Coase, Ronald and Ning Wang. *How China Became Capitalist.*
New York: Palgrave MacMillan, 2012.

Collier, Paul. *The Bottom Billion: Why the Poorest Countries Are Failing and
What Can Be Done about It.* Oxford: Oxford University Press, 2007.

Cushman, Thomas. "Intellectuals and Resentment toward Capitalism."
Society 49, no. 3 (2012): 247–255.

Dahrendorf, Ralf. *Society and Democracy in Germany.*
New York: Doubleday, 1967.

Delsol, Jean-Philippe. "The Great Process of Equalization of Conditions."
In *Anti-Piketty: Capital for the 21st Century*, edited by Jean-Philippe
Delsol, Nicholas Lecaussin and Emmanuel Martin, 5–17.
Washington, DC: Cato Institute, 2017.

Delsol, Jean-Philippe, Nicholas Lecaussin and Emmanuel Martin, eds.
Anti-Piketty: Capital for the 21st Century.
Washington, DC: Cato Institute, 2017.

Dietrich, Johannes. "Afrika liebt Champagner." *Der Westen* (29 April 2017).
Accessed 20 June 2016. https://www.derwesten.de/panorama/afri-
ka-liebt-champagner-id7896047.html

Dikötter, Frank. *Mao's Great Famine: The History of China's Most
Devastating Catastrophe, 1958–62.* London: Bloomsbury, 2010.

Drazen, Allan and Vittorio Grilli. "The Benefit of Crisis for Economic
Reforms." *American Economic Review* 83, no. 3 (1993): 598–607.

Easterly, William. *The White Man's Burden: Why the West's Efforts
to Aid the Rest Have Done So Much Ill and So Little Good.*
Oxford: Oxford University Press, 2006.

Eberle, Henrik. *Mit sozialistischem Gruß: Eingaben, Briefe und Mitteilungen an die DDR-Regierung.* Berlin: Edition Berolina, 2016.

Edwards, Chris. "Margaret Thatcher's Privatization." *Cato Journal* 37, no. 1 (2017): 89–101.

Ehringfeld, Klaus. "Venezuela droht der Kollaps." *Spiegel* (30 May 2017). Accessed 20 June 2018. www.spiegel.de/wirtschaft/venezuela-droht-der-kollaps-a-1149662.html.

Eltis, Walter. "The Key to Higher Living Standards." In *CPS Policy Study* no. 148. London: Centre for Policy Studies, 1996.

Enders, Stefan. "Investment in Afrika: Chinas und Indiens planvolle Präsenz." *IHK* (19 June 2017). Accessed 20 June 2018. www.subsahara-afrika-ihk.de/blog/2017/06/19/investment-in-afrika-chinas-und-indiens-planvolle-praesenz.

Erhard, Ludwig. *Wohlstand für alle.* Düsseldorf: Econ, 1990.

European Commission, "SPECIAL EUROBAROMETER 353: The EU and Africa: Working towards closer partnership", November 2010, accessed 20 June 2016, http://ec.europa.eu/commfrontoffice/publicopinion/archives/ebs/ebs_353_en.pdf.

Feuchtwanger, Lion. *Moscow 1937: My Visit Described for My Friends.* New York: Viking Press, 1937.

Fleckenstein, William A. and Frederick Sheehan. *Greenspan's Bubbles: The Age of Ignorance at the Federal Reserve.* New York: McGraw-Hill Professional, 2008.

Flossbach, Bert and Philipp Vorndran. *Die Schuldenlawine: Eine Gefahr für unsere Demokratie, unseren Wohlstand und ihr Vermögen.* Munich: FinanzBuch Verlag, 2012.

Frank, Rüdiger. *Nordkorea: Innenansichten eines totalen Staates,* 2nd ed. Munich: Deutsche Verlags-Anstalt, 2017.

Freytag, Andreas. "Ist Afrikas wirtschaftliche Entwicklung nachhaltig?" In *Praxishandbuch Wirtschaft in Afrika,* edited by Thomas Schmidt, Kay Pfaffenberger and Stefan Liebing, 31–40. Wiesbaden: Springer Gabler, 2017.

Friedman, Milton. "The Chicago Boys." In *Up for Debate: Reform without Liberty: Chile's Ambiguous Legacy* (nd). Accessed 20 June 2018. www.pbs.org/wgbh/commandingheights/shared/minitextlo/ufd_reform-liberty_full.html.

Friedman, Milton and Rose D. Friedman. *Two Lucky People: Memoirs.* Chicago: University of Chicago Press, 1998.

"Für deutsche Ohren mag es nach Überwachungsstaat klingen." *Süddeutsche Zeitung* (10 September 2014). Accessed 20 June 2018. www.sueddeutsche. de/wirtschaft/schweden-steuererklaerung-per-sms-1.1728167–2.

Gallegos, Raúl. *Crude Nation: How Oil Riches Ruined Venezuela.* Lincoln, NE: Potomac Books, 2016.

Georgetown University. "U2's Bono: Budget Cuts Can Impact Social Enterprise, Global Change" (13 November 2012). Accessed 20 June 2018. https://www.georgetown.edu/news/bono-speaks-at-gu.html.

Gilder, George. *Wealth and Poverty.* New York: Basic Books, 1981.

Gillies, Peter. "Ludwig Erhard: Ökonom der Freiheit." In Peter Gillies, Daniel Koerfer and Udo Wengst, *Ludwig Erhard,* 123–153. Berlin: Be.bra Wissenschaft Verlag, 2010.

Gillies, Peter, Daniel Koerfer and Udo Wengst. *Ludwig Erhard.* Berlin: Be.bra Wissenschaft Verlag, 2010.

Greenspan, Alan. *The Age of Turbulence: Adventures in a New World.* New York: Penguin, 2007.

Gregg, Samuel. *Becoming Europe: Economic Decline, Culture, and How America Can Avoid a European Future.* New York: Encounter Books, 2013.

Gwartney, James. "Freiheit und Wohlfahrt: Ein globaler Zusammenhang." In *Das Ende der Armut: Chancen einer globalen Marktwirtschaft,* edited by Christian Hoffmann and Pierre Bessard, 23–42. Zürich: Liberales Institut Zürich, 2012.

Gwartney, James D., Richard L. Stroup, Dwight R. Lee, Tawni H. Ferrarini and Joseph P. Calhoun. *Common Sense Economics: What Everyone Should Know about Wealth and Prosperity,* 3rd ed. New York: St. Martin's Press, 2016.

Habermann, Gerd. *Der Wohlfahrtsstaat: Die Geschichte eines Irrwegs.* Frankfurt: Propyläen Verlag, 1994.

Hammarberg, Daniel. *The Madhouse: A Critical Study of Swedish Society.* Daniel Hammarberg, 2011.

Harberger, Arnold. "The Miracle of Chile." In *Up for Debate: Reform without Liberty: Chile's Ambiguous Legacy* (nd). Accessed 20 June 2018. www.pbs.org/wgbh/commandingheights/shared/minitextlo/ufd_reform-liberty_full.html.

Hartmann, Michael. *Der Mythos von den Leistungseliten: Spitzenkarrieren und soziale Herkunft. in Wirtschaft, Politik, Justiz und Wissenschaft,* Frankfurt: Campus Verlag, 2002.

Hausmann, Ricardo and Francisco Rodríguez, eds. *Venezuela before Chávez: Anatomy of an Economic Collapse.* University Park: Pennsylvania State University Press, 2014.

Hausmann, Ricardo and Francisco Rodríguez. "Why Did Venezuelan Growth Collapse?" In *Venezuela before Chávez: Anatomy of an Economic Collapse,* edited by Ricardo Hausmann and Francisco Rodríguez, 15–50. University Park: Pennsylvania State University Press, 2014.

Hayek, Friedrich August von. *The Constitution of Liberty: The Definitive Edition.* Chicago: University of Chicago Press, 2011.

Hayek, Friedrich August von. *The Intellectuals and Socialism* [1949]. Reprinted from The University of Chicago Law Review (Spring 1949), The University of Chicago Press; George B. de Huszar ed., *The Intellectuals: A Controversial Portrait* (Glencoe, Illinois: the Free Press, 1960) pp. 371-84.

Hayek, Friedrich August von. *The Road to Serfdom.* London: Routledge, 2001.

Hayek, Friedrich August von. "Rules, Perception and Intelligibility." In *Studies in Philosophy, Politics and Economics,* 43–65. London: Routledge & Kegan Paul, 1967.

Hegel, Georg Wilhelm Friedrich. *Lectures on the Philosophy of History.* London: George Bell and Sons, 1902.

Heritage Foundation. *2018 Index of Economic Freedom.* Washington, DC: Institute for Economic Freedom, 2018.

Heritage Foundation. "Explore the Data." In *2018 Index of Economic Freedom* (2018), accessed 20 June 2018, https://www.heritage.org/index/explore.

Hermann, Rudolf. "Finanzministerin Blind im 'Budget-Maserati'." *Neue Zürcher Zeitung* (14 April 2016). Accessed 20 June 2018. https://www.nzz.ch/wirtschaft/wirtschaftspolitik/kraeftiges-wirtschaftswachstum-schweden-auf-der-ueberholspur-ld.13596.

Hiller von Gaertringen, Christian. "Afrikas junge Unternehmer." In *Praxishandbuch Wirtschaft in Afrika,* edited by Thomas Schmidt, Kay Pfaffenberger and Stefan Liebing, 1–14. Wiesbaden: Springer Gabler, 2017.

Hiller von Gaertringen, Christian. *Afrika ist das neue Asien: Ein Kontinent im Aufschwung.* Hamburg: Hoffmann und Campe Verlag, 2014.

Hoffmann, Christian and Pierre Bessard, eds. *Das Ende der Armut: Chancen einer globalen Marktwirtschaft.* Zürich: Liberales Institut Zürich, 2012.

Hollander, Paul. *From Benito Mussolini to Hugo Chavez: Intellectuals and a Century of Political Hero Worship.* Cambridge: Cambridge University Press, 2016.

Hollander, Paul. *Political Pilgrims: Western Intellectuals in Search of the Good Society.* Piscataway: Transaction, 1998.

Horkheimer, Max et al. „*Wirtschaft, Recht und Staat im Nationalsozialismus: Analysen des Instituts für Sozialforschung 1939–1942*, edited by Helmut Dubiel and Alfons Söllner, Frankfurt: Europäische Verlags-Anstalt, 1981.

Horn, Karen Ilse. *Die Soziale Marktwirtschaft: Alles, was Sie über den Neoliberalismus wissen sollten.* Frankfurt: Frankfurter Allgemeine Buch, 2010.

Horn, Karen Ilse, ed. *Verlockungen zur Unfreiheit: Eine kritische Bibliothek von 99 Werken der Geistesgeschichte.* Zürich: Frankfurter Allgemeine Buch, 2015.

Hummler, Konrad. "Von der Gier zum Anstand." In *Der Liberalismus: Eine zeitlose Idee – Nationale, europäische und globale Perspektiven*, edited by Gerd Habermann and Marcel Studer, 205–221. Munich: Olzog, 2011.

Hutchinson, Martin. "Rückkehr zum Vollblutkapitalismus." *Handelsblatt* (19 January 2010). Accessed 20 June 2018. https://www.handelsblatt. com/meinung/kolumnen/chile-rueckkehr-zum-vollblutkapitalis-mus/3348842.html.

Institut für Marxismus-Leninismus beim ZK der SED. *Revolutionäre deutsche Parteiprogramme: Vom Kommunistischen Manifest zum Programm des Sozialismus.* Berlin: Dietz Verlag, 1967.

International Monetary Fund. *Global Financial Stability Report* (October 2017). Accessed 20 June 2018. https://www.imf.org/en/ Publications/GFSR/Issues/2017/09/27/global-financial-stability-report-october-2017.

ITU. *Mobile-cellular subscriptions* (2000-2016). Accessed 20 June 2018. https://www.itu.int/en/ITU-D/Statistics/Documents/statistics/2018/ Mobile_cellular_2000-2016.xls

Jasay, Anthony de. "Über Umverteilung." In *Wider die Wohlstandsdiktatur: Zehn liberale Stimmen*, edited by Roland Baader, 19–56. Munich: Resch-Verlag, 1995.

Johnson, Paul M. *Intellectuals: From Marx and Tolstoy to Sartre and Chomsky.* New York: HarperCollins, 2007.

Jungbluth, Rüdiger. *Die elf Geheimnisse des IKEA-Erfolges.* Bergisch Gladbach: Bastei Lübbe (Bastei Verlag), 2008.

Kahan, Alan S. *Mind vs. Money: The War between Intellectuals and Capitalism.* New Brunswick: Transaction, 2010.

Kahn, Richard W. "A Tale of Two Economies." *Washington Times* (2 July 2013). Accessed 20 June 2018. https://www.washingtontimes.com/news/2013/jul/2/a-tale-of-two-economieschile-has-employed-free-mar.

Kappeler, Beat. "Wege und Irrwege der Entwicklungspolitik." In *Das Ende der Armut: Chancen einer globalen Marktwirtschaft*, edited by Christian Hoffmann and Pierre Bessard, 77–82. Zürich: Liberales Institut Zürich, 2012.

Kern, Thomas. "Südkoreas Bildungs- und Forschungssystem." In *Südkorea und Nordkorea: Einführung in Geschichte, Politik, Wirtschaft und Gesellschaft*, edited by Thomas Kern and Patrick Köllner, 149–167. Frankfurt: Campus Verlag, 2005.

Kern, Thomas and Patrick Köllner, eds. *Südkorea und Nordkorea: Einführung in Geschichte, Politik, Wirtschaft und Gesellschaft.* Frankfurt: Campus Verlag, 2005.

Knight Frank. *The Wealth Report 2016* (2016). Accessed 20 June 2016. https://content.knightfrank.com/research/83/documents/en/wealth-report-2016-3579.pdf.

Koenen, Gerd. *Die Farbe Rot: Ursprünge und Geschichte des Kommunismus.* Munich: C. H. Beck, 2017.

Koerfer, Daniel. "Ludwig Erhard: Der vergessene Gründervater." In Peter Gillies, Daniel Koerfer and Udo Wengst, *Ludwig Erhard*, 12–67. Berlin: Be.bra Wissenschaft Verlag, 2010.

Köhler, Wolfgang. *Wall Street in Panik.* Murnau: Mankau Verlag, 2008.

Köllner, Patrick. "Südkoreas politisches System." In *Südkorea und Nordkorea: Einführung in Geschichte, Politik, Wirtschaft und Gesellschaft*, edited by Thomas Kern and Patrick Köllner, 50–70. Frankfurt: Campus Verlag, 2005.

Kooperation International. "Bildungslandschaft: Republik Korea (Südkorea)" (nd). Accessed 20 June 2018. www.kooperation-international.de/laender/asien/republik-korea-suedkorea/bildungs-forschungs-und-innovationslandschaft/bildungslandschaft.

Lanz, Martin. "Je mehr Wohlstand, desto weniger anteilige Ausgaben für Essen: Ein positiver Zusammenhang?" *Neue Zürcher Zeitung* (2 November 2017). Accessed 20 June 2018. https://www.nzz.ch/wirtschaft/je-hoeher-der-wohlstand-desto-kleiner-der-anteil-der-essensausgaben-ein-uneingeschraenkt-positiver-zusammenhang-ld.1321011?mktcid=nled&mktcval=107_2017-11-2.

Lawson, Nigel. *The New Britain: The Tide of Ideas from Attlee to Thatcher.* London: Centre for Policy Studies, 1988.

Lee, Felix. *Macht und Moderne: Chinas großer Reformer Deng Xiaoping – Die Biographie*. Berlin: Rotbuch Verlag, 2014.

Lenin, Vladimir I. "What Is To Be Done? Burning Questions of Our Movement." In *Lenin's Collected Works*, Vol. 5, 347–517. Moscow: Foreign Languages Publishing House, 1961.

Lilla, Mark. *The Reckless Mind: Intellectuals and Politics*. New York: New York Review Books, 2001.

Lindbeck, Assar. "The Swedish Experiment." *Journal of Economic Literature* 35, no. 3 (1997): 1273–1319.

Lindbeck, Assar, Per Molander, Torsten Persson, Olof Petersson, Agnar Sandmo, Birgitta Swedenborg and Niels Thygesen. *Turning Sweden Around*. Cambridge, MA: MIT Press, 1994.

Lundberg, Ferdinand. *The Rich and the Super-Rich: A Study in the Power of Money Today*. New York: Lyle Stuart, 1968.

Luttwak, Edward N. *Strategy and Politics: Collected Essays*. Piscataway: Transaction, 1980.

Mahajan, Vijay. *Africa Rising: How 900 Million African Consumers Offer More than You Think*. New Jersey: Prentice Hall, 2009.

Makura, Moky. *Africa's Greatest Entrepreneurs*. Century City, CA: Penguin, 2008.

Mares, Detlev. *Margaret Thatcher: Die Dramatisierung des Politischen*. Gleichen: Hans Hansen-Schmidt, 2014.

Marx, Karl. *A Contribution to the Critique of Political Economy*, translated by S. W. Ryazanskaya. Moscow: Progress Publishers, 1859.

Mayer, Thomas. *Die neue Ordnung des Geldes: Warum wir eine Geldreform brauchen*, 3rd ed. Munich: FinanzBuch Verlag, 2015.

Mehrtens, Philip. *Staatsschulden und Staatstätigkeit: Zur Transformation der politischen Ökonomie Schwedens*. Frankfurt: Campus Verlag, 2014.

Meller, Patricio. *The Unidad Popular and the Pinochet Dictatorship: A Political Economy Analysis*. London: Palgrave Macmillan, 2000.

Mises, Ludwig von. *The Anti-capitalist Mentality*, edited by Bettina Bien Greaves. Indianapolis: Liberty Fund, 2006.

More, Thomas. *Utopia*, edited by William P. Weaver. London: Broadview Press, 2011.

Moses, Carl. "Der Öl-Caudillo." *Frankfurter Allgemeine Zeitung* (27 February 2007). Accessed 20 June 2018. www.faz.net/aktuell/wirtschaft/wirtschaftspolitik/hugo-chavez-der-oel-caudillo-1118662.html.

Moyo, Dambisa. *Dead Aid: Why Aid Is Not Working and How There Is a Better Way for Africa.* New York: Farrar, Straus & Giroux, 2009.

Moyo, Dambisa. *Winner Take All: China's Race for Resources and What It Means for the World.* New York: Basic Books, 2012.

"M-Pesa Has Completely Transformed Kenya's Economy, This Is How..." *CNBC Africa* (4 January 2017). Accessed 20 June 2018. https://www.cnbcafrica.com/news/east-africa/2017/01/04/mpesa-economic-impact-on-kenya.

Neuber, Harald. "Billiges Heizöl für 16 US-Bundesstaaten." *Amerika21* (12 December 2007). Accessed 20 June 2018. https://amerika21.de/nachrichten/inhalt/2007/dez/heizoel-fuer-usa.

Neuweg, Georg Hans. *Könnerschaft und implizites Wissen: Zur lehr- und lerntheoretischen Bedeutung der Erkenntnis- und Wissenstheorie Michael Polanyis.* Münster: Waxmann, 2001.

Niemietz, Kristian. "Der Mythos vom Globalisierungsverlierer: Armut im Westen." In *Das Ende der Armut: Chancen einer globalen Marktwirtschaft,* edited by Christian Hoffmann and Pierre Bessard, 141–159. Zürich: Liberales Institut Zürich, 2012.

Niemietz, Kristian. *Redefining the Poverty Debate: Why a War on Markets Is No Substitute for a War on Poverty.* London: Institute of Economic Affairs, 2012.

Niskanen, William A. *Reaganomics: An Insider's Account of the Policies and the People.* New York: Oxford University Press, 1988.

Niskanen, William A. and Stephen Moore. "Supply-Side Tax Cuts and the Truth about the Reagan Economic Record." *Cato Policy Analysis* no. 261 (22 October 1996).

Nohlen, Dieter and Hartmut Sangmeister, eds. *Macht, Markt, Meinungen: Demokratie, Wirtschaft und Gesellschaft in Lateinamerika.* Wiesbaden: VS Verlag für Sozialwissenschaften, 2004.

Norberg, Johan. *Financial Fiasco: How America's Infatuation with Home-ownership and Easy Money Created the Economic Crisis.* Washington, DC: Cato Institute, 2009.

Nozick, Robert. "Why Do Intellectuals Oppose Capitalism?" In *Socratic Puzzles.* Cambridge, MA: Harvard University Press, 1997.

Oguz, Fuat. "Hayek on Tacit Knowledge." *Journal of Institutional Economics* 6, no. 2 (2010): 145–165.

Organisation for Economic Co-operation and Development.
  PISA 2015: PISA Results in Focus (2018). Accessed 20 June 2018.
  https://www.oecd.org/pisa/pisa-2015-results-in-focus.pdf.
Palmer, Tom G. "Foreword." In *Anti-Piketty: Capital for the 21st Century*,
  edited by Jean-Philippe Delsol, Nicholas Lecaussin and Emmanuel
  Martin, xi–xvi. Washington, DC: Cato Institute, 2017.
Pascha, Werner. "Südkoreas Wirtschaft." In *Südkorea und Nordkorea:
  Einführung in Geschichte, Politik, Wirtschaft und Gesellschaft*, edited by
  Thomas Kern and Patrick Köllner, 87–120. Frankfurt: Campus Verlag, 2005.
Pfaffenberger, Kay. "Die Bedeutung regionaler Besonderheiten für das
  Geschäftsleben." In *Praxishandbuch Wirtschaft in Afrika*, edited by
  Thomas Schmidt, Kay Pfaffenberger and Stefan Liebing, 55–67.
  Wiesbaden: Springer Gabler, 2017.
Piketty, Thomas. *Capital in the Twenty-First Century.*
  Boston: Harvard University Press, 2014.
Pohlmann, Markus C. "Südkoreas Unternehmen." In *Südkorea und Nordkorea:
  Einführung in Geschichte, Politik, Wirtschaft und Gesellschaft*, edited by
  Thomas Kern and Patrick Köllner, 121–148. Frankfurt: Campus Verlag, 2005.
Polanyi, Michael. *The Tacit Dimension.* London: Routledge, 1966.
Poller, Horst. *Mehr Freiheit statt mehr Sozialismus: Wie konservative Politik
  die Krisen bewältigt, die sozialistisches Wunschdenken schafft.*
  Munich: Olzog, 2010.
Pollock, Friedrich. "Ist der Nationalsozialismus eine neue Ordnung?"
  In Max Horkheimer et al., *Wirtschaft, Recht und Staat im Nationalsozia-
  lismus: Analysen des Instituts für Sozialforschung 1939–1942*,
  edited by Helmut Dubiel and Alfons Söllner, 111–128.
  Frankfurt: Europäische Verlags-Anstalt, 1981.
Rand, Ayn. *For the New Intellectual: The Philosophy of Ayn Rand.*
  New York: Random House, 1961.
Ravier, Adrian and Peter Lewin. "The Subprime Crisis." *Quarterly Journal of
  Austrian Economics* 15, no. 1 (2012): 45–74.
Reagan, Ronald. "The President's News Conference." *The American
  Presidency Project* (12 August 1986). Accessed 20 June 2018.
  www.presidency.ucsb.edu/ws/?pid=37733.
"Reaktionen: Wagenknecht preist Chávez' Arbeit." *Handelsblatt*
  (3 March 2013). Accessed 20 June 2018. www.handelsblatt.com/
  politik/deutschland/reaktionen-wagenknecht-preist-wirtschaftsmod-
  ell-von-chvez/7887454.html.

Riley, Jason L. *Please Stop Helping Us: How Liberals Make It Harder for Blacks to Succeed.* New York: Encounter Books, 2014.

Rinke, Stefan. *Kleine Geschichte Chiles.* Munich: C. H. Beck, 2007.

Rogoff, Kenneth S. and Carmen M. Reinhart. *This Time Is Different: Eight Centuries of Financial Folly.* Princeton: Princeton University Press, 2009.

Rommel, Alexander. "Sozialstruktur, Armut, Ungleichheit und soziale Klassen." In *Venezuela heute: Politik, Wirtschaft, Kultur,* edited by Andreas Boeckh, Friedrich Welsch and Nikolaus Werz, 51–76.
Frankfurt: Vervuert Verlagsgesellschaft, 2011.

Rüb, Matthias. "Telenovela über Hugo Chávez: Er konnte Menschen verführen." *Frankfurter Allgemeine* (1 February 2017).
Accessed 20 June 2018. www.faz.net/aktuell/feuilleton/medien/el-comandante-eine-serie-ueber-hugo-chavez-14799710.html.

Rüesch, Andreas. "Wieso es in Russland wieder salonfähig ist, Stalin zu verehren." *Neue Zürcher Zeitung* (24 October 2017).
Accessed 20 June 2018. https://www.nzz.ch/international/stalin-und-die-sehnsucht-nach-der-starken-hand-ld.1323741?mktcid=nled&mktcval=107_2017–10–24.

Sahlén, Malin and Salim Furth. "Piketty Is Misleading about the Swedish Case." In *Anti-Piketty: Capital for the 21st Century,* edited by Jean-Philippe Delsol, Nicholas Lecaussin and Emmanuel Martin, 97–100. Washington, DC: Cato Institute, 2017.

Sanandaji, Nima. *Debunking Utopia: Exposing the Myth of Nordic Socialism.* Washington, DC: WND Books, 2016.

Sanders, Bernie. *Our Revolution: A Future to Believe In.*
New York: Thomas Dunne Books, 2016.

Schaller, Michael. *Ronald Reagan.* Oxford: Oxford University Press, 2011.

Schaller, Sven. "Wandel durch Persistenz (Teil 1): Eine Analyse der Wirtschaftspolitik von Hugo Chávez," *Quetzal* (March 2013). Accessed 20 June 2018. www.quetzal-leipzig.de/lateinamerika/venezuela/venezuela-wirtschaftspolitik-hugo-chavez-erdoel-wirtschaftsstruktur-19093.html.

Scheen, Thomas. "Ein Reformwunder mit Schönheitsfehlern." *Frankfurter Allgemeine Zeitung* (7 January 2017). Accessed 20 June 2018. www.faz.net/aktuell/wirtschaft/afrika-im-umbruch/ruanda-reformwunder-mit-schoenheitsfehlern-14592400.html.

Schmidt, Thomas, Kay Pfaffenberger and Stefan Liebing, eds.
Praxishandbuch Wirtschaft in Afrika. Wiesbaden: Springer Gabler, 2017.

Schmieding, Holger. "Vor Thatcher war Großbritannien ein Trümmerhaufen." *Die Welt* (9 April 2013). Accessed 20 June 2018.
https://www.welt.de/wirtschaft/article115147486/Vor-Thatch-
er-war-Grossbritannien-ein-Truemmerhaufen.html.

Schneidewind, Dieter. *Wirtschaftswunderland Südkorea.*
Wiesbaden: Springer Gabler, 2013.

Schoeck, Helmut. *Envy: A Theory of Social Behaviour.*
Indianapolis: Liberty Fund, 1966.

Schöllgen, Gregor. *Gerhard Schröder: Die Biografie.*
Munich: Deutsche Verlags-Anstalt, 2015.

Schröder, Gerhard. Byline article for *Handelsblatt* (16 December 2002).

Schroeder, Klaus and Monika Deutz-Schroeder. *Gegen Staat und Kapital – für
die Revolution! Linksextremismus in Deutschland: Eine empirische Studie.*
Frankfurt: Peter Lang / Internationaler Verlag der Wissenschaften, 2015.

Schumpeter, Joseph. *Capitalism, Socialism and Democracy.*
London: George Allen & Unwin, 1976.

Schumpeter, Joseph. *Theory of Economic Development.*
London: Routledge, 1981.

Schwarz, Hans-Peter. *Die Ära Adenauer: Gründerjahre der Republik
1949–1957.* Stuttgart: Deutsche Verlags-Anstalt, 1981.

Schweizer, Thomas. "So regiert Maduro sein Land in den Abgrund."
Wirtschaftswoche (25 May 2017). Accessed 20 June 2018.
https://www.wiwo.de/politik/ausland/venezuela-so-regiert-madu-
ro-sein-land-in-den-abgrund/19850212.html.

Scruton, Roger. *Fools, Frauds and Firebrands: Thinkers of the New Left.*
London: Bloomsbury, 2016.

Sennholz, Hans F. "Über den Abbau von Armut und Ungleichheit."
In *Wider die Wohlstandsdiktatur: Zehn liberale Stimmen,* edited by
Roland Baader, 121–133. Munich: Resch-Verlag, 1995.

Shane, Scott. "A Political Gadfly Lampoons the Left via YouTube."
New York Times (18 September 2009). Accessed 20 June 2018.
www.nytimes.com/2009/09/19/us/19sting.html.

Sharma, Ruchir. *The Rise and Fall of Nations: Forces of Change in the
Post-crisis World.* New York: Allen Lane, 2016.

Shiller, Robert J. *Irrational Exuberance,* 3rd ed.
Princeton: Princeton University Press, 2015.

Sieren, Andreas and Frank Sieren. *Der Afrika-Boom: Die große Überraschung des 21. Jahrhunderts.* Munich: Carl Hanser Verlag, 2015.

Signer, David. "Entwicklungshilfe statt Entwicklung? Die fragwürdige Bilanz eines überholten Konzeptes." In *Das Ende der Armut: Chancen einer globalen Marktwirtschaft*, edited by Christian Hoffmann and Pierre Bessard, 85–98. Zürich: Liberales Institut Zürich, 2012.

Sinn, Hans-Werner. *Die Target-Falle: Gefahren für unser Geld und unsere Kinder*. Munich: Carl Hanser Verlag, 2012.

Sommer, Rainer. *Die Subprime-Krise: Wie einige faule US-Kredite das internationale Finanzsystem erschüttern*. Hanover: Heisoft, 2008

Soto, Hernando de. "Eigentumsrechte und Märkte." *LI-Paper* (May 2016). Accessed 29 June 2018. www.libinst.ch/publikationen/LI-Paper-De-Soto-Eigentum.pdf.

Soto, Hernando de. "Die Fiktion des edlen Wilden: Warum die Armen sicheres Eigentum brauchen." In *Das Ende der Armut: Chancen einer globalen Marktwirtschaft*, edited by Christian Hoffmann and Pierre Bessard, 101–123. Zürich: Liberales Institut Zürich, 2012.

Spoerer, Mark and Jochen Streb. *Neue deutsche Wirtschaftsgeschichte des 20. Jahrhunderts*. Munich: De Gruyter Oldenbourg, 2013.

"Staatsquote im internationalen Vergleich" (2012). Accessed 20 June 2018. https://www.tu-chemnitz.de/wirtschaft/vwl2/downloads/material/Staatsquote_2012.pdf.

Steiner, André. *Von Plan zu Plan: Eine Wirtschaftsgeschichte der DDR*. Berlin: Aufbau Taschenbuch, 2007.

Stiglitz, Joseph. *The Great Divide: Unequal Societies and What We Can Do about Them*. New York: W. W. Norton & Company, 2015.

Stoisser, Hans. *Der Schwarze Tiger: Was wir von Afrika lernen können*. Munich: Kösel-Verlag, 2015.

"Storm over Venezuela Oil Speech." *BBC News* (4 November 2006). Accessed 7 November 2006. http://news.bbc.co.uk/1/hi/world/americas/6114682.stm.

Sundberg, Jacob. "Die schwedische Hochsteuergesellschaft: Eine Herausforderung an den Rechtsstaat." In Lothar Bossle and Gerhard Radnitzky, *Selbstgefährdung der offenen Gesellschaft*, 173–210. Würzburg: Naumann, 1982.

Tempelman, Jerry H. "Austrian Business Cycle Theory and the Global Financial Crisis: Confessions of a Mainstream Economist." *Quarterly Journal of Austrian Economics* 13, no. 1 (2010): 3–15.

Ten Brink, Tobias. *Chinas Kapitalismus: Entstehung, Verlauf, Paradoxien*. Frankfurt: Campus Verlag, 2013.

Thatcher, Margaret. *The Downing Street Years.* London: Harper Collins, 1993.

Thomas, Cal. "Millennials Are Clueless about Socialism (Call It the 'Bernie Sanders effect')." *Fox News Opinion* (20 October 2016). Accessed 20 June 2018. www.foxnews.com/opinion/2016/10/20/millennials-are-clueless-about-socialism-call-it-bernie-sanders-effect.html.

Transparency International. *Corruption Perceptions Index* 2017 (2018). Accessed 29 May 2018. https://www.transparency.org/news/feature/corruption_perceptions_index_2017.

United Nations Development Programme. *Human Development Report 2016.* New York: United Nations, 2016.

Urech, Fabian. "Das Öl hat der Regierung den Kopf verdreht." *Neue Zürcher Zeitung* (11 August 2015). Accessed 20 June 2018. https://www.nzz.ch/international/afrika/das-oel-hat-der-regierung-den-kopf-verdreht-1.18593317.

Velten, Robert. "Die Soziologie der antiken Reichtumsphilosophie." In *Reichtum und Vermögen: Zur gesellschaftlichen Bedeutung der Reichtums- und Vermögensforschung,* edited by Thomas Druyen, Wolfgang Lauterbach and Matthias Grundmann, 242–254. Wiesbaden: Verlag für Sozialwissenschaften, 2009.

Venezuela's Tragic Meltdown: Hearing before the Subcommittee on the Western Hemisphere of the Committee on Foreign Affairs House of Representatives, 115th Congress, 1st Session (28 March 2017), serial no. 115-13.

"Venezuela: Von Hunger und Sterben" [broadcast]" *NDR* (17 July 2017).

Voegeli, William. *Never Enough: America's Limitless Welfare State.* New York: Encounter Books, 2010.

Wagner, Thomas. *Die Angstmacher: 1968 und die Neuen Rechten.* Berlin: Aufbau Verlag, 2017.

Wasike, Nambuwani. "M-PESA and Kenya's GDP Figures: The Truth, the Lies and the Facts." *LinkedIn Pulse* (2 March 2015). Accessed 20 June 2018. https://www.linkedin.com/pulse/m-pesa-kenyas-gdp-figures-truths-lies-facts-wasike-phd-student-.

Weede, Erich. "Wirtschaftliche Freiheit: Hintergrundbedingungen, Auswirkungen und Gefährdungen." *Wirtschaftspolitische Blätter* 3–4 (2014): 443–455.

Wemheuer, Felix. *Der große Hunger: Hungersnöte unter Stalin und Mao.* Berlin: Rotbuch Verlag, 2012.

Wirner, Stefan. "Die deutsche Linke nimmt sich Chávez als Vorbild." *Die Welt* (29 November 2007). Accessed 20 June 2018. https://www.welt.de/politik/article1412494/Die-deutsche-Linke-nimmt-sich-Chavez-als-Vorbild.html.

Wittmann, Walter. *Soziale Marktwirtschaft statt Wohlfahrtsstaat: Wege aus der Krise.* Zürich: Orell Füssli, 2013.

Wolle, Stefan. *Der große Plan: Alltag und Herrschaft in der DDR 1949–1951.* Berlin: Ch. Links Verlag, 2013.

Woods, Thomas E., Jr. *Meltdown: A Free-Market Look at Why the Stock Market Collapsed, the Economy Tanked, and Government Bailouts Will Make Things Worse.* Washington, DC: Regnery, 2009.

World Bank, *Time Required to start a Business (days),* accessed on 20 June 2018, https://data.worldbank.org/indicator/IC.REG.DURS?view=chart

World Food Programme. "Zero Hunger." Accessed 20 June 2018. http://de.wfp.org/hunger/hunger-statistik.

Zeyer, René. *Armut ist Diebstahl: Warum die Armen uns ruinieren.* Frankfurt: Campus Verlag, 2013.

Zhang Weiying. *The Logic of the Market: An Insider's View of Chinese Economic Reform.* Washington, DC: Cato Institute, 2015.

Zitelmann, Rainer. *Hitler: The Policies of Seduction.* London: London House, 1999.

Zitelmann, Rainer. "Träume vom neuen Menschen." In *Hat die politische Utopie eine Zukunft?,* edited by Richard Saage, 27–33. Darmstadt: Wissenschaftliche Buchgesellschaft, 1992.

Zitelmann, Rainer. *The Wealth Elite: A Groundbreaking Study of the Psychology of the Super Rich.* London: LID Publishing, 2018.

Index of Persons

About the Author

DR. RAINER ZITELMANN

Rainer Zitelmann holds doctorates in History and Sociology. He is the author of 21 books. After working as a historian at the Freie Universität Berlin, he later served as section head at the daily newspaper Die Welt. In 2000, he founded his own company, which he subsequently sold in 2016. Today he lives in Berlin as an investor and publicist.

Sharing knowledge since 1993

- 1993 Madrid
- 2008 Mexico DF and Monterrey
- 2010 London
- 2011 New York and Buenos Aires
- 2012 Bogotá
- 2014 Shanghai